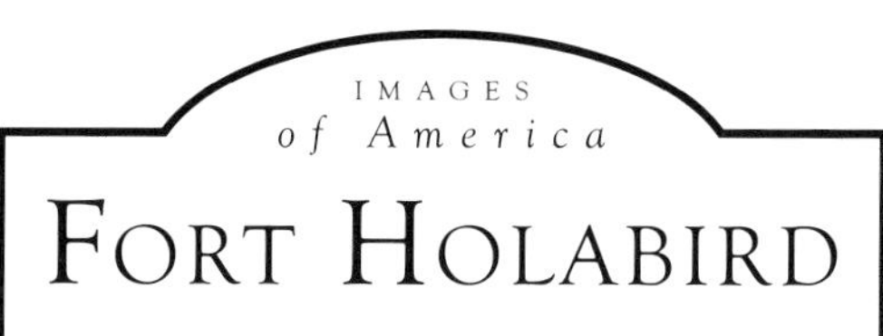
IMAGES
of America
FORT HOLABIRD

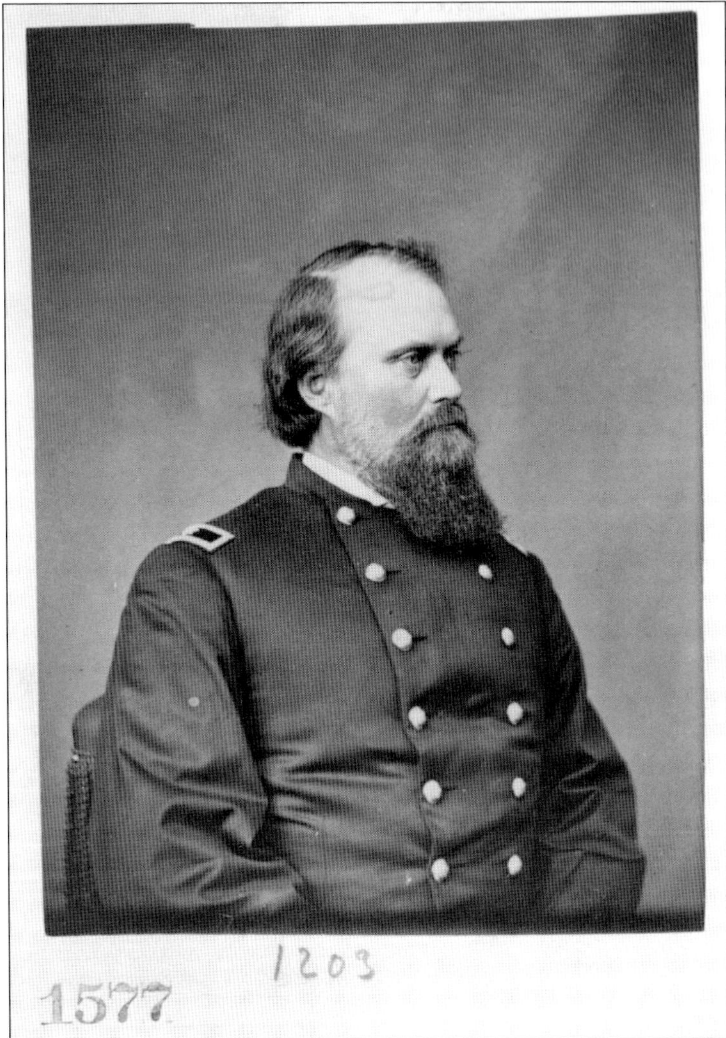

Fort Holabird was originally named Camp Holabird in honor of Brig. Gen. Samuel Beckley "S.B." Holabird. Brigadier General Holabird was a Quartermaster Corps officer who served from 1849 until 1890. He was a Civil War veteran who served during the Battle of Antietam. In 1883, he was promoted to the position of Army quartermaster general. (Courtesy NARA.)

ON THE COVER: In this August 10, 1941, photograph, there are three versions of a versatile Dodge three-fourth-ton military truck. From left to right are a WC-52 Command Car, WC-52 Cargo Truck, and WC-54 Ambulance version. The drivers stand at attention by their vehicles while a film crew gets ready. (Courtesy NARA.)

IMAGES
of America

FORT HOLABIRD

David B. Lari

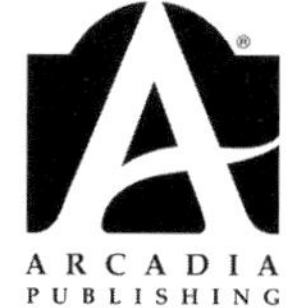

ISBN 9781-4671-6083-4

Published by Arcadia Publishing
Charleston, South Carolina

Printed in the United States of America

Library of Congress Control Number: 2023945173

For all general information, please contact Arcadia Publishing:
Telephone 843-853-2070
Fax 843-853-0044
E-mail sales@arcadiapublishing.com

Visit us on the Internet at www.arcadiapublishing.com

This book is dedicated to the generations of soldiers who passed through Holabird's gates during its 55-year history.

Contents

Acknowledgments

This book would not have been possible without the kind assistance of the staff of the National Archives, the US Army Heritage and Education Center, the National WWI Museum and Memorial, the Dundalk-Patapsco Neck Historical Society & Museum, the Kansas Historical Society, and the editors of Arcadia Publishing.

INTRODUCTION

The land that became Fort Holabird has an interesting history. Lying east of Baltimore on the banks of Colgate Creek, the land that became Holabird was first populated by Native Americans. Archeological evidence exists of activity by the Iroquoian-speaking Susquehannock in and around what became Baltimore, Maryland.

Colgate Creek was named for colonial land grant holder Col. Richard Colgate. He held a land grant of 7,000 acres that undoubtedly included the land that became Fort Holabird. When he died in 1722, he was buried on his estate where Colgate Creek meets the Patapsco River. When his heirs sold the remaining estate to the Canton Company in 1870, Colonel Colgate was reinterred at Mount Carmel Cemetery near Baltimore, Maryland.

In later years, the Colgate Creek area was home to farms and summer retreats colloquially called "shore shacks." It was a popular place for swimming and fishing, and excursion boats from Baltimore brought tourists to clubs and picnic grounds on the creek.

Early residents recall the area that became Fort Holabird was farms, pastures, and woods. Some remembered trapping muskrats in the marshes along the creek.

There were also some industrial sites including a brick factory, a bone grinding plant, and a distillery.

The north end of Fort Holabird, between Colgate Creek and Dundalk Avenue, was home to an African American community of farm workers. The community was demolished to make way for the fort; no trace of the community survives today.

One

World War I

The precursor to Camp Holabird was Mechanical Repair Shop Unit No. 306 at 1421 I Street, Northwest, Washington, DC. In March 1918, the Mechanical Repair Unit 306 moved to the newly created Camp Holabird, Maryland. The camp was named in honor of Brig. Gen. S.B. Holabird, who had served in the Quartermaster Corps. Camp Holabird opened in preparation for World War I. Holabird trained vehicle drivers and mechanics and served as a depot testing and shipping military motor vehicles. Holabird has an amazing history, beginning as a training center for a relatively new military technology: the motor vehicle.

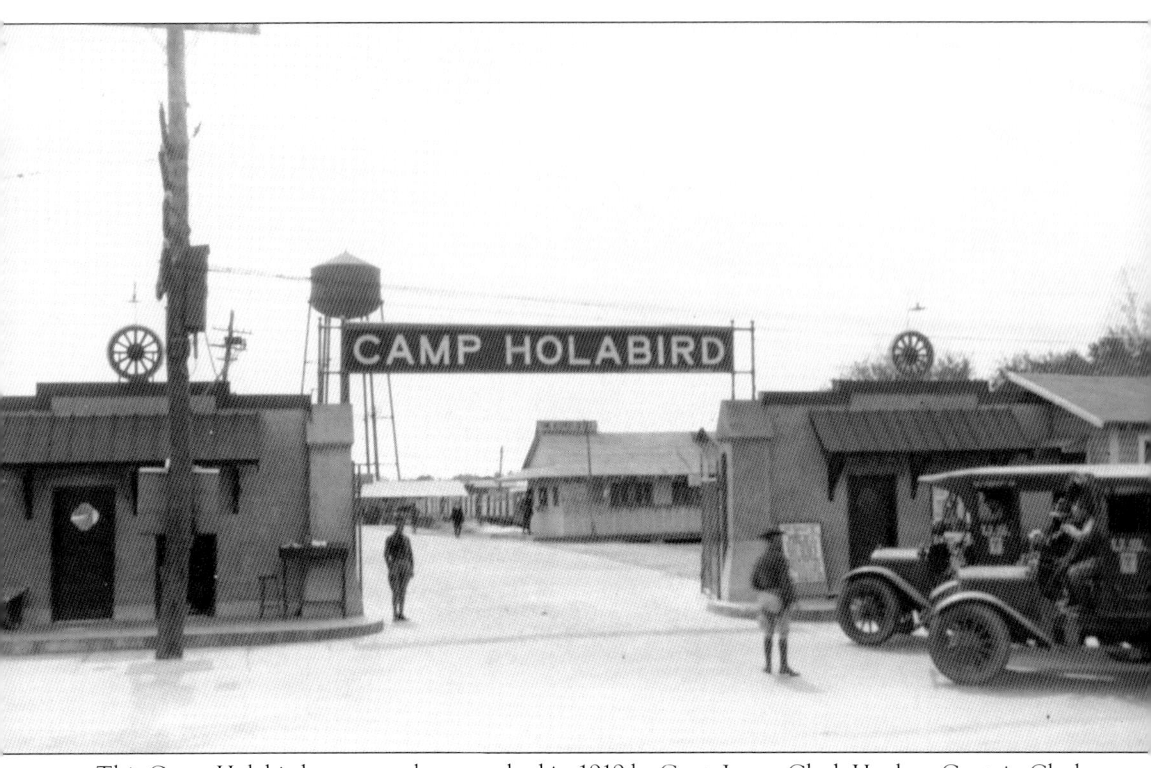

This Camp Holabird gate was photographed in 1919 by Capt. James Clark Hughes. Captain Clark was a World War I veteran. He was stationed at Camp Holabird for six months while at the Motor Transport School, departing in February 1920. Captain Clark was an avid photographer, which was an unusual hobby in 1919. (Courtesy Kansas Historical Society.)

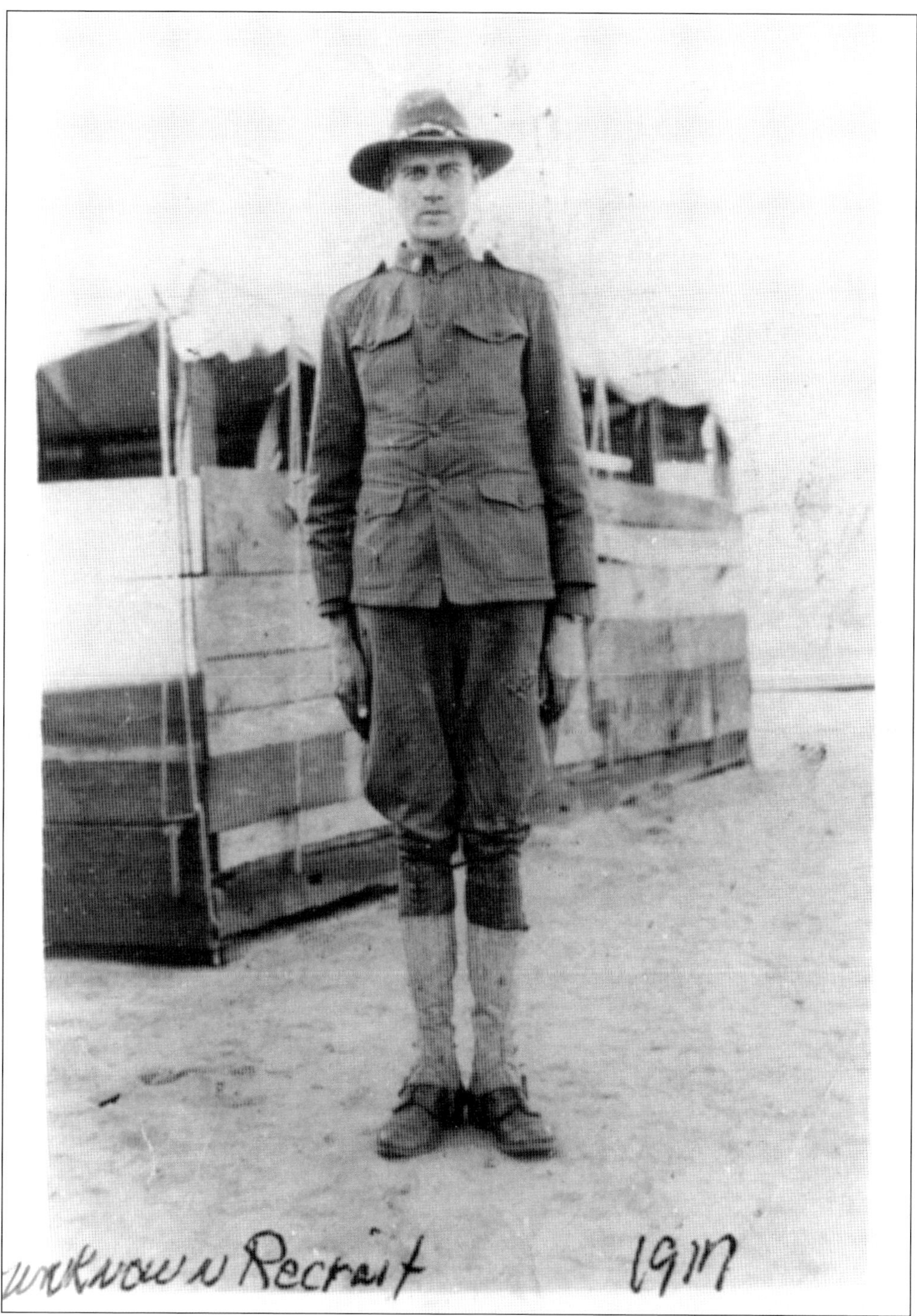

One of the earliest photographs of Camp Holabird, this 1917 image shows an "Unknown Recruit." He appears to be wearing the 1917 boot, which would soon be replaced by the legendary 1918 trench boot colloquially known as the Pershing boot. The tears in his trousers indicate a work uniform. Given that Camp Holabird officially opened in 1918, this soldier may have been part of the work crews setting up the new facility. (Courtesy Dundalk-Patapsco Neck Historical Society & Museum.)

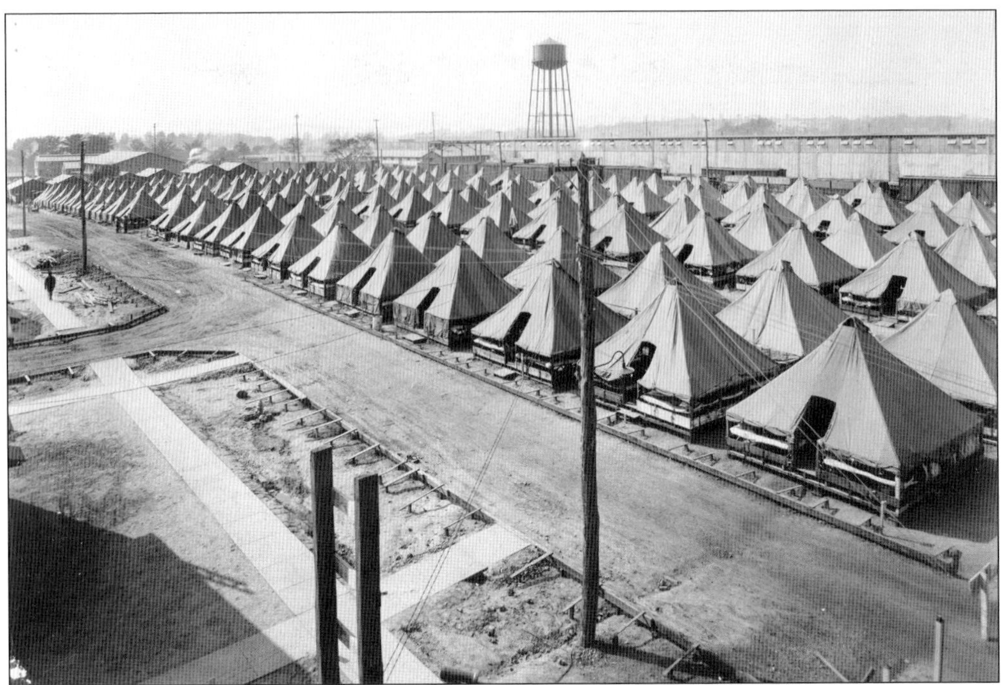

This April 26, 1919, photograph shows rows of spike tents where Holabird soldiers were housed. This was shortly after the end of World War I. If some of the soldiers were veterans of trench warfare, they may have found these accommodations quite comfortable. (Courtesy National Archives and Records Administration [NARA].)

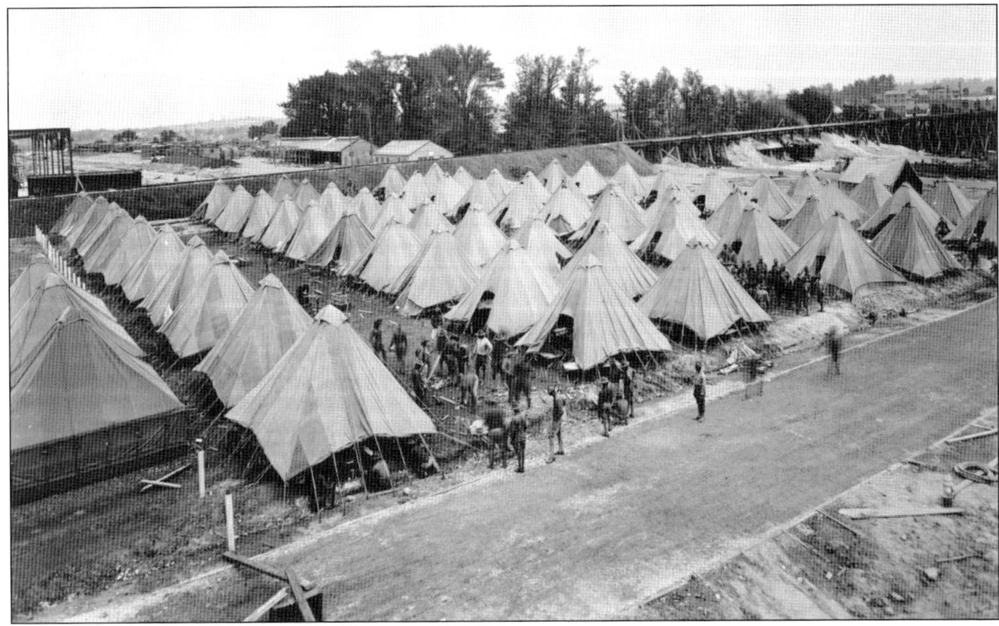

This 1919 photograph shows soldiers living in tents at Holabird, giving a peek into camp life. Soldiers are lying on cots while others are gathered in and around the tents. The soldiers in this image appear to be African American. The Army was segregated in 1919, and these tents may have been the barracks for Holabird's African American soldiers. (Courtesy NARA.)

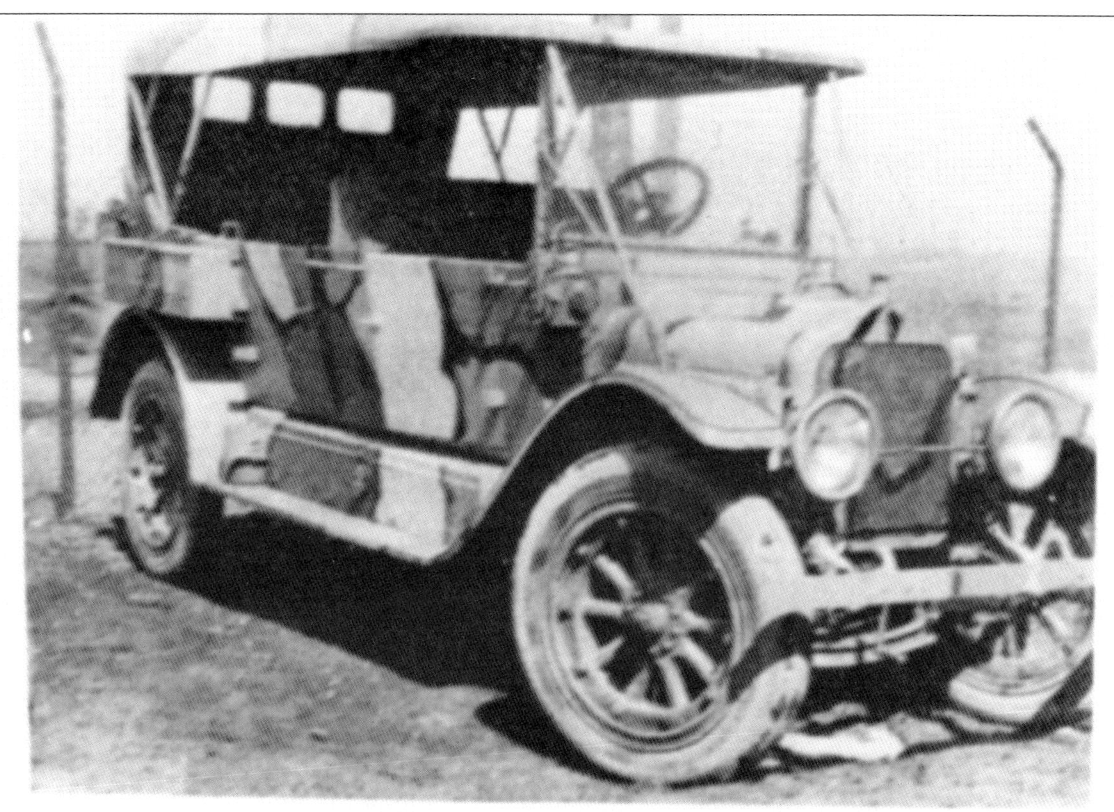

General Pershing's Locomobile

Shown here is "General Pershing's Locomobile." This was apparently his staff car. The early use of camouflage paint indicates it was intended for use in combat areas. The photograph is undated, so it is not known if it is being prepared to deploy or returning from combat. General Pershing was known to operate near the front, so a camouflage staff car would come in handy. (Courtesy Dundalk-Patapsco Neck Historical Society & Museum.)

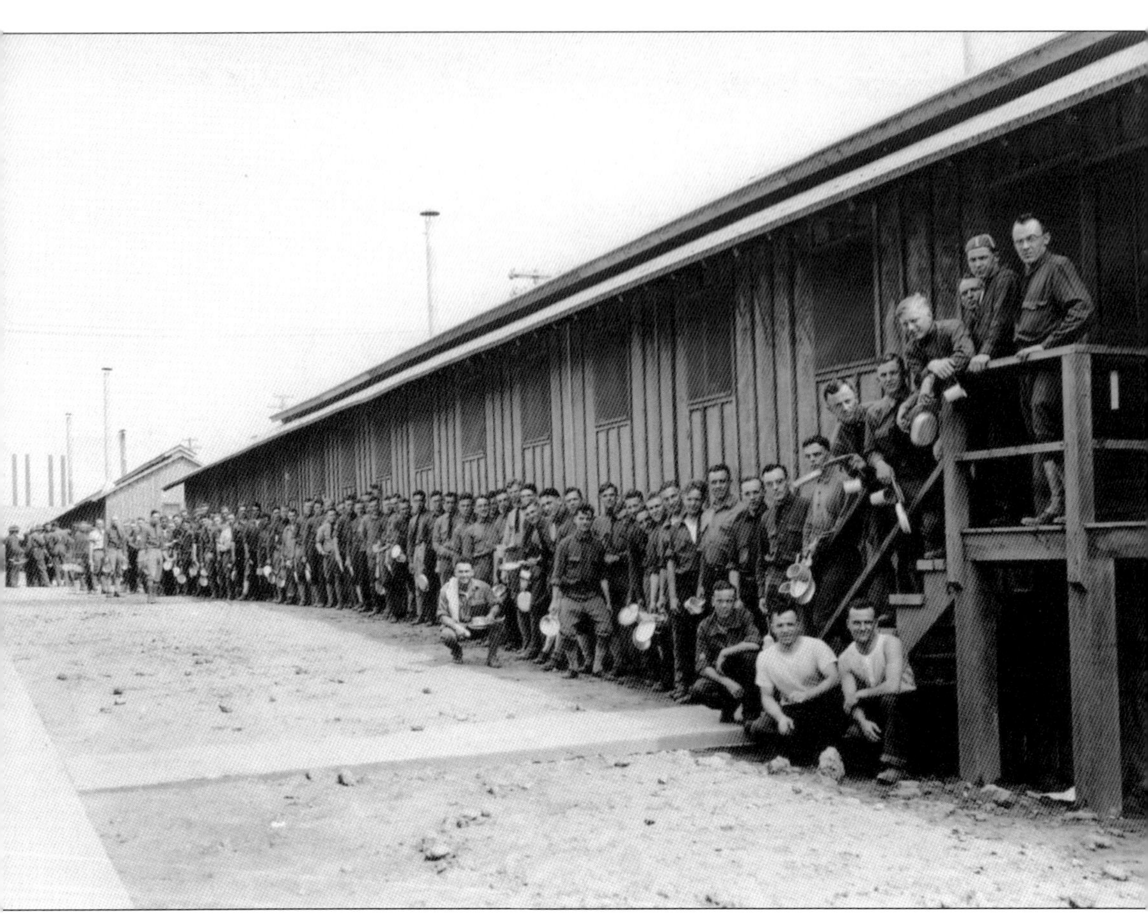

This 1918 photograph depicts a line of soldiers, mess kits and canteen cups in hand, outside a Holabird mess hall. The mess kits appear to be the M1910 "meat can" model. It came in two halves that separated into dining surfaces and came with utensils with a leather sheath for each. The entire kit fit into a haversack. The two soldiers crouching by the stairs may have been pulling KP (kitchen patrol) duty that day. Judging from the turnout, this is one bugle call nobody minded. (Courtesy NARA.)

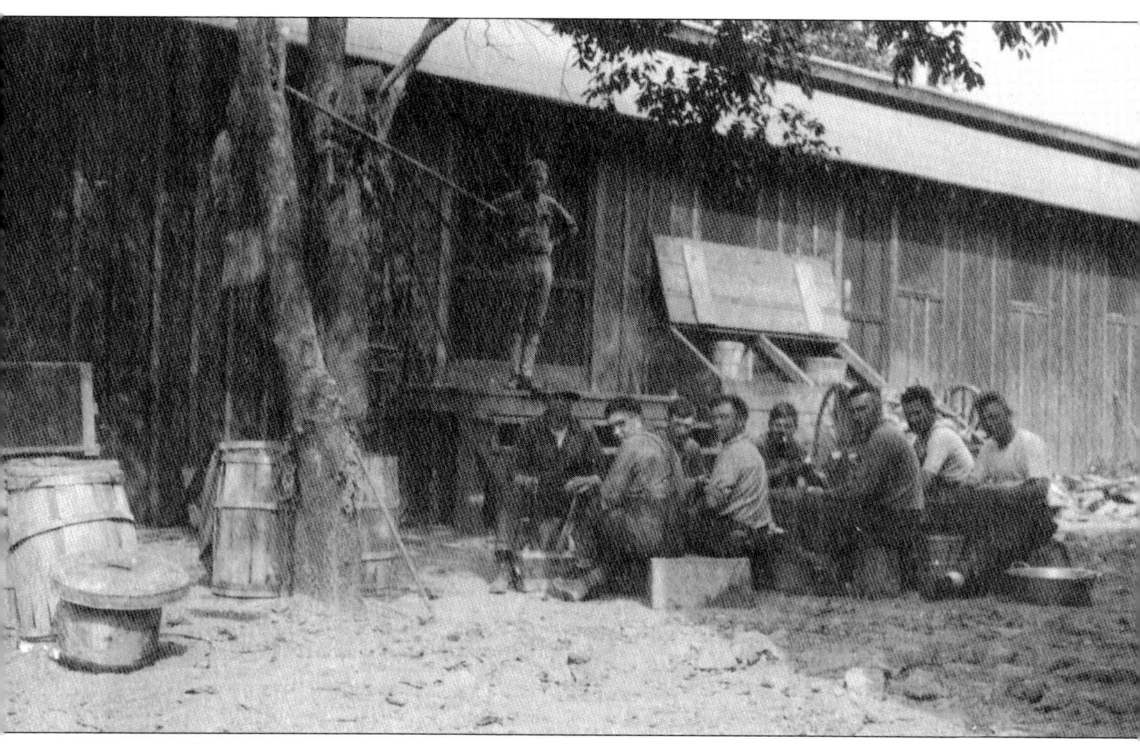

KP was a task most soldiers dreaded. It was ignoble and unglamorous but a vitally necessary task to keep an army that moves on its stomach moving. These soldiers have the stereotypical KP task of peeling potatoes. The soldier in the background smoking a pipe is most likely a noncommissioned officer whose task was to keep the kitchen patrol on task. (Courtesy National WWI Museum and Memorial.)

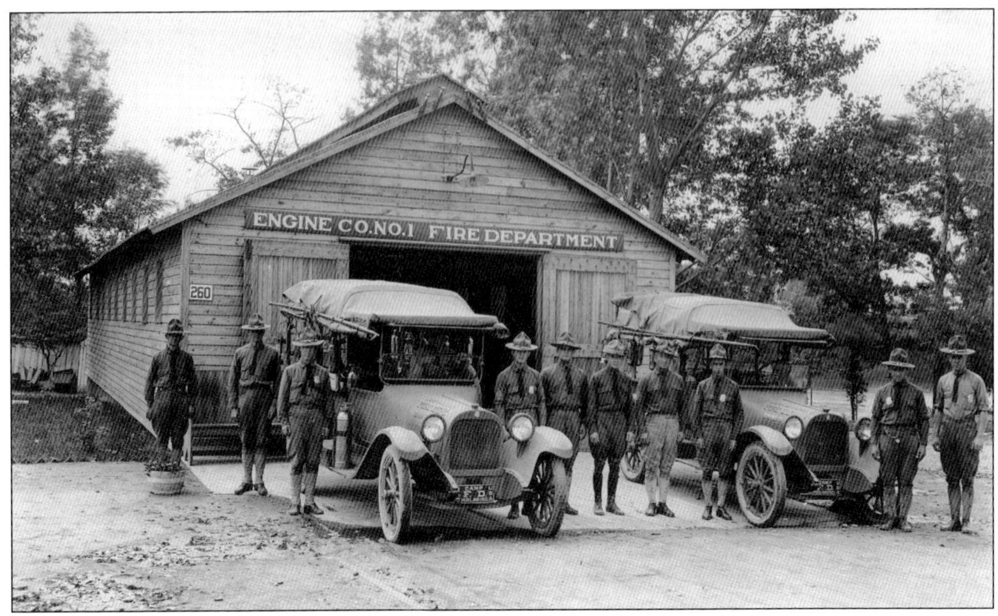

This photograph dated April 26, 1919, shows Camp Holabird Engine Co., No. 1 Fire Department consisting of two trucks and personnel. The trucks are equipped with a fire extinguisher and other equipment. The trucks appear to be Dodge Model 30, which were marketed for firefighting purposes from 1914 to 1922. (Courtesy NARA.)

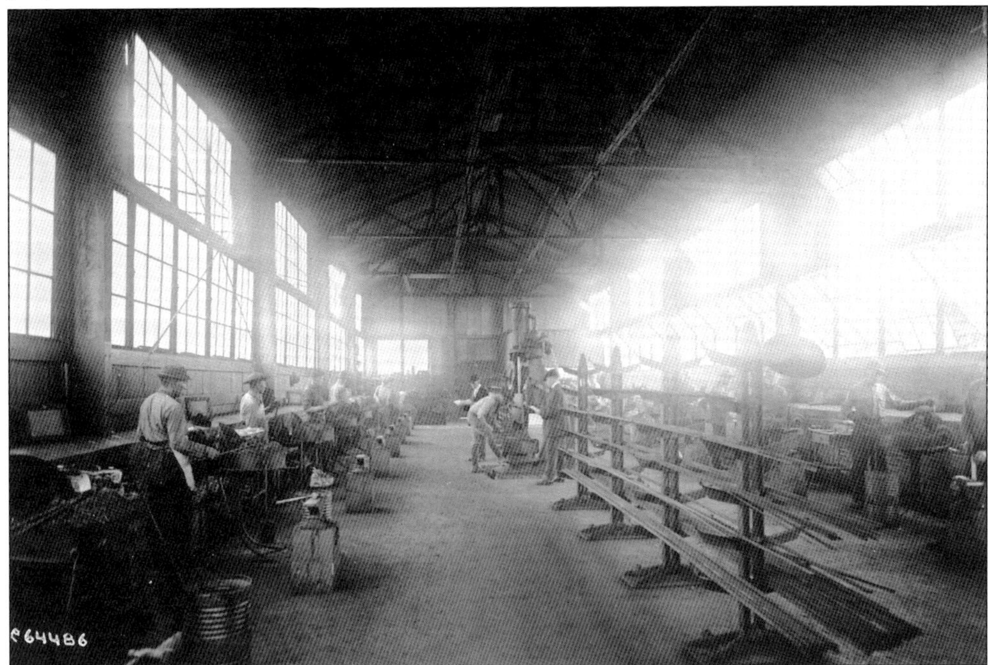

Holabird was a motor training post when the motor vehicle was still a relatively new technology. This class of blacksmithing students illustrates how Holabird bridged the gap between two eras of military technology. One cannot help but feel sorry for the blacksmithing students. They were probably overjoyed to learn a marketable trade in the Army, but it was a trade whose days were numbered. (Courtesy NARA.)

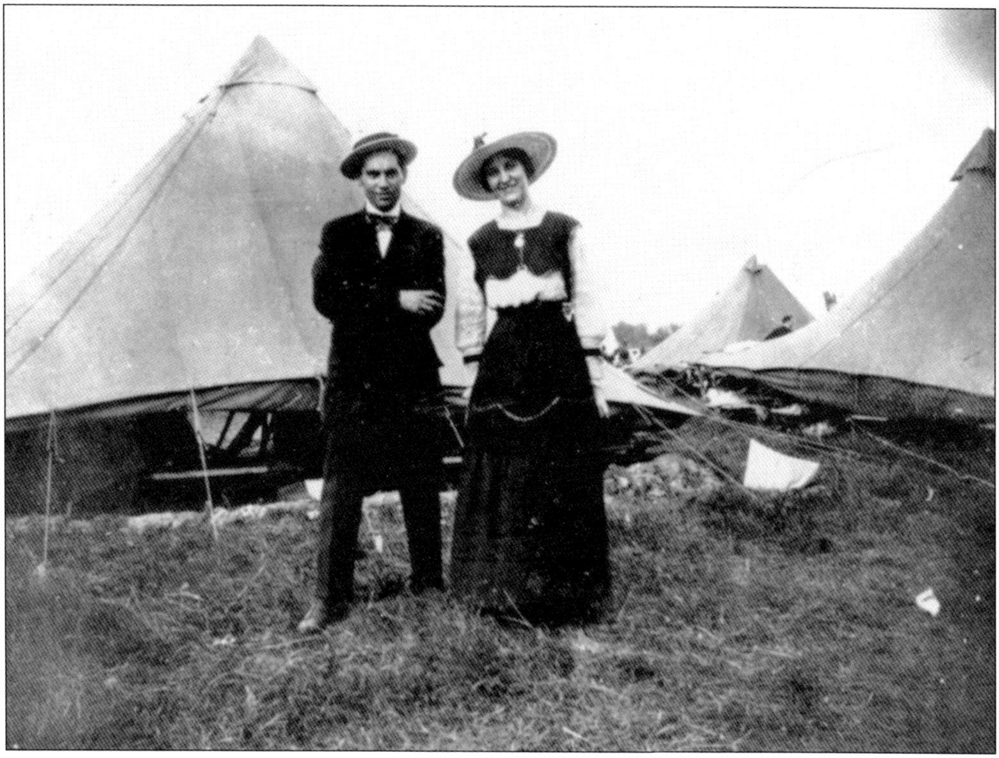

Couple visiting Camp Holabird during the early years. These tents were made of cotton duck, and they were intended to sleep eight soldiers. This image offers a look at how crowded tent life must have been. Someone wrote on the back of the photograph, "Probably His Last Day of Civilian Life." Their identities are unknown, but they are certainly well-dressed for the occasion. (Courtesy Dundalk-Patapsco Neck Historical Society & Museum.)

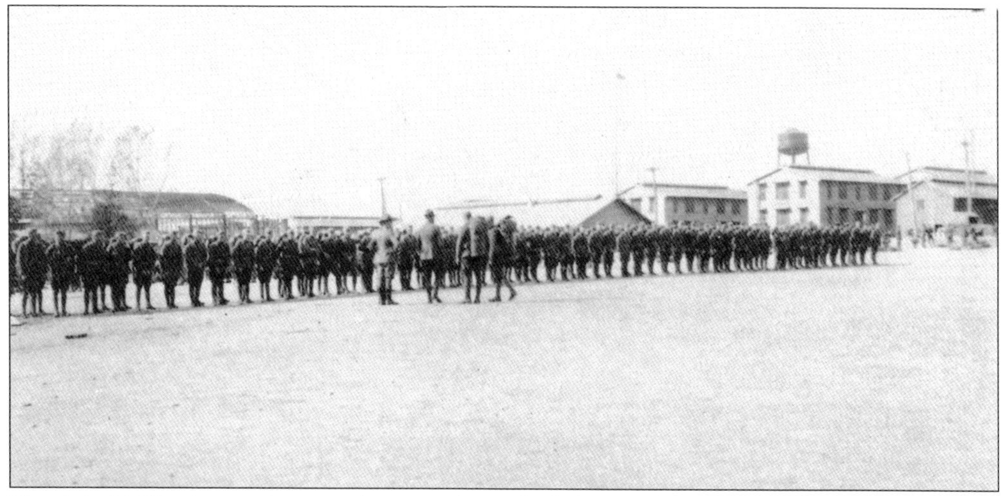

This World War I–era photograph is titled simply "Black and white photograph of soldiers at Camp Holabird, Baltimore, Maryland conducting drills." The soldiers are lined up in formation with wooden barracks in the background. Two soldiers in front of the formation have duffel bags indicating this might have been a training formation of some kind (Courtesy National WWI Museum and Memorial.)

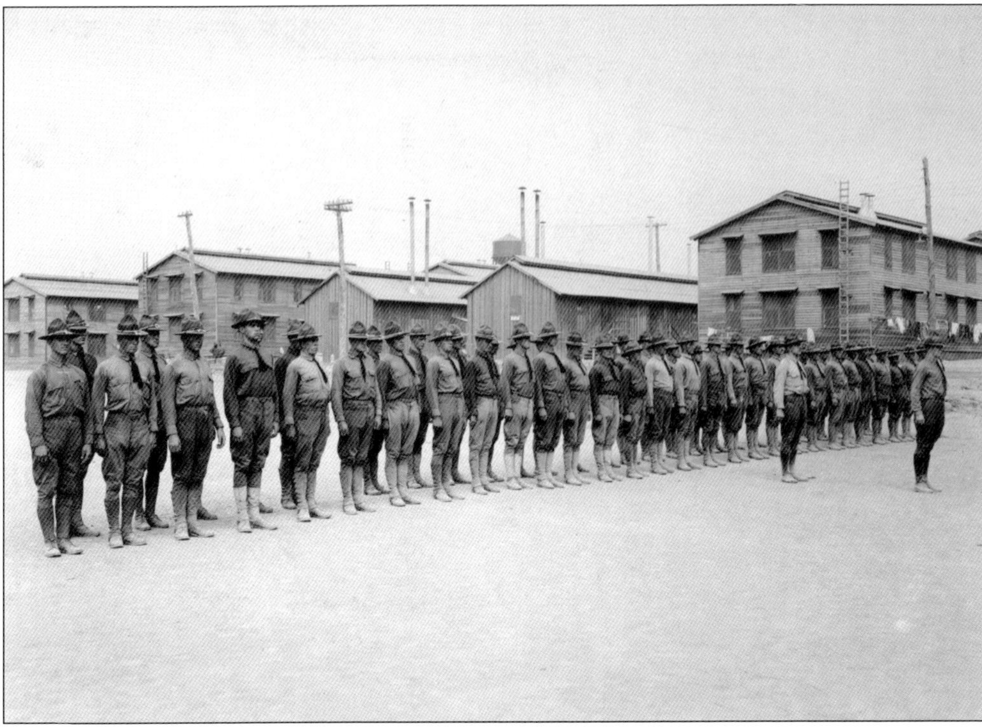

Soldiers lined up at attention in formation with a row of barracks in the background. There is laundry hanging outside one of the barracks. The presence of laundry indicates this was an ordinary formation and not an inspection day. The soldiers are wearing what appears to be the Pershing or trench boot. (Courtesy NARA.)

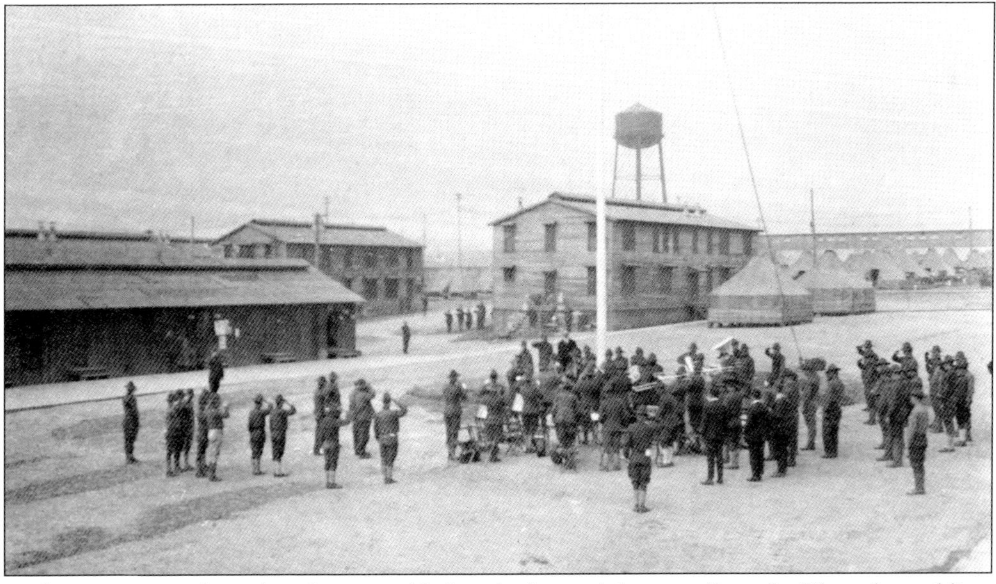

In this image, a military band is assembled at the base of the post flagpole. The other soldiers in the image are saluting while standing at attention. This indicates they are raising or striking the colors. In any event, these soldiers appear to be taking the matter quite solemnly. (Courtesy National WWI Museum and Memorial.)

POST EXCHANGE

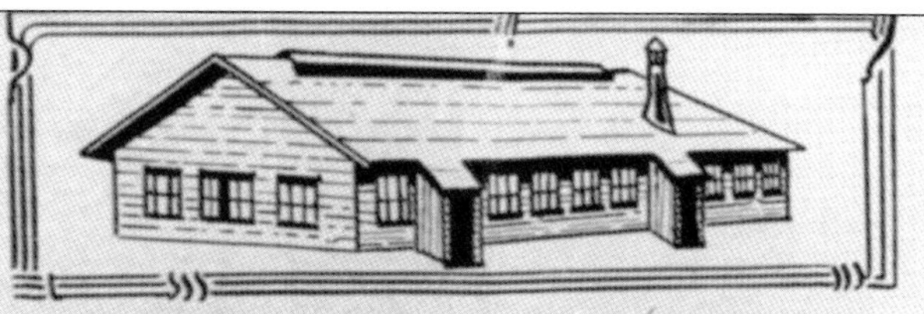

SUIT CASES, BAGS AND CANVAS LEGGINGS
AT YOUR OWN PRICES

LEATHER PUTTEES - FANCY PILLOW TOPS

Gold and Silver Insignia Rings and Pins

CIGARS, TOBACCOS AND CIGARETTES

CIGARETTE HOLDERS AT BARGAIN PRICES

SHOES A-PLENTY

NEW SUPPLY FOUNTAIN PENS, FLAGS, NOVELTIES FOR GIFTS

ALL SORTS OF GIFTS FOR THE GIRLS, FRIENDS AND PARENTS AT HOME

HEADQUARTERS FOR

Candies	Smoking Tobacco
Cakes	Chewing Tobacco
Drinks	Bath Towels
Cigars	Face Towels
Cigarettes	Wearing Apparel
Pipes	Cuff Leggings

Military Trunks, $8.50 to $10

COLD DRINK

ICE CREAM

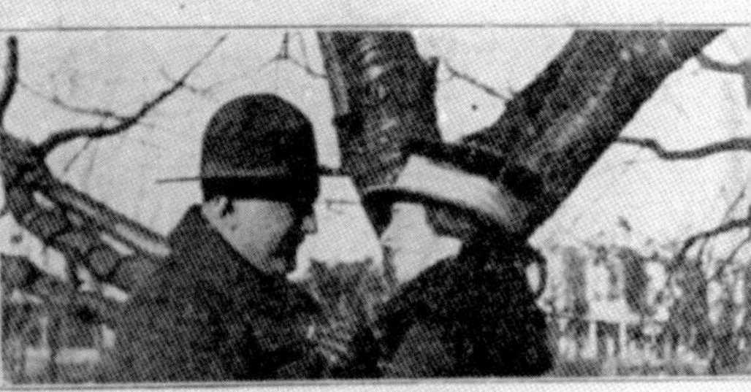

1919

27- This ad appeared in the 1919 issue of the Camp's paper named "The Spark". Note popular items then, such as canvas leggings, leather puttees, cuff leggings, and "all sorts of gifts for the girl, friends and parents at home."

This image is an ad from a 1919 issue of the Camp Holabird newspaper known as the *Spark*. The ad includes the multitude of items available at the reliable old PX. Later, post newspapers were the *Holabird Exhaust* and the *Holabird Herald*. No surviving copies of the World War I–era Spark were found for this publication. (Courtesy Dundalk-Patapsco Neck Historical Society & Museum.)

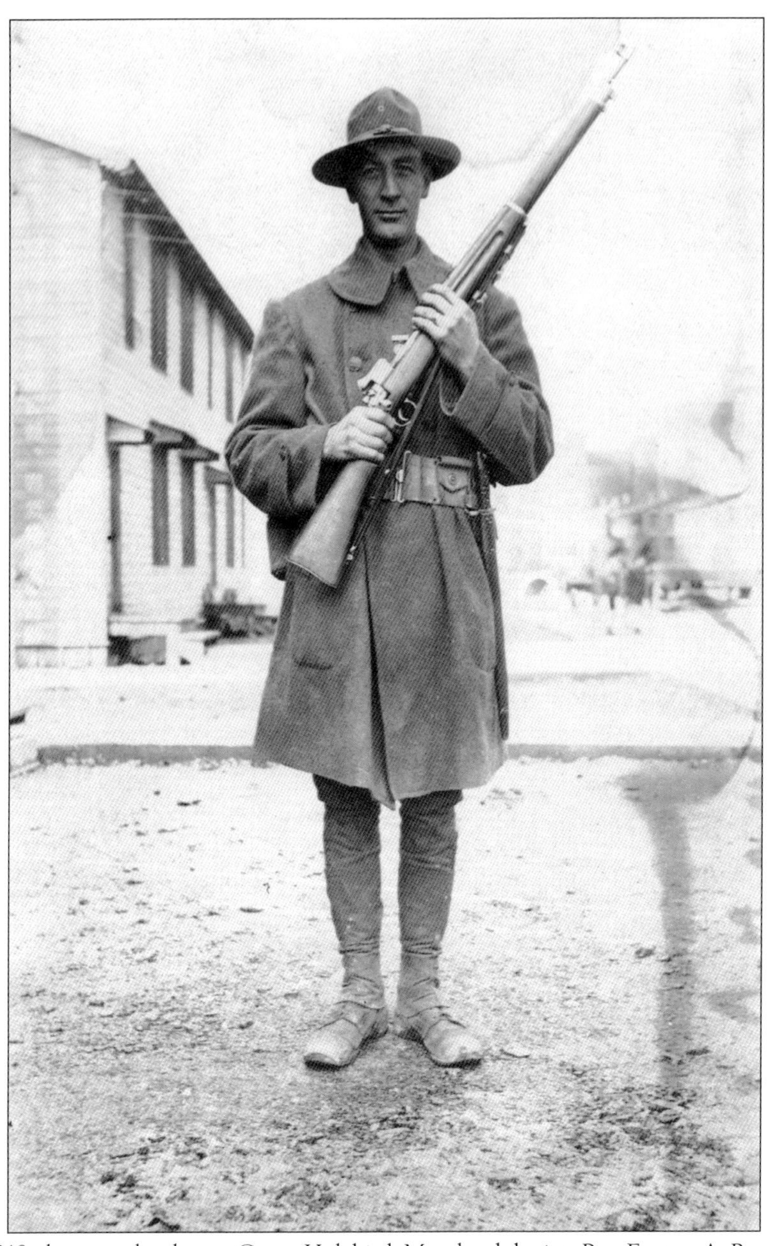

This July 1918 photograph taken at Camp Holabird, Maryland depicts Pvt. Everett A. Rexroat. There is a caption on the back that reads, "Everett at Camp Holabird/Baltimore Maryland July 1918." Private Rexroat is holding an M1917 Rifle. This rifle has an interesting history. Before the United States entered the war, US manufacturers were making versions of the British Enfield Model 1914 rifle. They also made a Model 1913 bayonet compatible with this rifle. When the United States entered the war in 1917, The 1914 rifle and 1913 bayonets were issued to US troops as the M1917 rifle and bayonet. Since it was modeled on the British Enfield, the US version was colloquially known as "the Enfield." He is wearing what appears to be an M1910-pattern infantry belt. His belt is equipped with an ammo pouch and what is most likely an M1917 bayonet. Behind his rifle, a badge is visible, perhaps a marksmanship badge he earned. The state of his uniform and footgear are evidence of the drudgery of camp life. (Courtesy National WWI Museum and Memorial.)

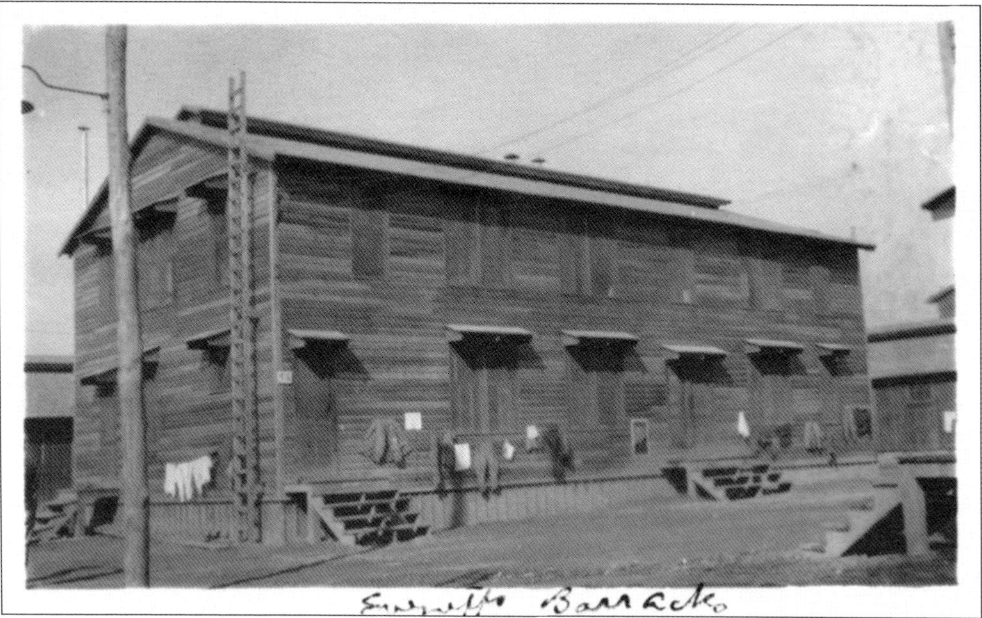

This is a photograph of a humble wooden barracks labeled "Everetts Barracks." This photograph is from the Everett Rexroat collection, and it is safe to assume this was his barracks. Outside the barracks, laundry is hung out to dry. It is not a five-star suite, but it was home to several soldiers while they served at Holabird. (Courtesy National WWI Museum and Memorial.)

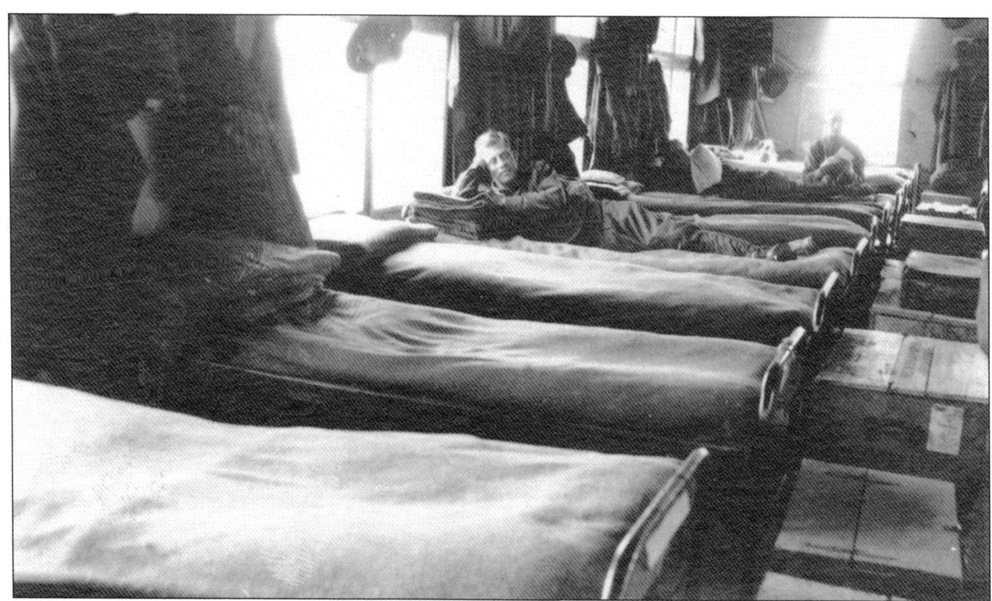

This image gives a glimpse into World War I barracks life. The row of bunks had limited space to hang hats, uniforms, and outer garments. The soldier's living area consisted of a bunk, hooks to hang items on, and a trusty footlocker. (Courtesy National WWI Museum and Memorial.)

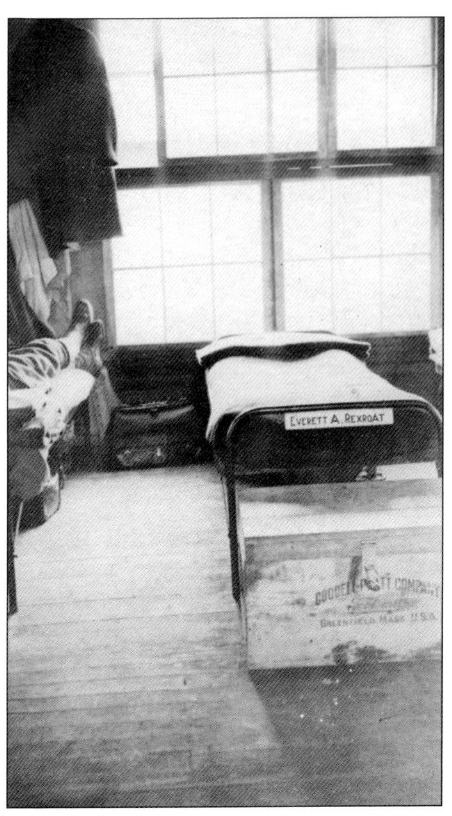

This photograph of Everett A. Rexroad's bunk and footlocker provides a close-up of an individual soldier's living area. Most of his belongings would be stored in the footlocker. Some uniform items, including an overcoat and campaign hat, would be hung on the window frame. To the left, a soldier lounges on an adjacent bunk. (Courtesy National WWI Museum and Memorial.)

This April 20, 1919, image juxtaposes a man on horseback in front of a row of military trucks. The image is symbolic of the motor vehicle replacing the horse in warfare. When Holabird first opened, blacksmithing was a class offered. As a center for military vehicle testing, Holabird bridged the gap between two eras of military technology. (Courtesy NARA.)

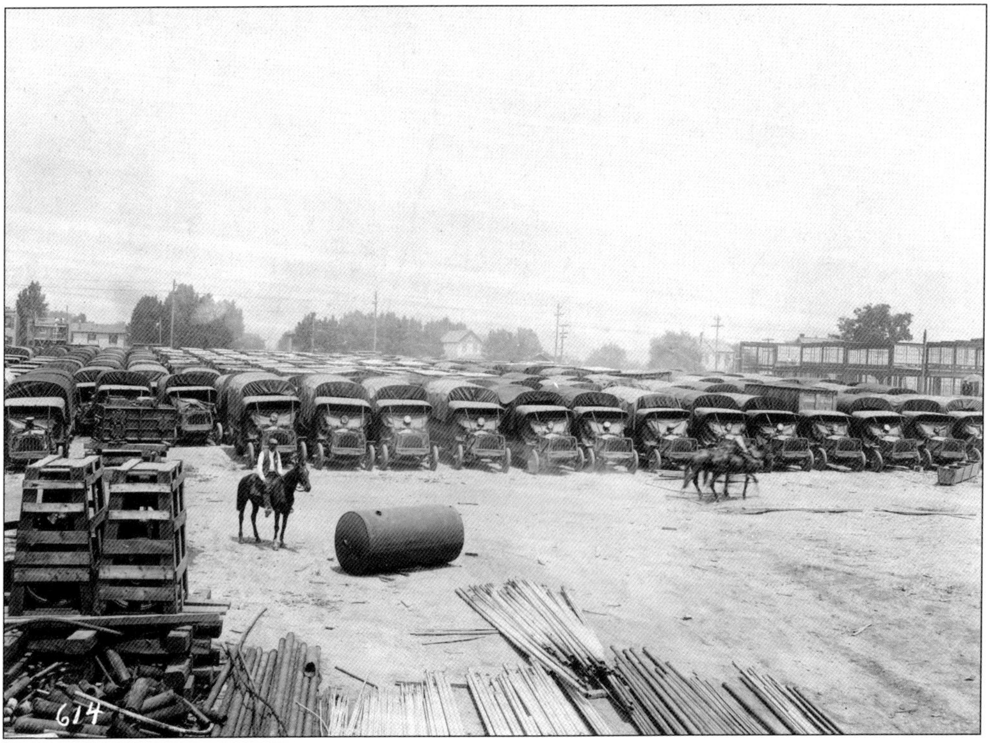

This 1919 photograph shows rows of trucks under the protective roof of a wooded shed. Their rear wheels are off the ground indicating this is probably a storage facility of some kind. The image is labeled "Motor Transport Service Trucks," and the sign on the building reads, "School of Motor Transportation." (Courtesy NARA.)

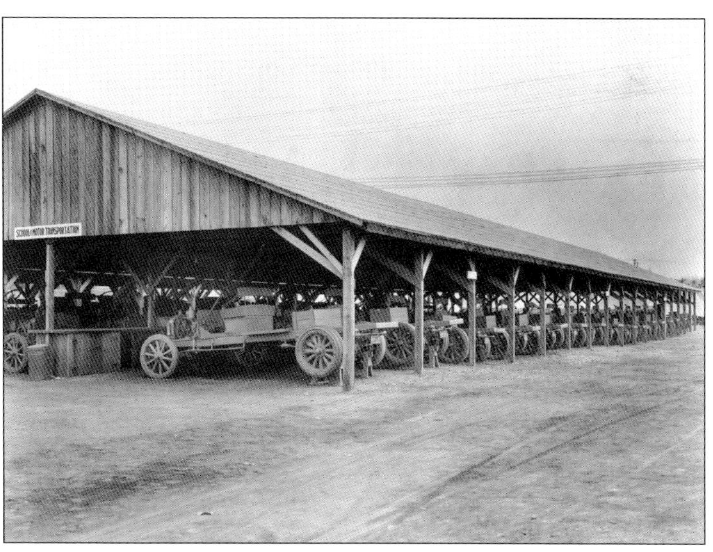

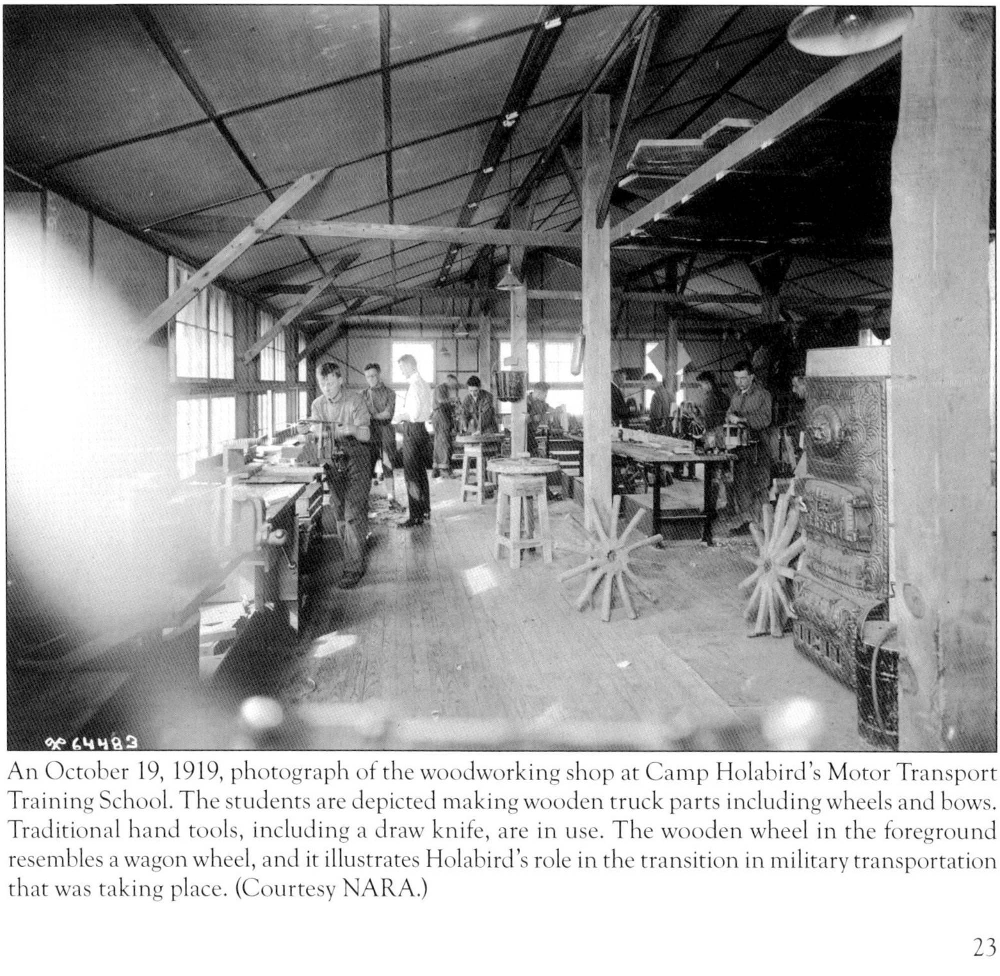

An October 19, 1919, photograph of the woodworking shop at Camp Holabird's Motor Transport Training School. The students are depicted making wooden truck parts including wheels and bows. Traditional hand tools, including a draw knife, are in use. The wooden wheel in the foreground resembles a wagon wheel, and it illustrates Holabird's role in the transition in military transportation that was taking place. (Courtesy NARA.)

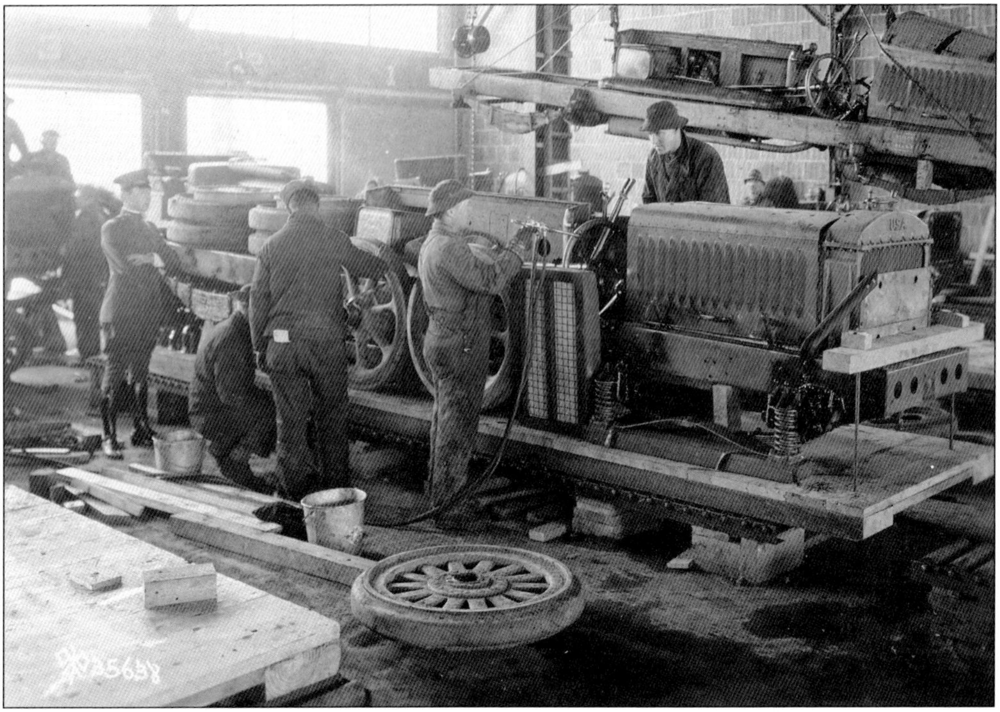

Holabird students are learning to crate a truck for shipment. The truck is partially disassembled in the process, and the pieces are carefully packed for safe shipment. The soldiers are learning under the watchful eye of an officer observing the scene. The intensity on the soldiers' faces indicates they took their work seriously. These students are crating what appears to be a Class B "Liberty Truck." (Courtesy NARA.)

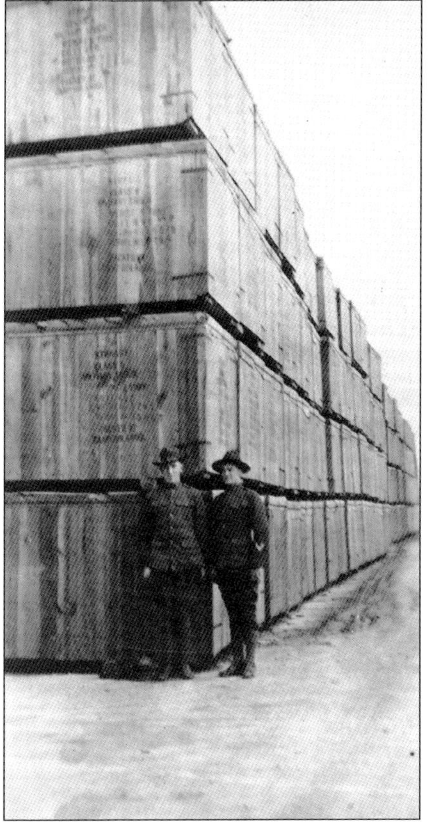

In this photograph, two soldiers stand by what might be the finished product of the truck crating class. The crates ready for shipment are stacked 20 feet by 20 feet by 65 feet and appear to be labeled "Storage Class B Military Truck." The two soldiers standing by the crates are unidentified, but one is a corporal and the other is a private. (Courtesy National WWI Museum and Memorial.)

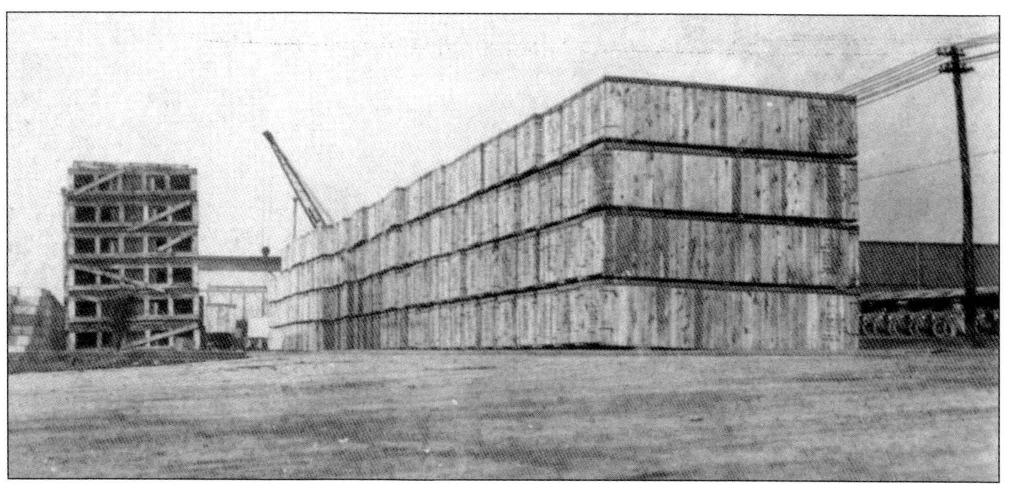

Here are still more crates, stacked four and six crates high. It is not possible to be sure what is in those crates, but most likely some of the Liberty Trucks from the crating class in the previous photograph are included in these outbound stacks. These crates would be shipped to units all over the country and perhaps overseas. (Courtesy NARA.)

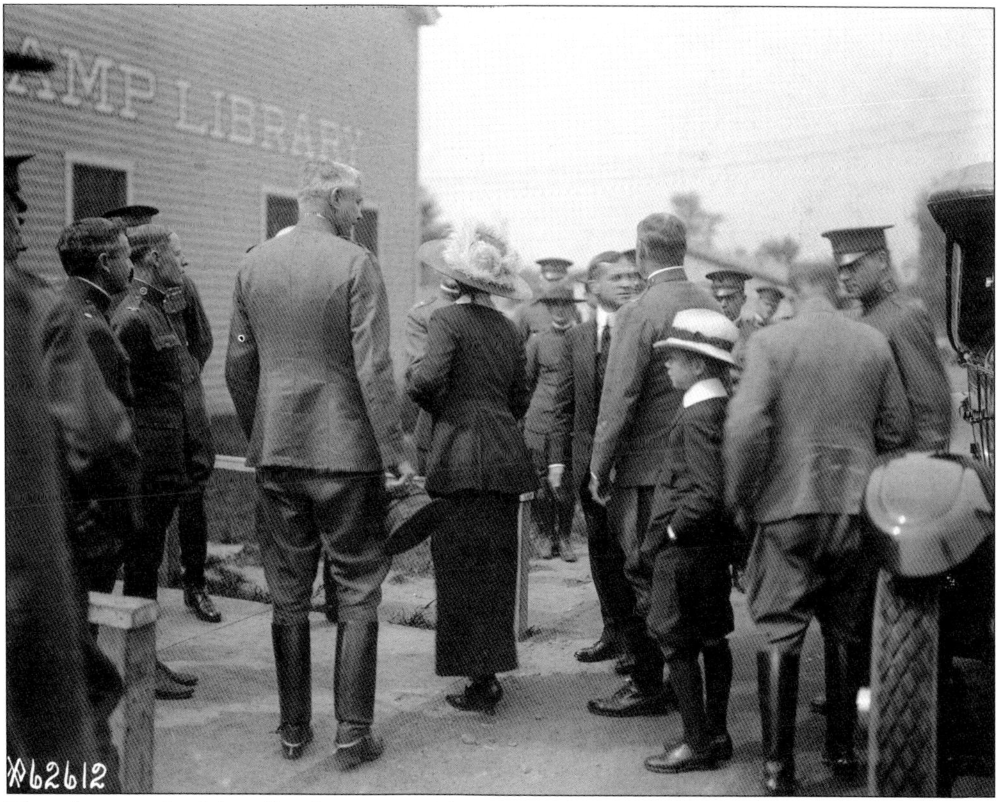

This photograph of the official opening of the Motor Transport Corps Training School was taken on September 5, 1919. In attendance were Secretary of War Newton D. Baker accompanied by his wife, Col. W.D. Chitty the commandant of Camp Holabird, and Brig. Gen. Charles Drake. During its existence from 1919 to 1926, the Motor Transport Corps Training School graduated 178 officers, 8 warrant officers, and 1,830 enlisted men. (Courtesy NARA.)

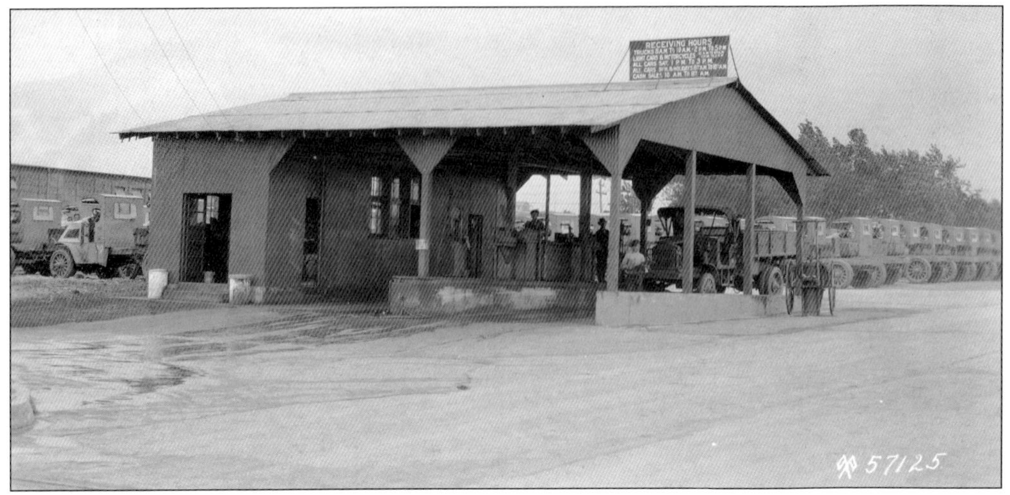

The Filling Station at Camp Holabird is seen here in 1919. As a motor transport post, the filing station must have been a busy place. The architecture is plain and rustic but efficient. One side is clearly marked "Out" to avoid traffic mishaps. The pumps appear to be very early manual pumps that the attendants would operate by hand. Evidence of the busy nature is the sign on the roof with rather complicated hours of operation. (Courtesy NARA.)

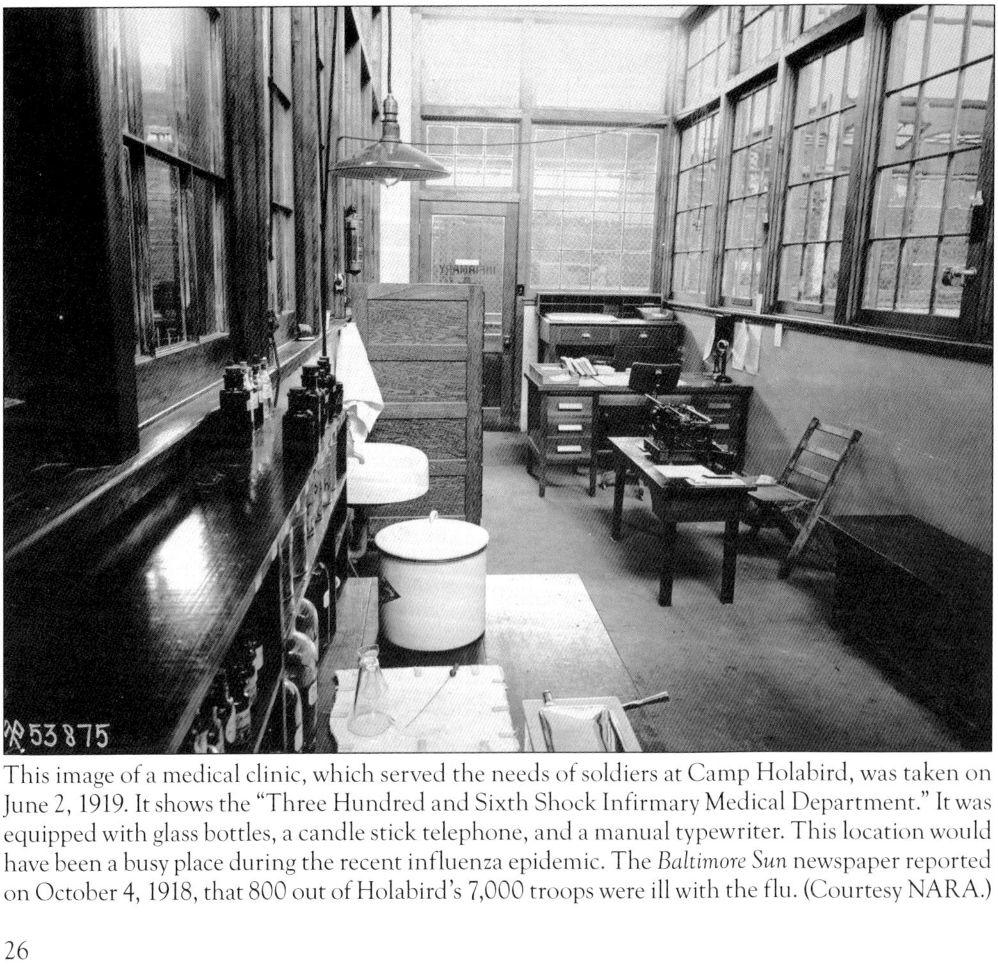

This image of a medical clinic, which served the needs of soldiers at Camp Holabird, was taken on June 2, 1919. It shows the "Three Hundred and Sixth Shock Infirmary Medical Department." It was equipped with glass bottles, a candle stick telephone, and a manual typewriter. This location would have been a busy place during the recent influenza epidemic. The *Baltimore Sun* newspaper reported on October 4, 1918, that 800 out of Holabird's 7,000 troops were ill with the flu. (Courtesy NARA.)

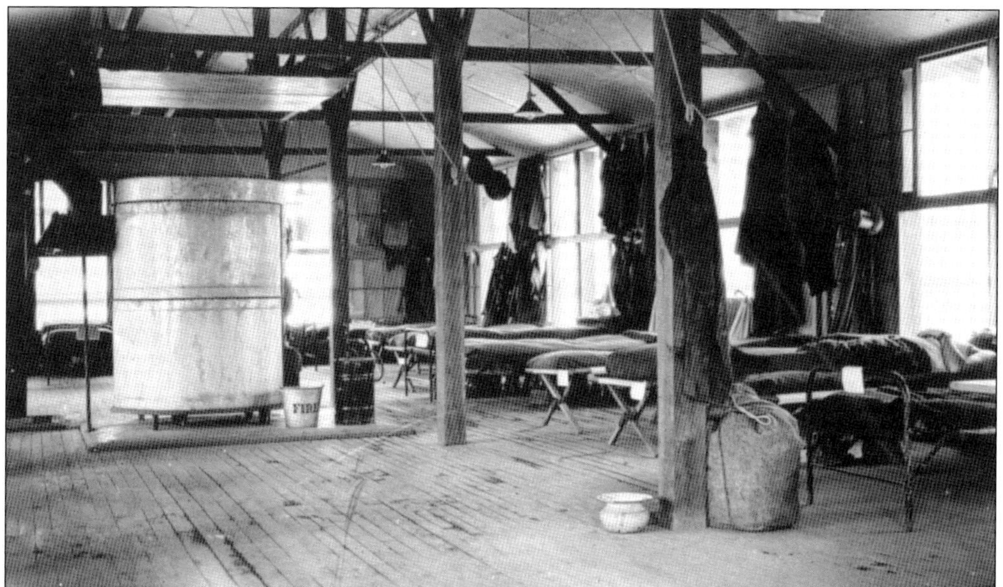

This World War I–era photograph shows the interior of a barracks. A large part of the floor space is occupied by a water heater. The soldiers' gear including hats, overcoats, and laundry bags are hung wherever there was space. In the foreground is a spittoon. One must pity the poor private whose job it was to clean the spittoon. (Courtesy National WWI Museum and Memorial.)

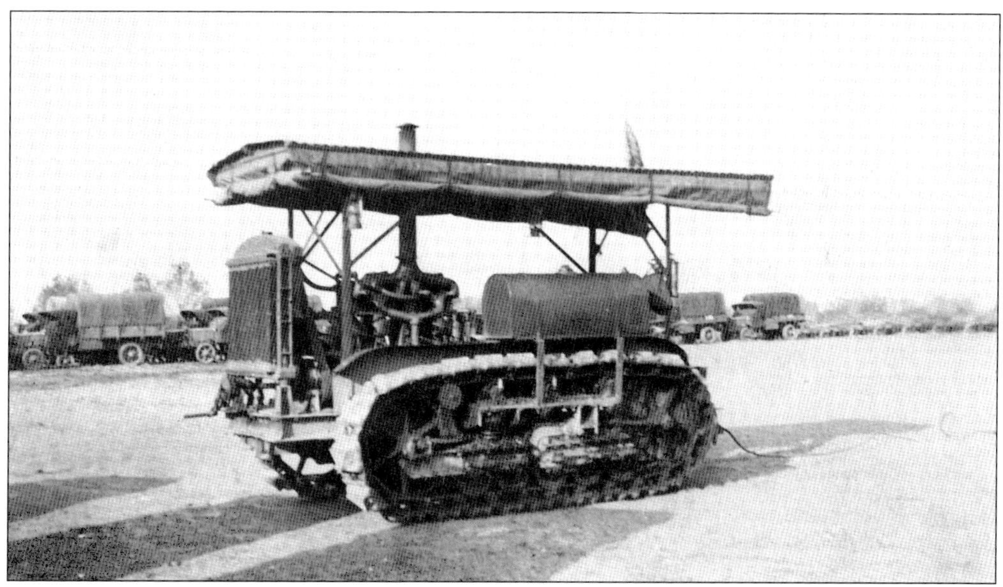

This photograph shows a World War I–era tractor. This powerful machine would be called upon for all kinds of duties in the United States and overseas. The drivers who operated the behemoth as well as the mechanics who maintained it were both trained at Camp Holabird Motor Transport School. (Courtesy National WWI Museum and Memorial.)

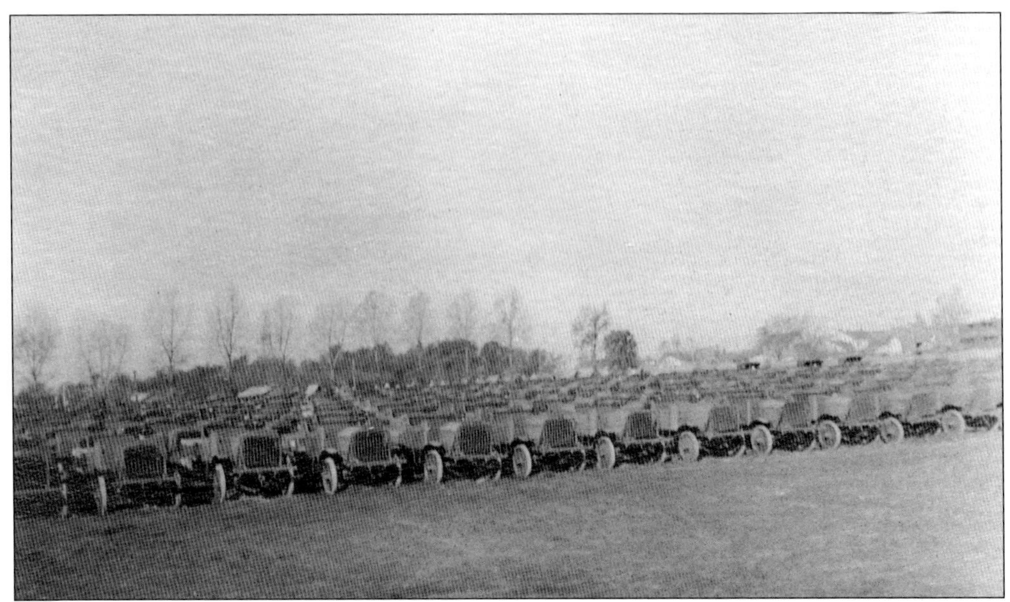

This World War I–era photograph is titled "Black and white photograph of hundreds of trucks to be shipped overseas (not yet crated) at Camp Holabird, Baltimore, Maryland." This indicates these vehicles are bound for the war in Europe. This field is full of row upon row of uncrated trucks. It is difficult to tell if they are Liberty Trucks or some other vehicle. (Courtesy National WWI Museum and Memorial.)

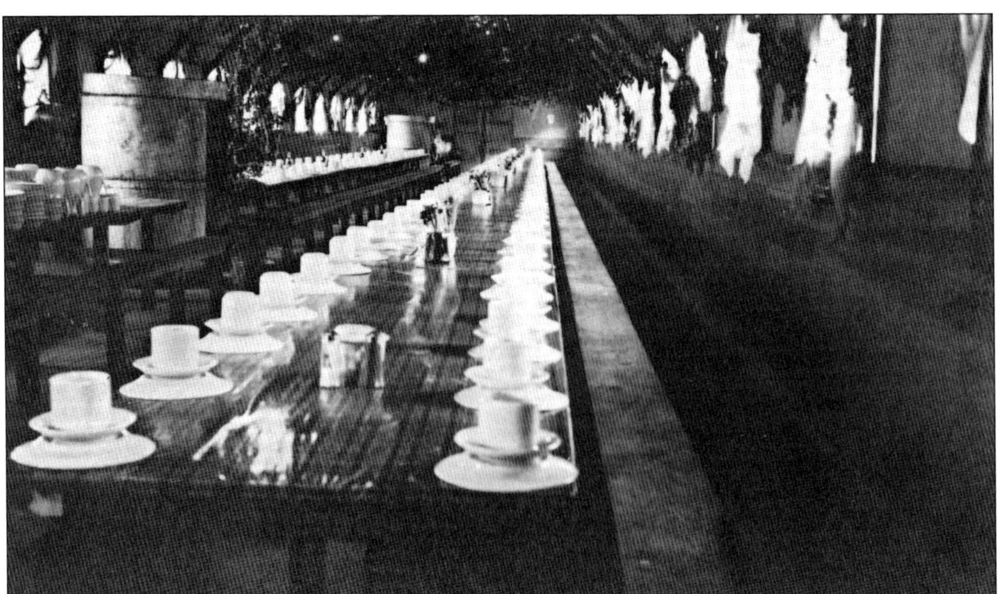

This World War I–era photograph shows the interior of a mess facility. It is clearly an officers' mess because the table is set with coffee cups, plates, and bowls. At this time at Camp Holabird, enlisted men and noncommissioned officers dined on M1910 mess kits. Rank has its privileges. (Courtesy National WWI Museum and Memorial.)

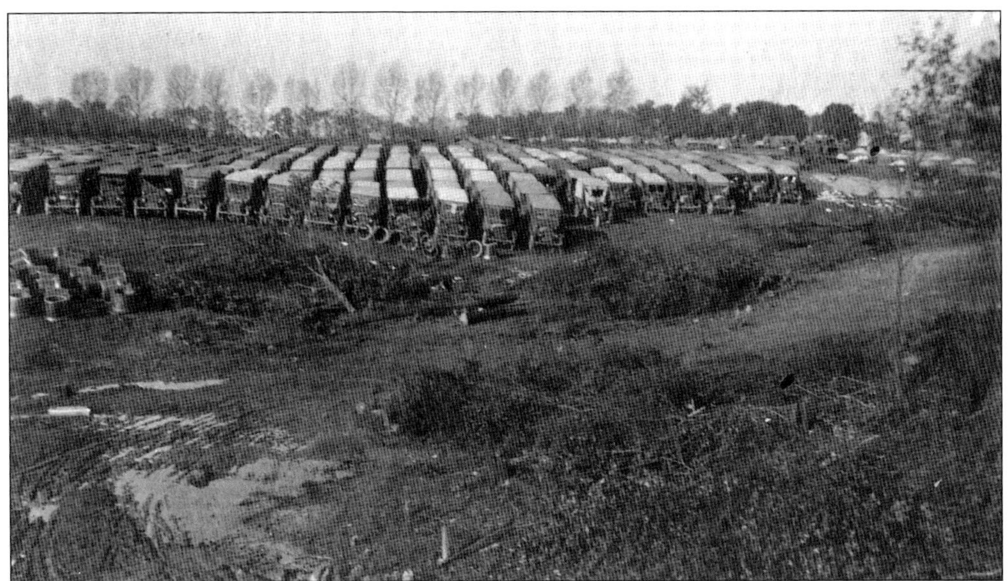

In this World War I–era image, more trucks are lined up in a field prepared "to be shipped overseas (not yet crated)." It is difficult to determine what kind of vehicles these are, but there is no question about where they are going. These trucks will see action in the war in Europe. (Courtesy National WWI Museum and Memorial.)

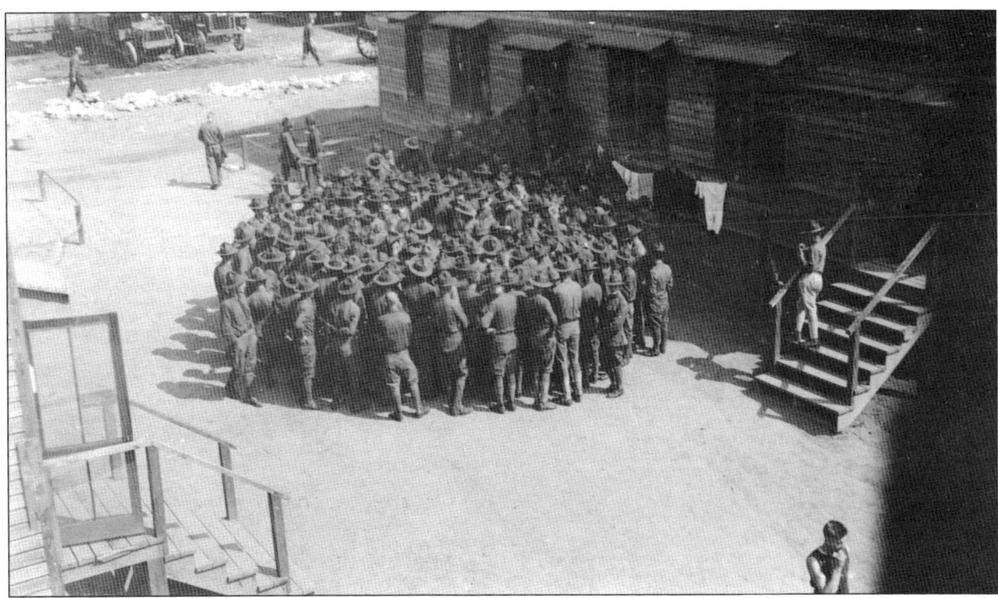

In this World War I–era photograph, there is what is described as a "large crowd of soldiers gathered in a circle." The event here is mail call, where soldiers hoped for letters from loved ones back home. With the exception of mess calls, it was probably the soldier's favorite time of day. (Courtesy National WWI Museum and Memorial.)

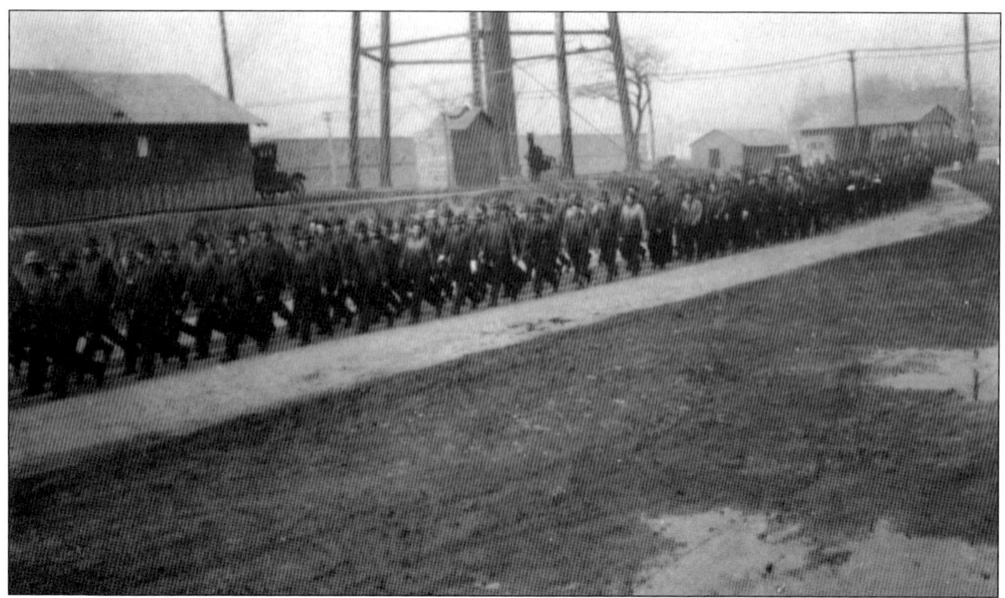

In this World War I–era image, a long line of soldiers are marching. With their mess kits in hand, it is clear that they are marching to or from the mess hall. Their work uniforms indicate that they are student mechanics. Many of them would soon be called upon to maintain vehicles overseas. (Courtesy National WWI Museum and Memorial.)

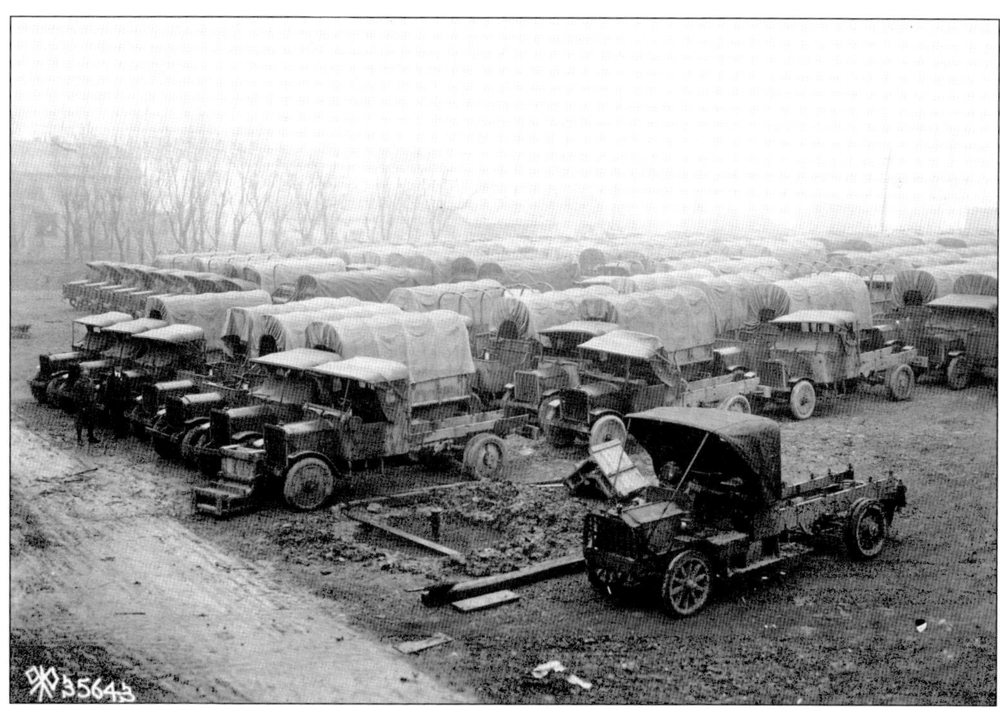

This World War I–era photograph was titled as trucks to be shipped. Given their appearance, it appears they have seen better days. Perhaps this is a scrap yard, and they are being shipped off as scrap. There are two men in the image, one is in a military uniform and the other is in a suit. The man in the suit may be a civilian bidder. (Courtesy NARA.)

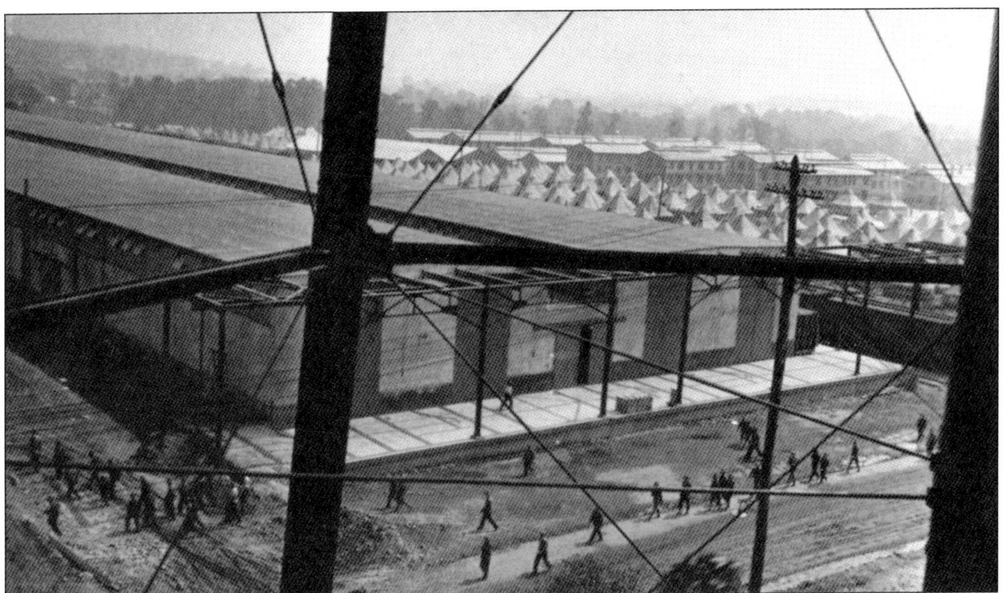

This is an image from the early days of Camp Holabird. It is titled "View of bivouac and storage building from above." The photograph appears to have been shot from the water tower. The image shows both spike tents, and in the background are wooden barracks. Holabird was in transition from tent to barracks accommodations. (Courtesy National WWI Museum and Memorial.)

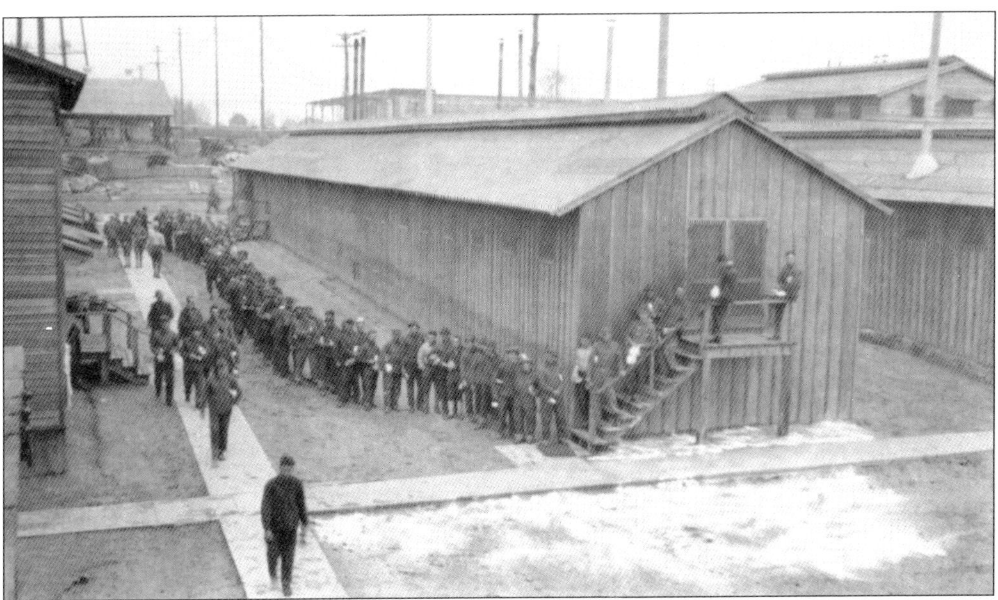

This World War I–era image is titled "Exterior view of a mess hall at Camp Holabird, Baltimore, Maryland. Line for mess extends around outside of building." It is similar architecture to the previous mess hall photograph. A key difference is this mess hall has an entrance on the end, not the side. (Courtesy National WWI Museum and Memorial.)

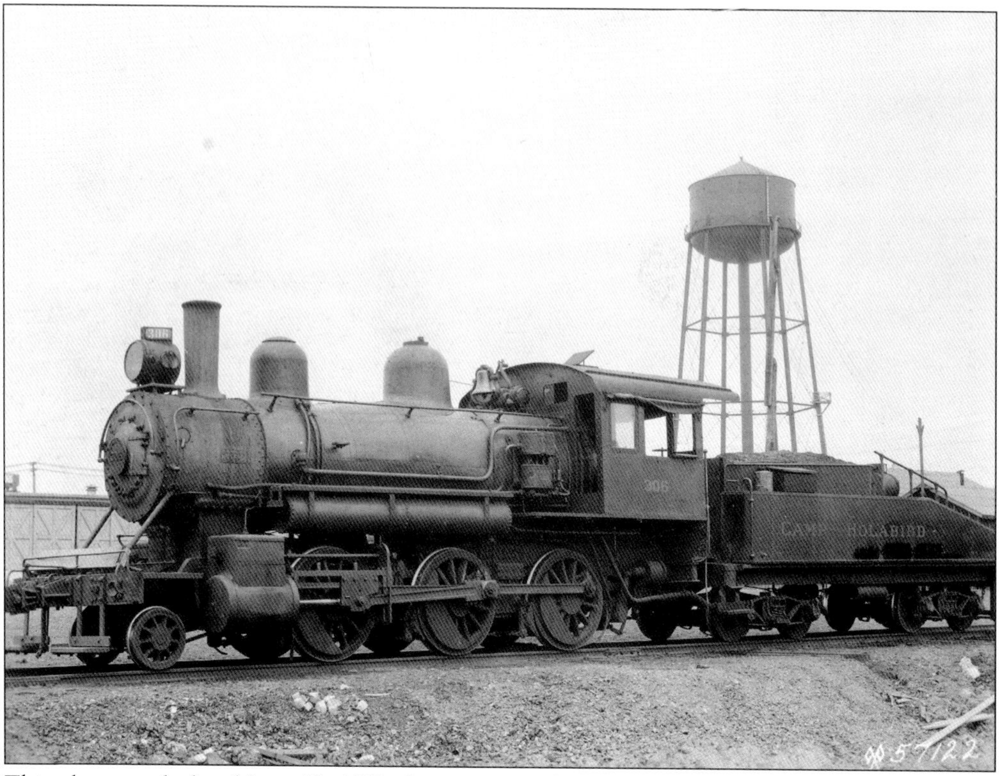

This photograph dated June 18, 1919, shows a steam locomotive. It is marked "Camp Holabird" and belongs to the Departments of Mechanical Repair Shop No. 306 and Yards at Camp Holabird. It is a yard service engine meaning it operated on Camp Holabird and did not belong to a civilian railroad. (Courtesy National WWI Museum and Memorial.)

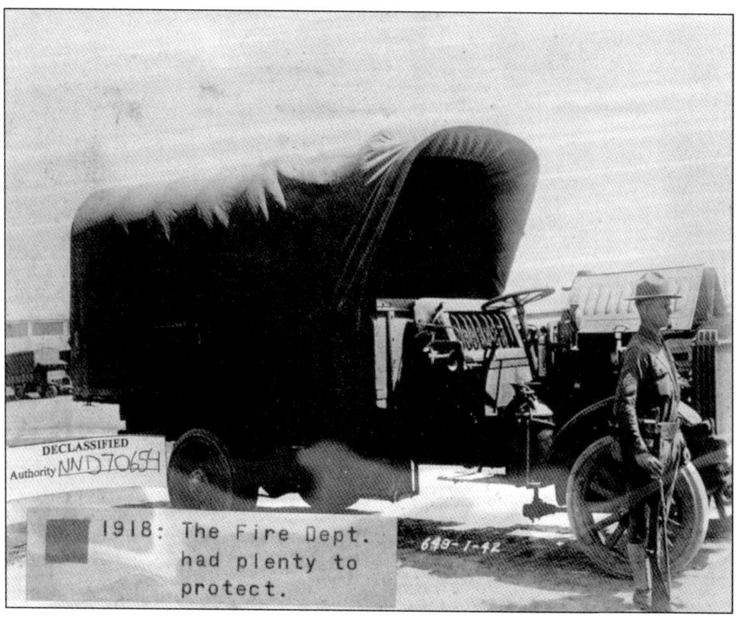

This 1918 image depicts a military truck, most likely a Liberty Truck. The canvas cargo cover resembles a Conestoga Wagon illustrating Holabird's unique position between the horse-drawn army and the motor-vehicle army. This sergeant stands at attention with his Springfield Rifle. Perhaps it was a vehicle inspection day. (Courtesy NARA.)

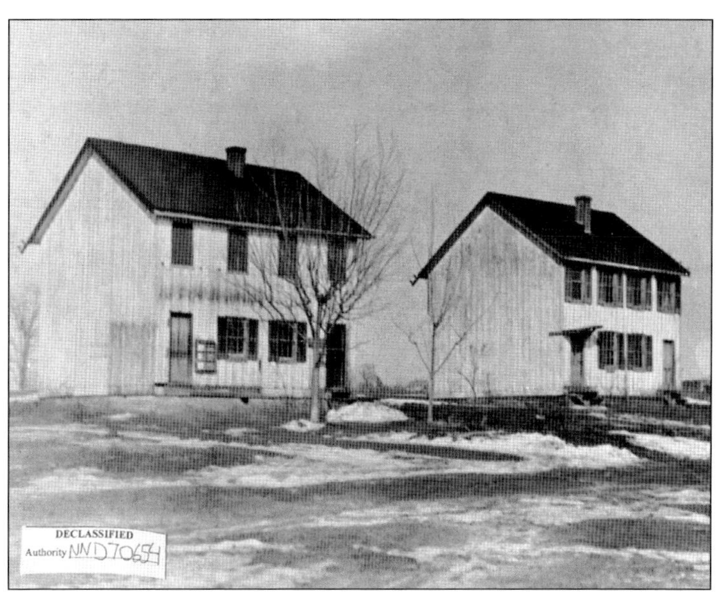

This image is believed to be from 1918. The image depicts two wooden-frame houses. They are duplex houses, which would indicate they were family housing for either noncommissioned officers or lower-ranking commissioned officers. In this era, every structure at Camp Holabird was made of wood or canvas. Steel and masonry buildings would come later. (Courtesy NARA.)

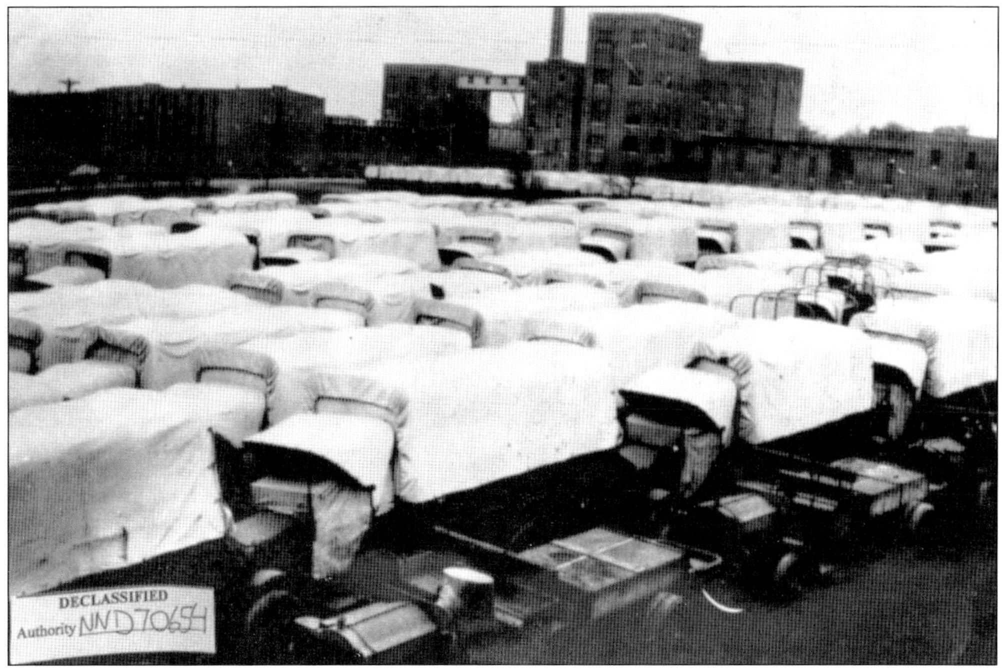

This 1918 photograph shows row upon row of trucks prepared to ship out to parts unknown. These appear to be Liberty Trucks with canvas cargo covers. Looking closely, the driver's seats are packed with goods. No space went wasted when military goods had to be shipped out to waiting Army units. (Courtesy NARA.)

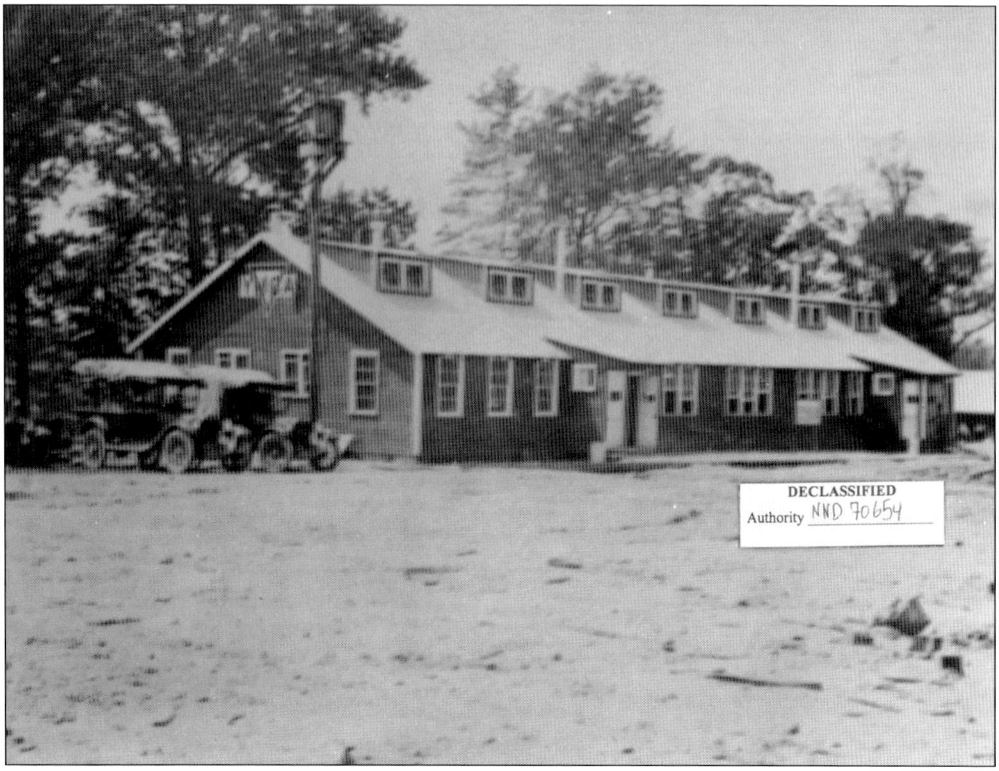

This 1918 photograph shows the Camp Holabird YMCA. It was a popular place for recreation for off-duty soldiers. The YMCA's mission was to make soldiers feel at home while away from home, many for the first time. The YMCA had games and dances. It was also a popular place to write letters home. (Courtesy NARA.)

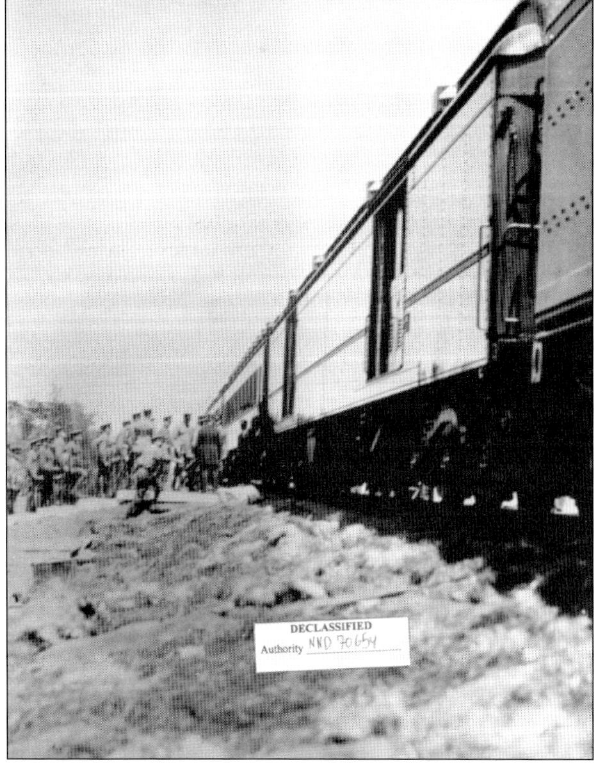

This 1918 photograph depicts several soldiers boarding a train passenger car. Camp Holabird was largely a training post for drivers and mechanics. Once trained, they were shipped out to units where they would apply their new skills. Camp Holabird was intersected by the Baltimore & Ohio Railroad (B&O) lines, which made shipping troops in and out easy. (Courtesy NARA.)

Two

World War II

World War II was highly mechanized, and Holabird was called upon again to test and ship vehicles and train both drivers and mechanics. Before the war was over, drivers and mechanics from Holabird had served in every theater of the war.

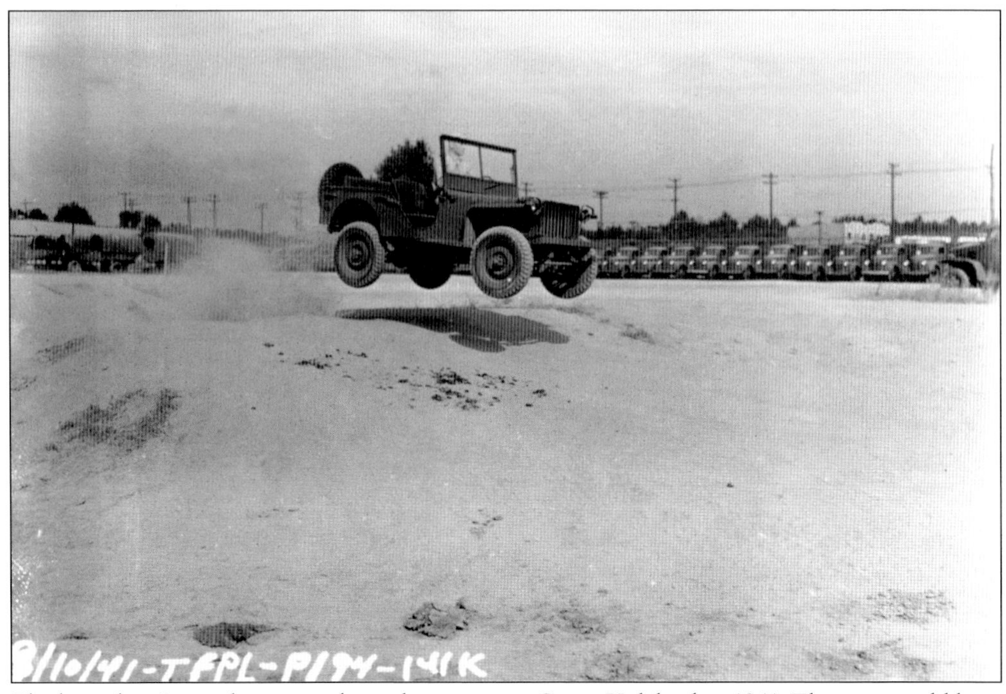

The legendary Jeep is being put through its paces at Camp Holabird in 1941. The jeep would have its mettle tested when the United States joined World War II, and it had to be a proven commodity. Holabird was a testing ground for various prototypes that became the Jeep. Perhaps this driver should have joined the Air Corps. (Courtesy NARA.)

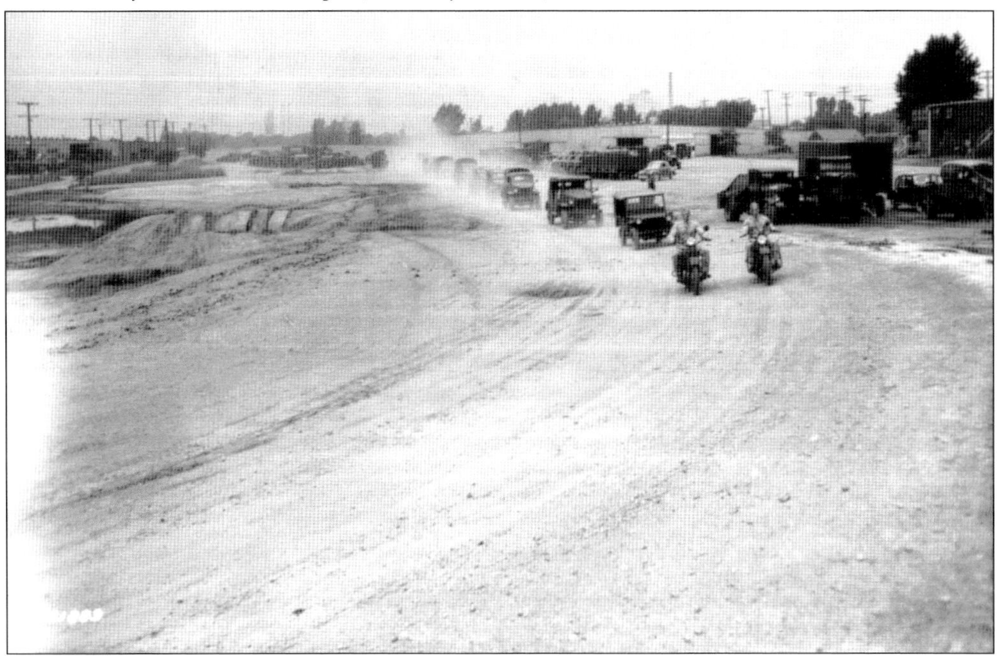

This photograph dated July 16, 1941, shows two motorcycles leading a procession of Holabird's vehicles including a jeep and trucks. In about five months, on a Sunday afternoon, the units at Camp Holabird would go on alert because a Navy base in Hawaii was under attack. (Courtesy NARA.)

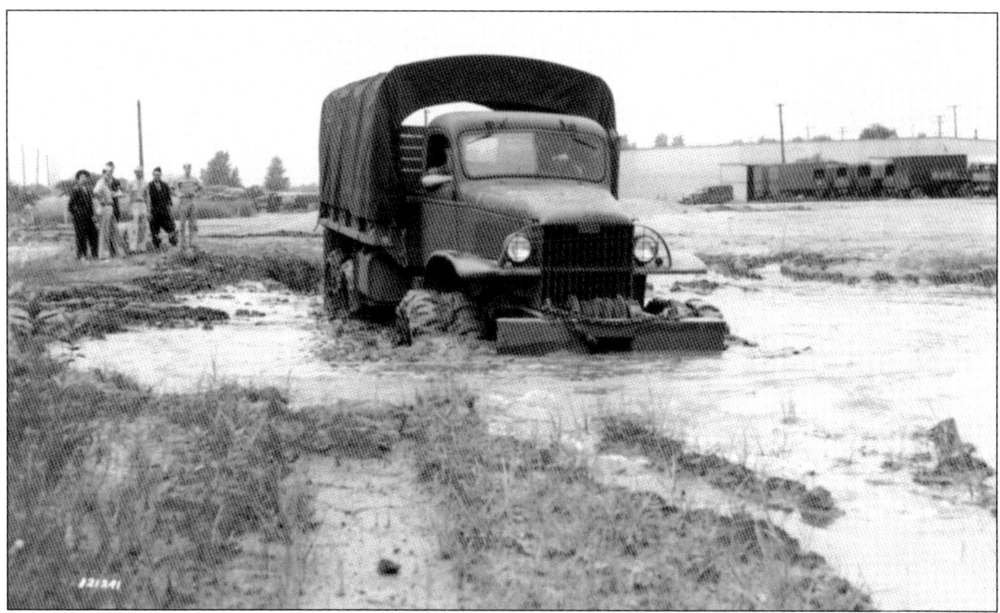

A "Deuce and a Half" truck wades into the water and mud for the water course at Holabird's Motor Transport School. The truck has tire chains attached, and it may well need them before this exercise is over. Several staff members are observing. This photograph was taken on July 16, 1941. In a few months, this truck and driver would be called upon to serve in far-flung places like North Africa or the South Pacific. (Courtesy NARA.)

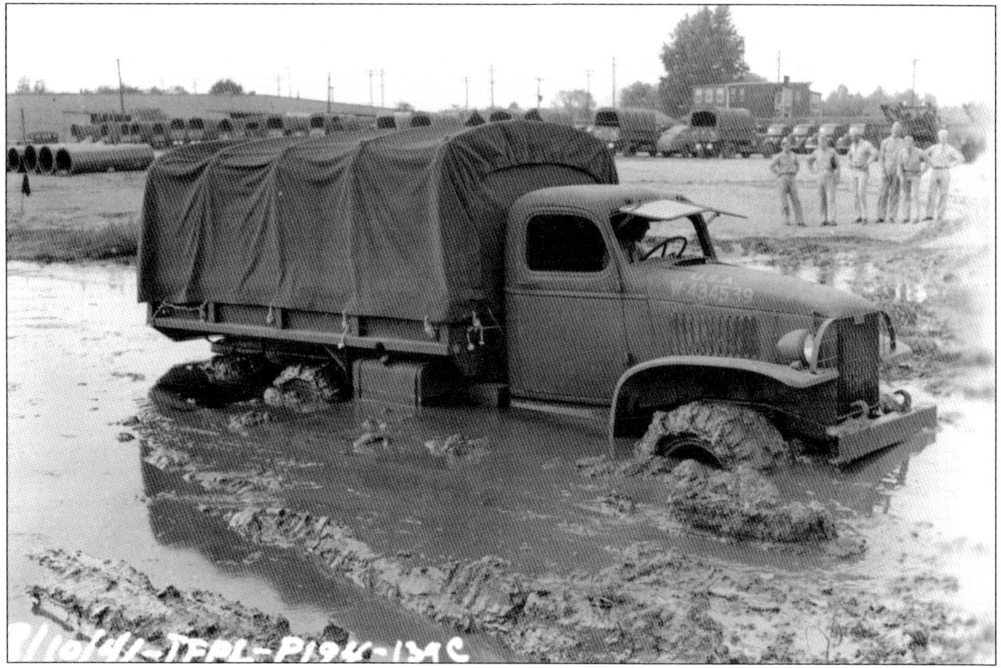

This August 10, 1941, photograph depicts a six-wheeled 2.5-ton truck at the water course. Six staff members observe its progress as it plows forward, axle-deep, through the Maryland mud. Dressed in khakis, they will not be much help if the six-drive wheels with tire chains attached are not up to the task. (Courtesy NARA.)

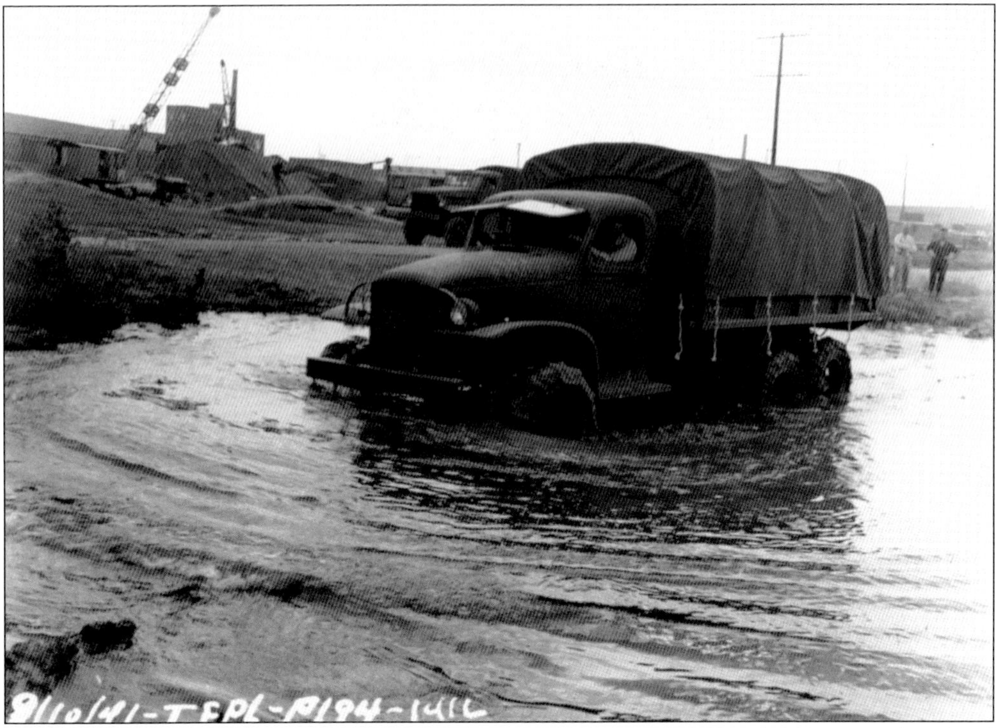

Appearing more boat than truck, this "Deuce" traverses the water course. This photograph is dated August 10, 1941. In a few months, both driver and truck would be in the Army of a nation at war. An infantry captain might be waiting for a truckload of ammo, rations, or medical supplies, and a puddle or creek could not be allowed to stand in the way. (Courtesy NARA.)

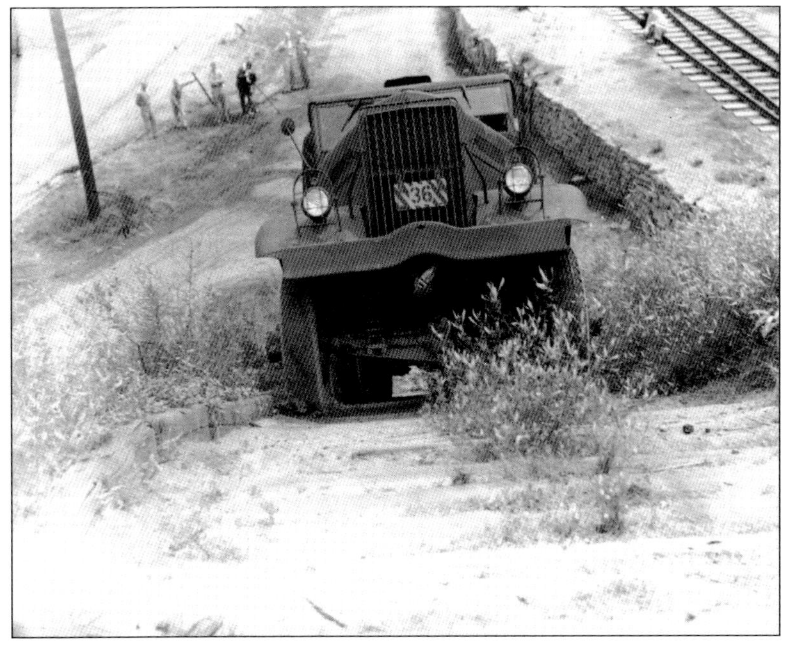

A Deuce and a Half ascends a steep rugged obstacle. These trucks were put through their paces at Holabird to be sure they were fit for combat duty. The "Deuce" saw action in every theatre of the war and was the mainstay of cargo units like the famed Red Ball Express. (Courtesy NARA.)

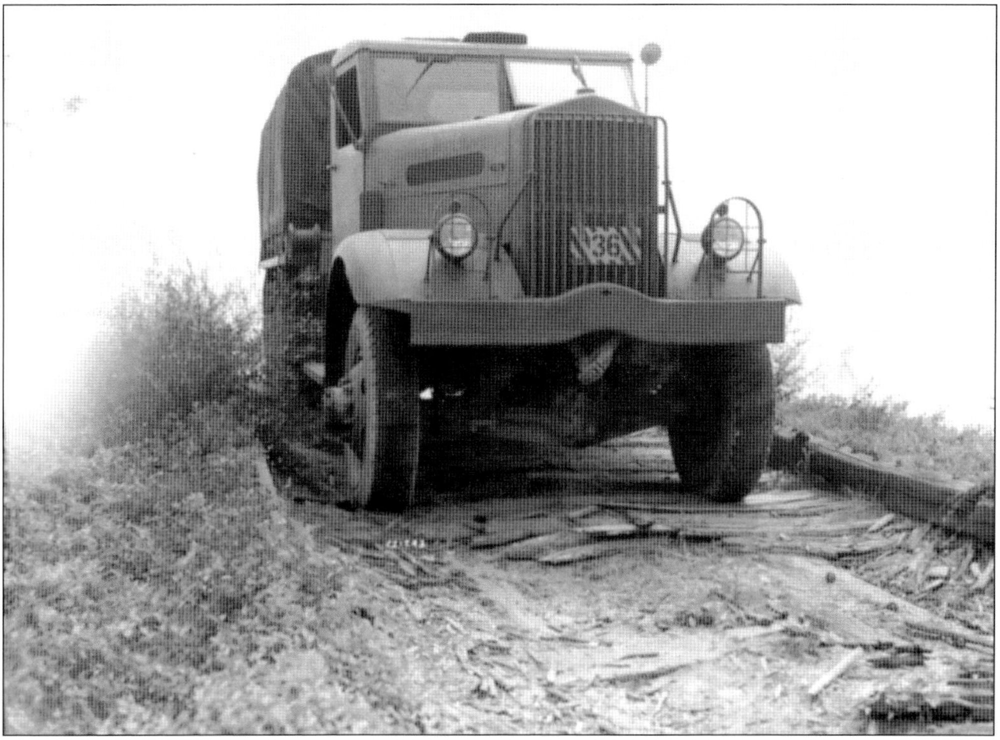

What goes up must come down. This "Deuce" is shown descending an obstacle at Holabird. This angle shows the front-drive axle that made this beast a 6x6. Before the war was over, she would be called upon to deliver vital cargo in all weather and road conditions. (Courtesy NARA.)

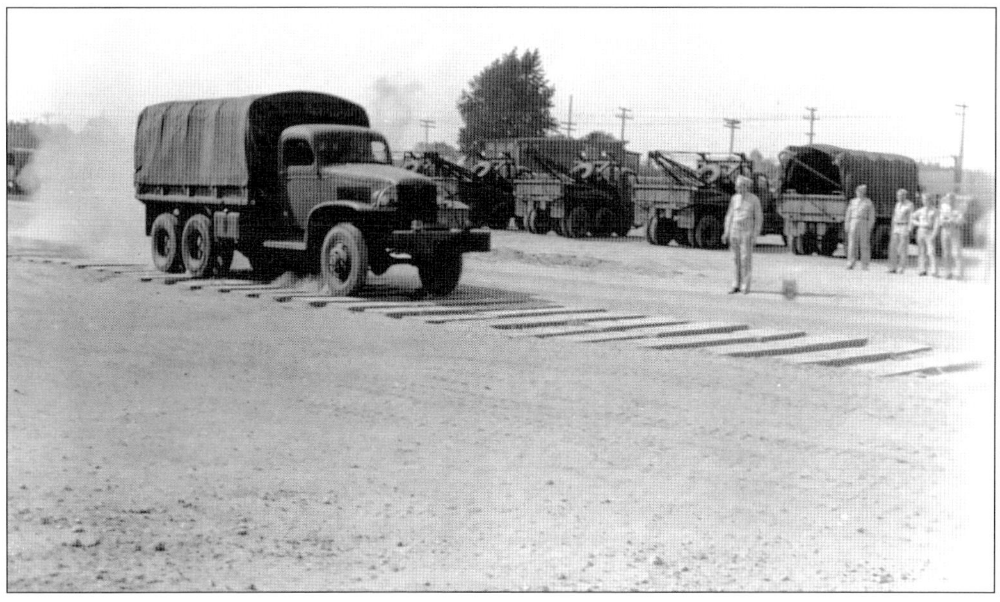

This rugged track tests both driver and vehicle. These test tracks at Holabird simulated conditions that the driver and vehicle might encounter in wartime, and here at Holabird, they tested their mettle and proved their merit. The wreckers standing by might indicate that some vehicles did not return under their own power. (Courtesy NARA.)

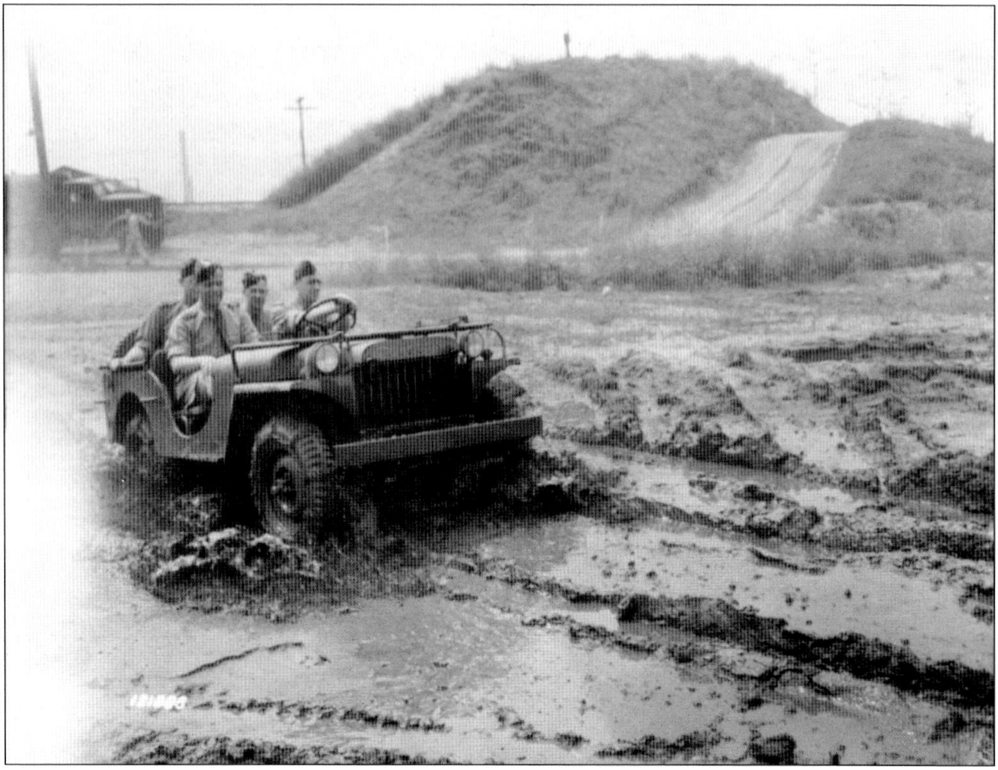

This July 16, 1941, photograph shows the legendary Jeep, being put "through its paces" at Camp Holabird. The photograph depicts four officers, all members of the Royal Canadian Ordinance Corps. They are, from left to right, Lt. R.H. Hodgson, Lt. H.V. Flett (front seat), Lt. R.H. Painter, and Lt. R.G. Farrell (rear seat). The officers are students at the US Army Motor Transport School. Many foreign troops were trained at Camp Holabird. This was because many of the vehicles their home countries used, through the Lend-Lease and other programs, were trained at Holabird. The vehicle appears to be the 1941 Willys MA. (Both, courtesy NARA.)

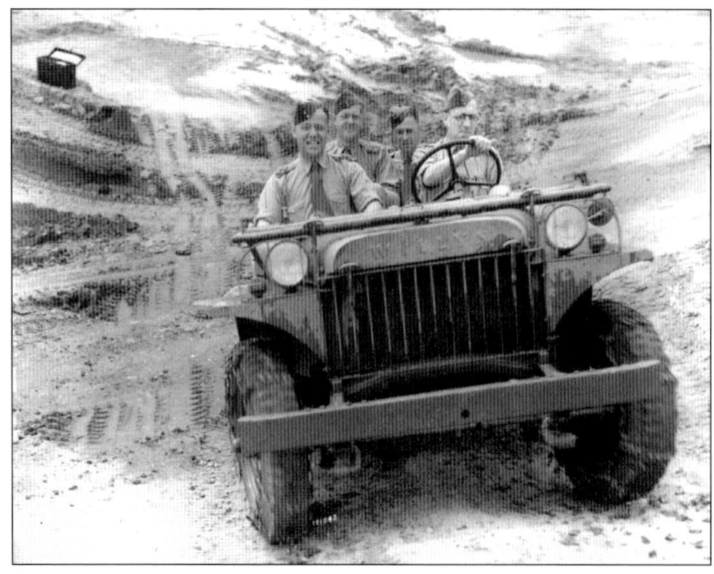

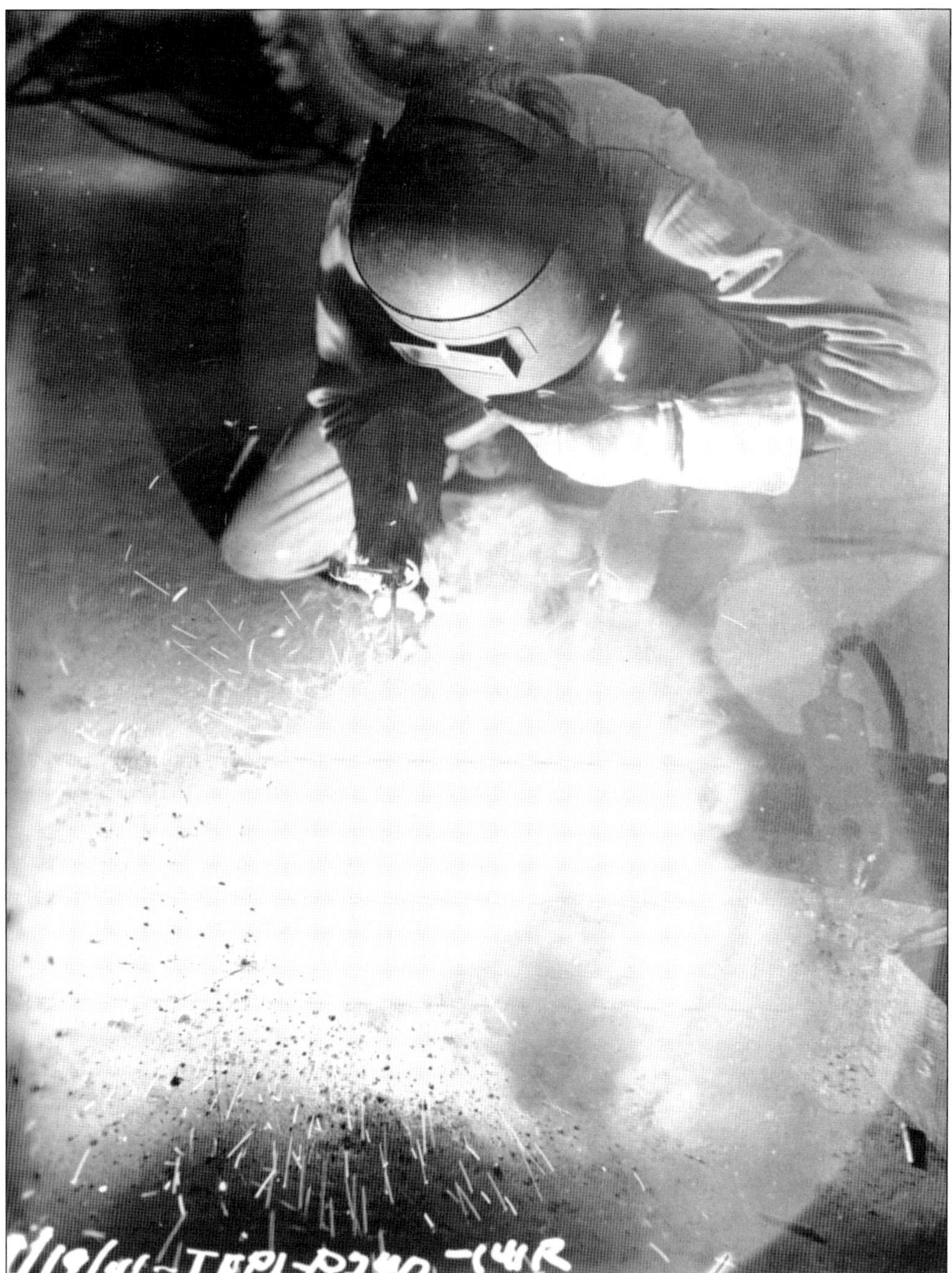

In this 1941 photograph, a welder is hard at work. The project is not clear, but he is well-equipped for the job with a helmet and protective gloves. With all the vehicles and trailers in daily use at Holabird, something was bound to break, and there was ample opportunity for a welder to put his skills to use. (Courtesy NARA.)

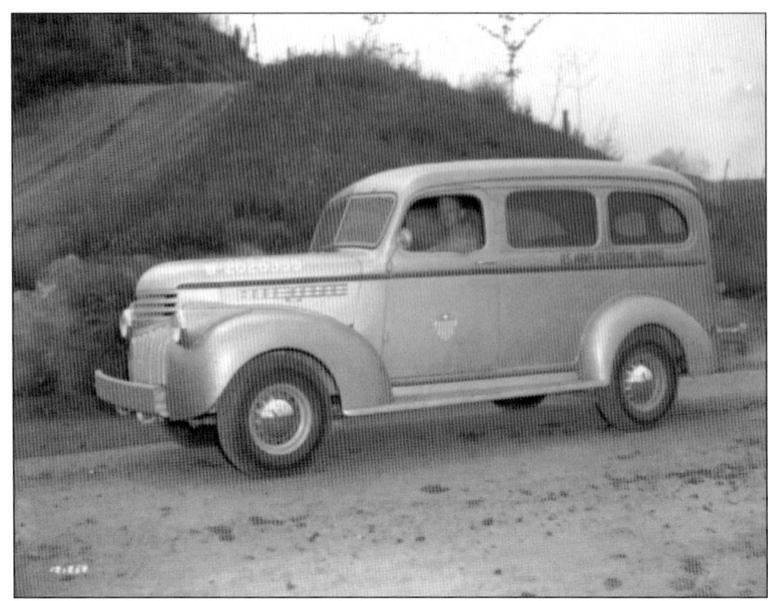

Not every vehicle at Holabird was destined for the front line. This humble sedan appears to be a Chevrolet. It had a vital role as part of the US Army Recruiting Service. The soldier who drove it and the mechanics who maintained it were both very likely trained at Holabird. (Courtesy NARA.)

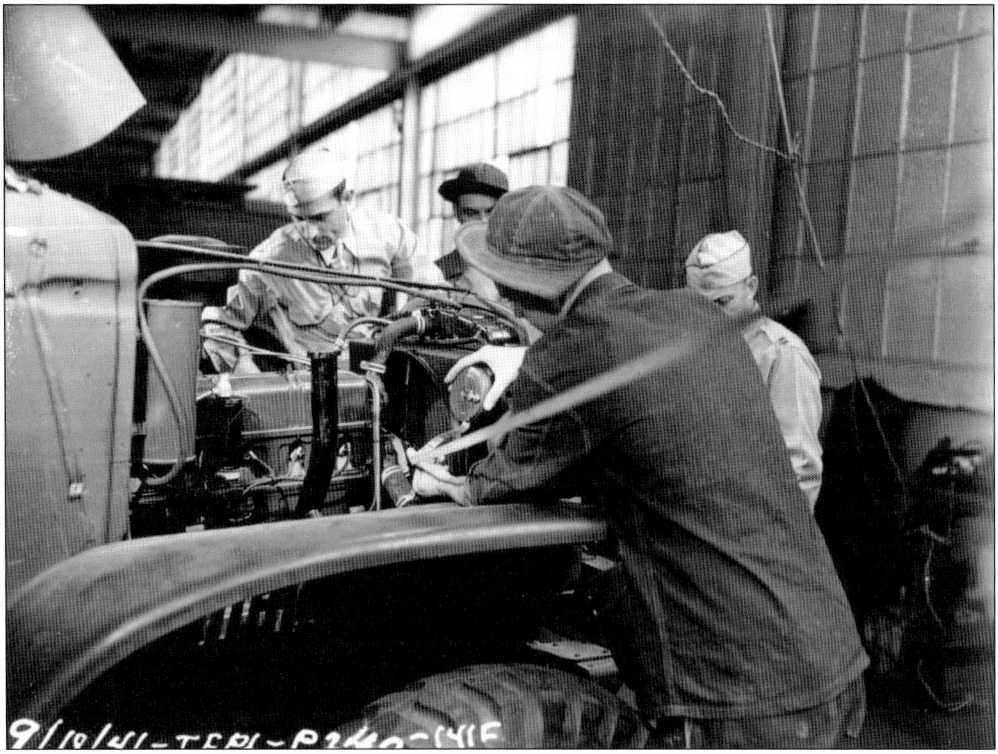

This 1941 photograph depicts a team working under the hood of a truck. One is a captain; the others appear to be enlisted men. Two are wearing mechanics' garb and may be students at US Army Motor Transport School. The enlisted man with his back to the camera appears to be using a tape measure. One of the men in khakis has something around his neck and tucked in his pocket, perhaps a whistle. A wise decision with all the moving parts under that hood. (Courtesy NARA.)

Mechanic working outdoors on a precursor to the jeep, the Bantam BRC-40. His trusty toolbox is nearby. This photograph was taken in 1941. The Bantam and the jeep were tested at Holabird, and they were new entries to the Army's vehicle inventory. This mechanic is deploying new skills on a state-of-the-art piece of equipment. (Courtesy NARA.)

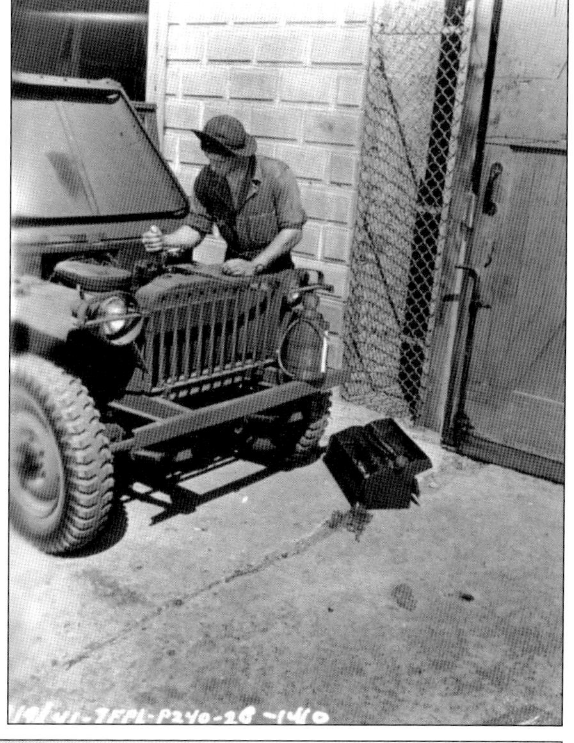

This September 10, 1941, photograph provides a nice view of the Bantam BRC-40, a precursor to the noble military jeep. The driver looks like he may be having trouble. A headlight is missing, so this Bantam may be in for repairs. Two motorcycles are visible in the background. (Courtesy NARA.)

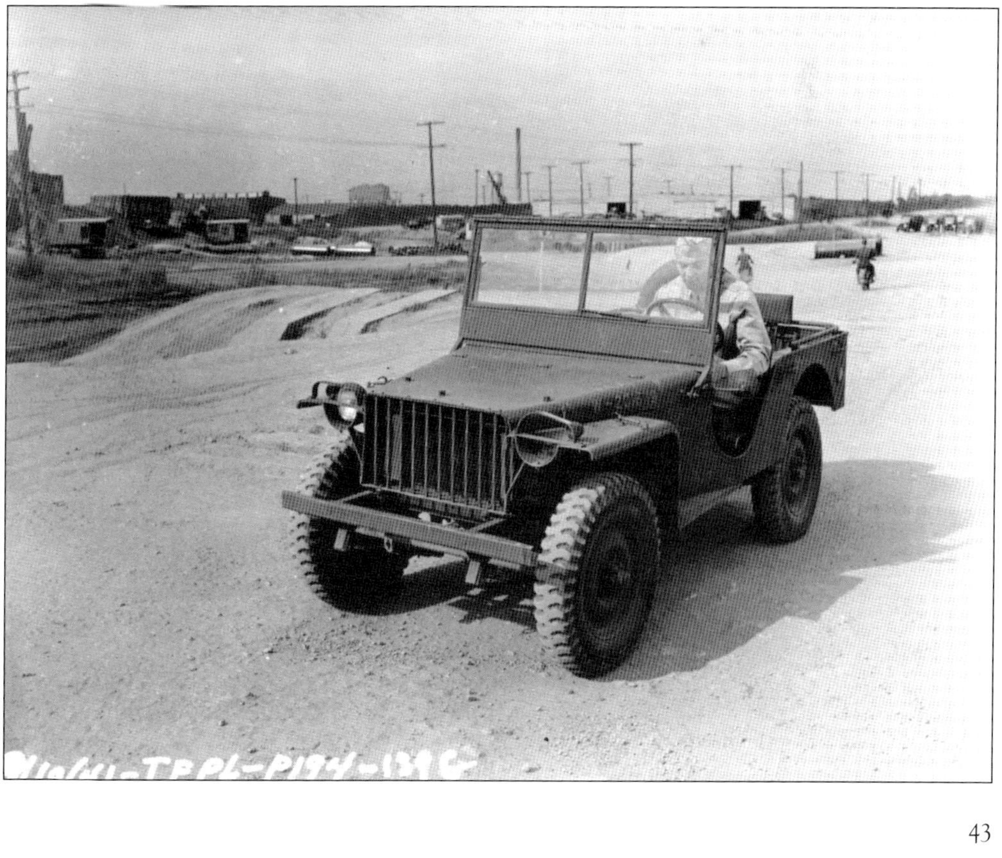

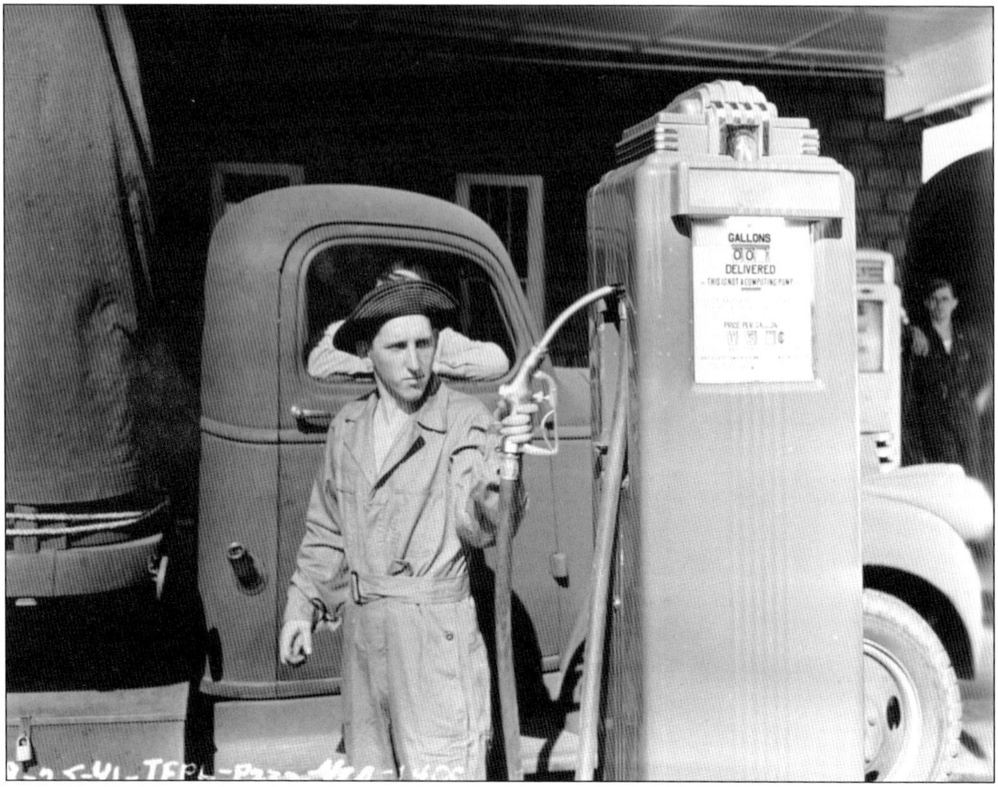

Just like in World War I, the filing station at Holabird during World War II must have been a busy place. Holabird was a vehicle training post, and World War II was a highly mechanized conflict. The 1919 filing station was made largely of wood and sheet metal, while the 1941 filing station was made of masonry. It seems the Army recognized the motor vehicle was a proven commodity in combat and was here to stay. (Courtesy NARA.)

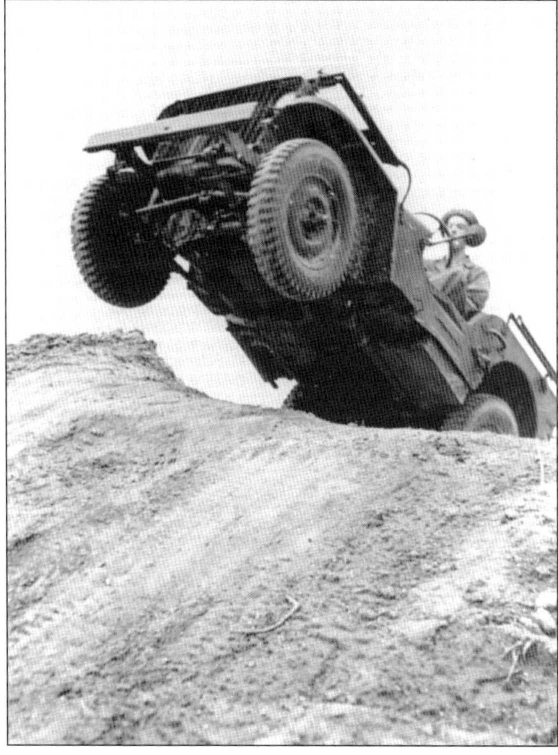

This World War II–era photograph shows a jeep being tested. The jeep appears to be a Willys MB model. This model jeep saw action all over the world during the war. This angle provides a good view of the front wheel drive assembly that made the jeep a 4x4 and a formidable wartime machine. (Courtesy Dundalk-Patapsco Neck Historical Society & Museum.)

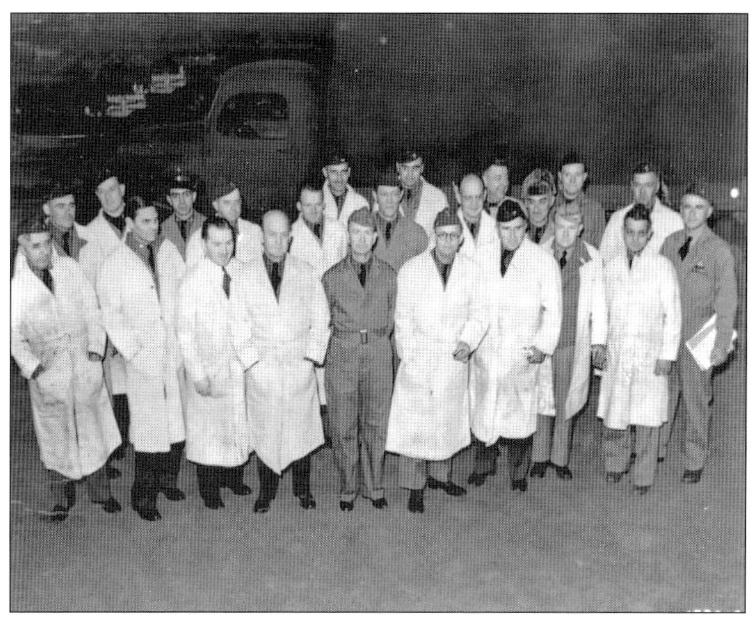

Looking like an assemblage of doctors in their lab coats, this 1942 photograph shows general and field grade officers in the "Course C Preventative Maintenance" at the Holabird Quartermaster Depot. The purpose of the course was to give commanders first-hand training on driving convoys and how to handle minor breakdowns. (Courtesy NARA.)

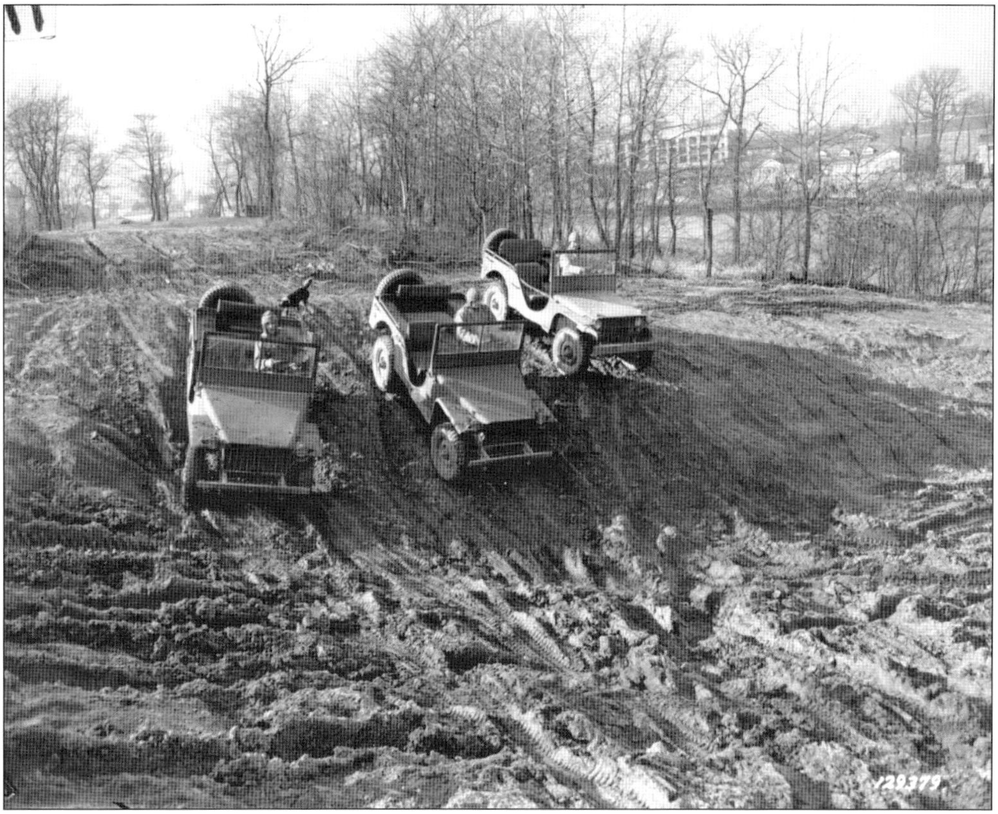

Pictured on February 25, 1942, three brigadier generals drive jeeps while participating in the two-week Course C Preventive Maintenance. The existence of this course for general grade officers illustrates the importance that the motor vehicle had taken in modern warfare. The generals are left to right Vernon E. Prichard, T.E. Marchant, and Joseph C. Hutchinson. (Courtesy NARA.)

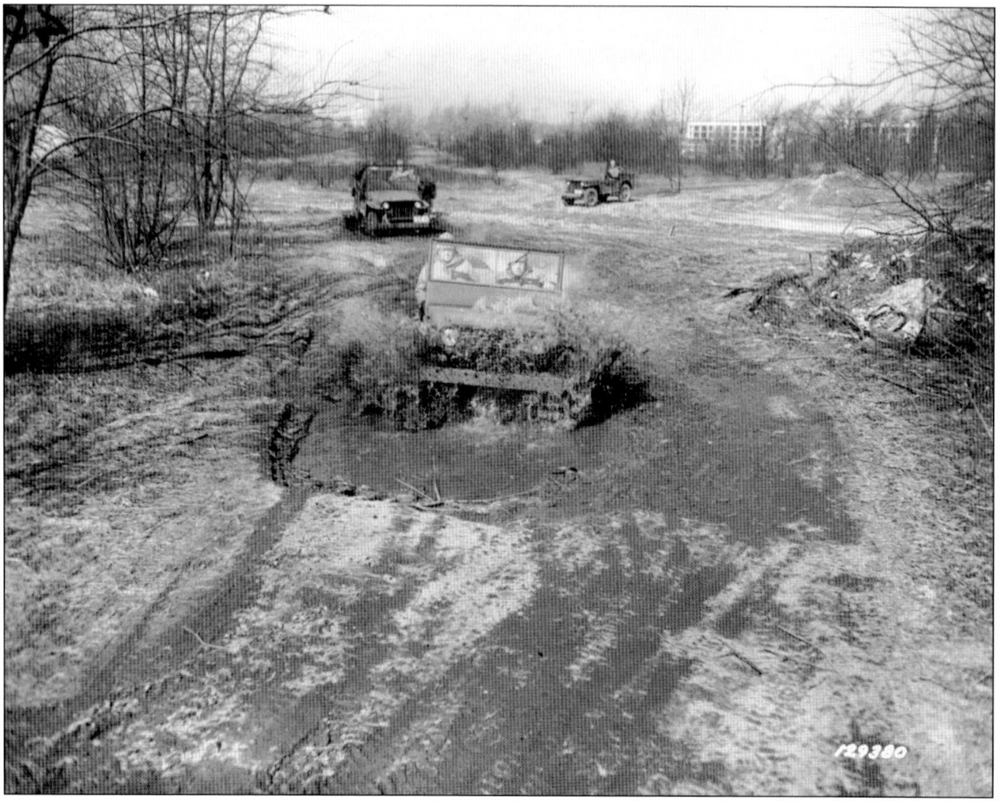

A jeep makes a splash at Camp Holabird. This February 25, 1942, photograph shows what might be a Willys Slat Grill jeep on a test course at the Holabird's Motor Transport School. It might look like fun, but it was serious business, as the United States had entered World War II just two months past. (Courtesy NARA.)

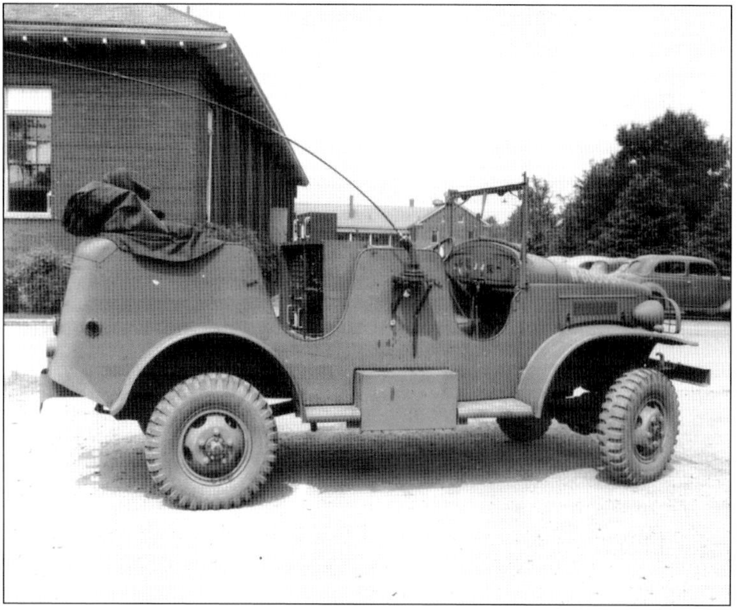

In this World War II–era photograph, what appears to be a Dodge W-6 reconnaissance car is shown. This vehicle may have been the precursor to the Dodge W-56 and was being tested at Holabird. The W-56 came in different models with different adaptations, including the command and the reconnaissance car. (Courtesy NARA.)

This May 19, 1941, photograph depicts Cpl. Arlie Gilbert of Chester, Pennsylvania. Corporal Gilbert was serving as a Holabird Quartermaster Depot garage dispatcher. He had been in the Army for eight months and was a corporal. Corporal Gilbert would later serve in the European Theater as part of the 3510th Quartermaster Truck Company under General Patton. (Courtesy NARA.)

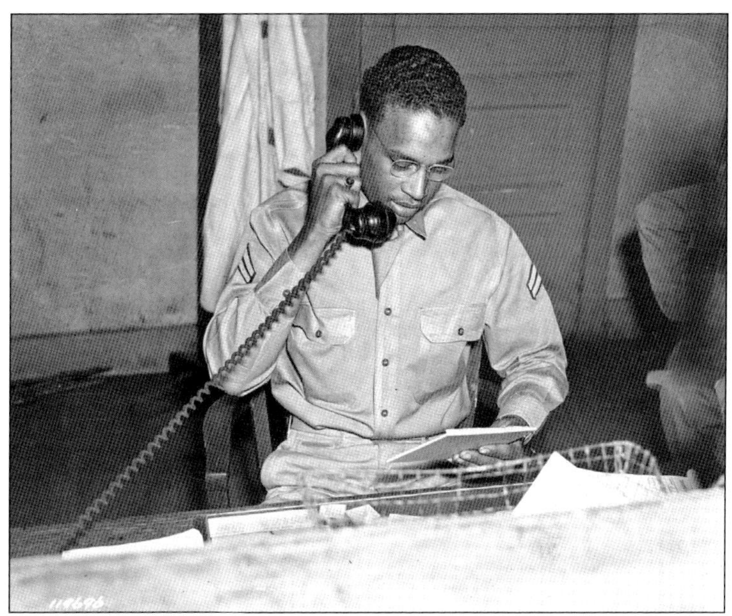

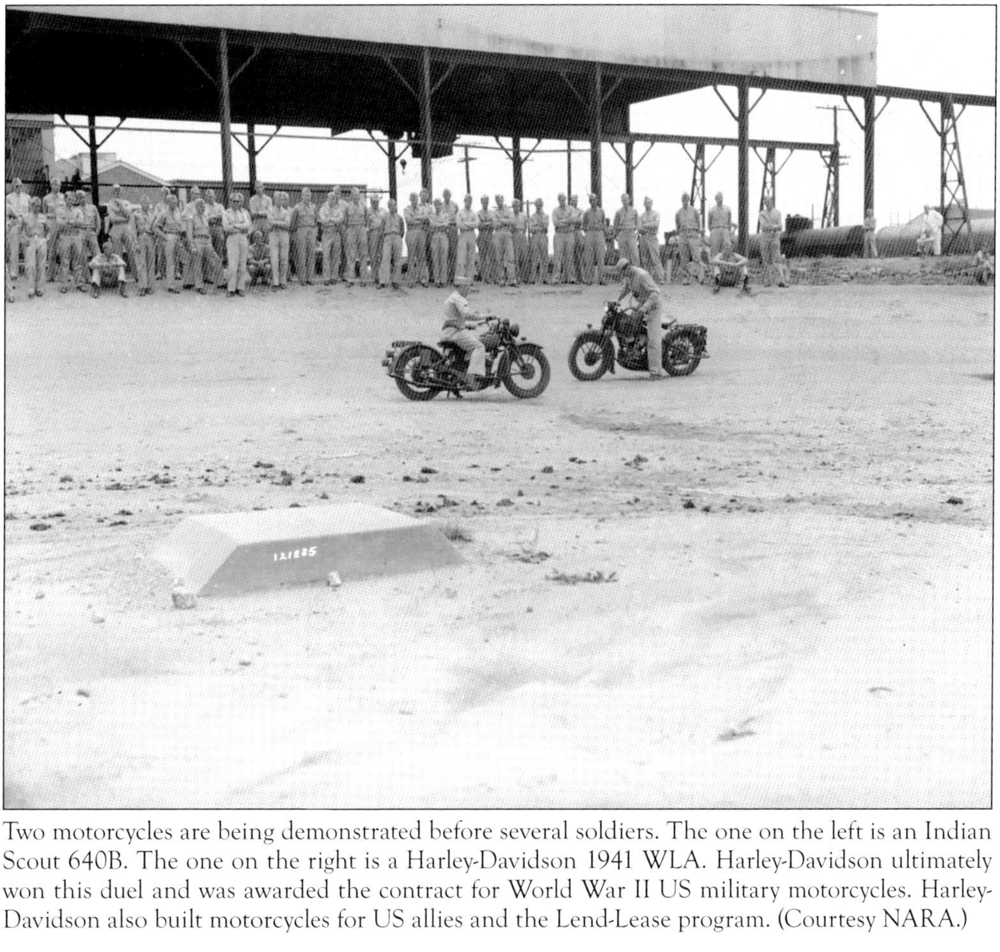

Two motorcycles are being demonstrated before several soldiers. The one on the left is an Indian Scout 640B. The one on the right is a Harley-Davidson 1941 WLA. Harley-Davidson ultimately won this duel and was awarded the contract for World War II US military motorcycles. Harley-Davidson also built motorcycles for US allies and the Lend-Lease program. (Courtesy NARA.)

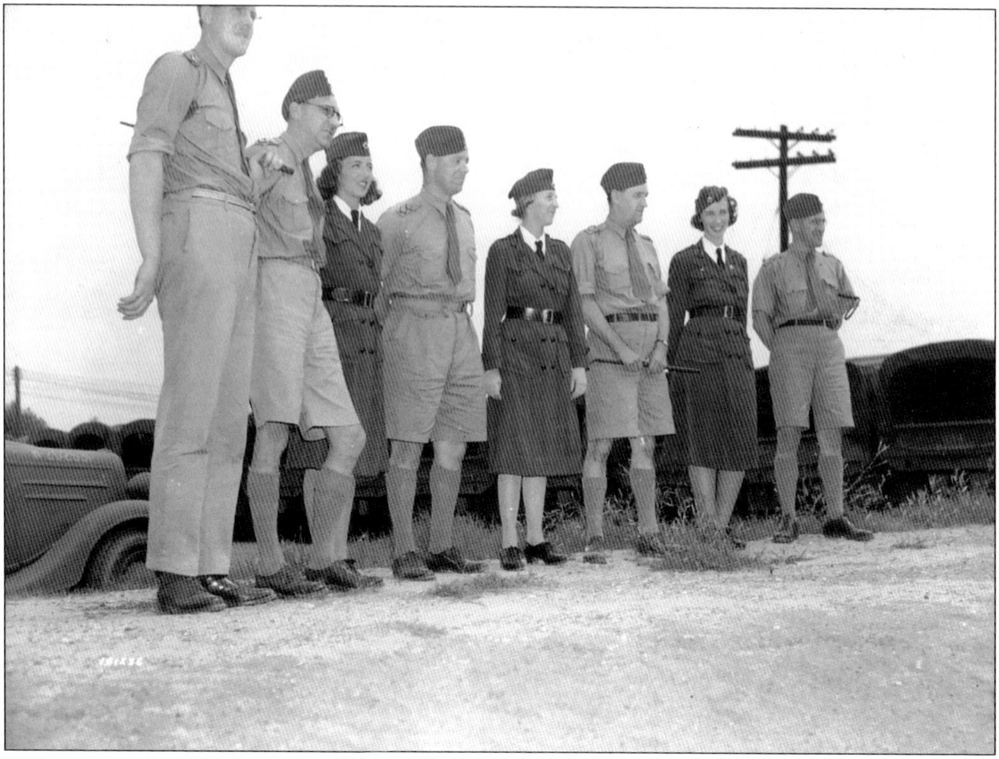

In this July 16, 1941, image, there are five Canadian Army officers and three Red Cross ambulance drivers at the Motor Transport School. Katherine Garrett of Baltimore, Maryland, second from the right, had already served in combat. According to the July 30, 1940, edition of the *Baltimore Sun* newspaper, Garrett served in 1940 as an ambulance driver with American Friends of France and came under enemy fire during the evacuation of the Meuse Valley. (Courtesy NARA.)

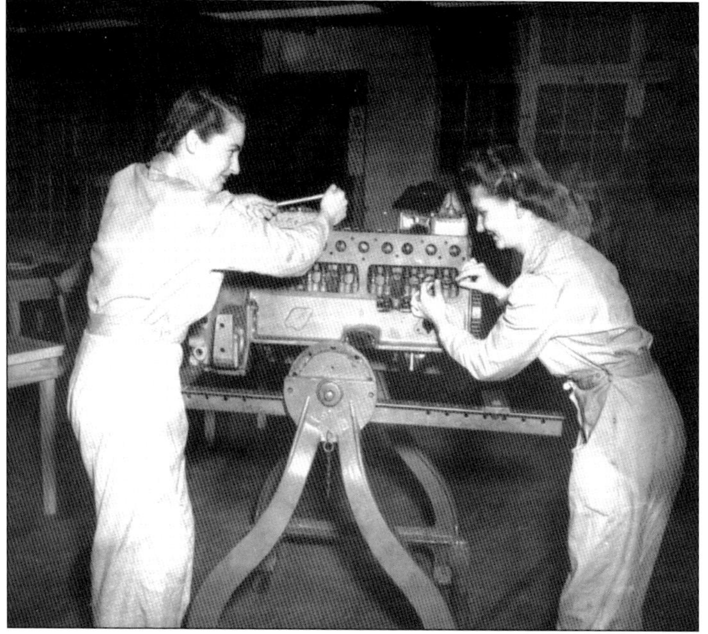

This 1942 photograph shows members of the Women's Army Auxiliary Corps (WAAC) working on an engine block in a mechanic class. The women in this photograph are 3rd Officers Eileen H. Knowles and Jesse V. Hogan. In 1943, the WAAC would become the Women's Army Corps (WAC). Other options for members of the WAAC included switchboard operator and baker. (Courtesy NARA.)

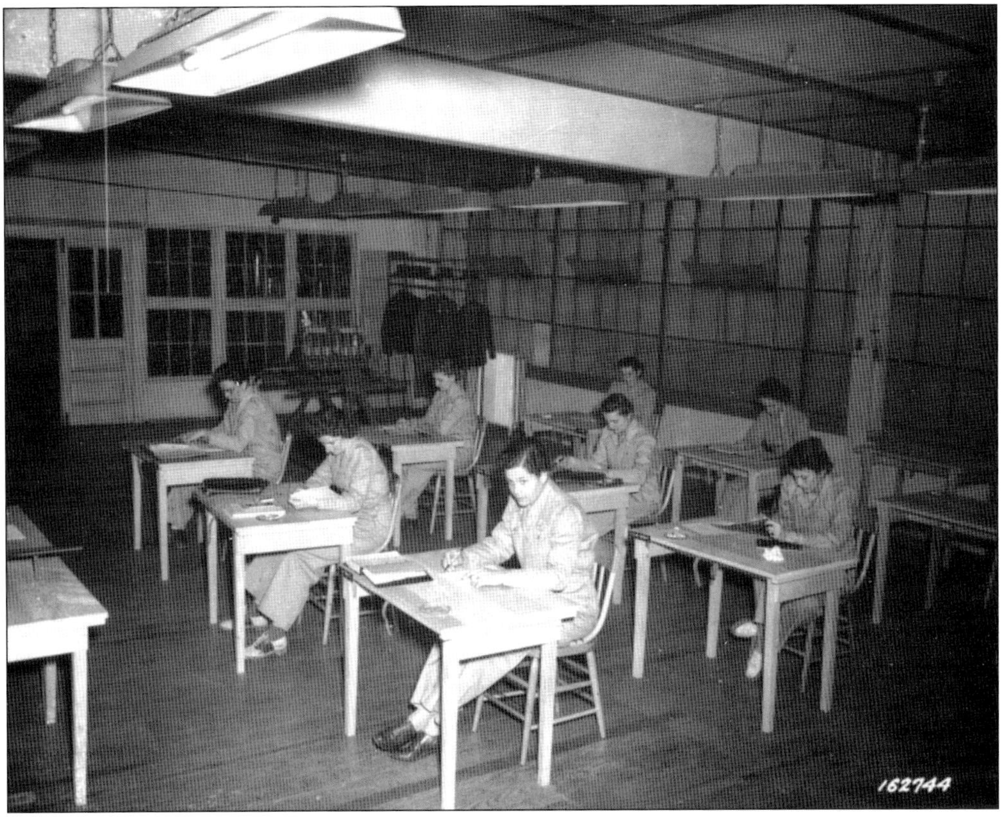

This photograph from January 1943 shows members of the Women's Army Auxiliary Corps (WAAC) in a classroom at Camp Holabird. At Holabird, these WAAC members would be in a mechanic class. In this photograph, they are in uniform but wearing civilian shoes. Leather was a war commodity and may have been allocated to combat boots and holsters. (Courtesy NARA.)

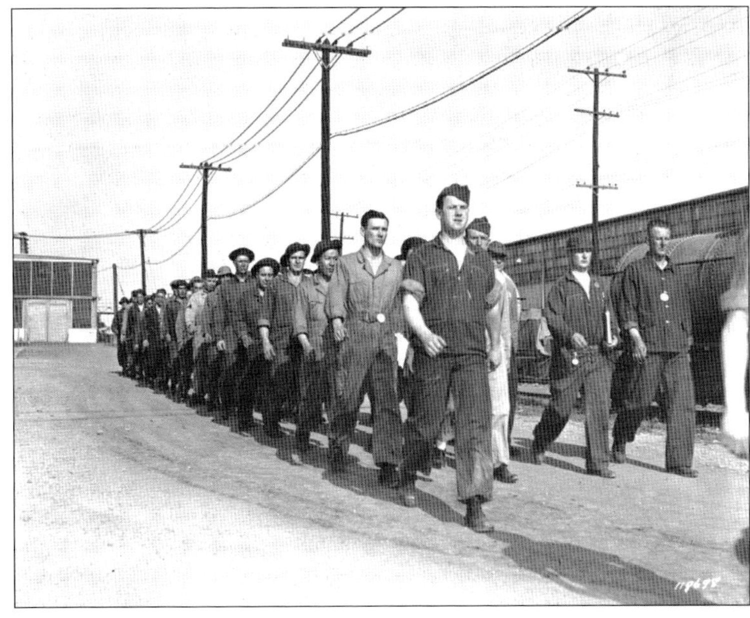

This photograph from May 19, 1941, shows a group of student mechanics returning to the barracks after a hard day of mechanical training. According to the caption, they are marching to "martial music." After a shower, it will be off to chow at the mess hall. In five months, they will graduate from the Motor Transport School. (Courtesy NARA.)

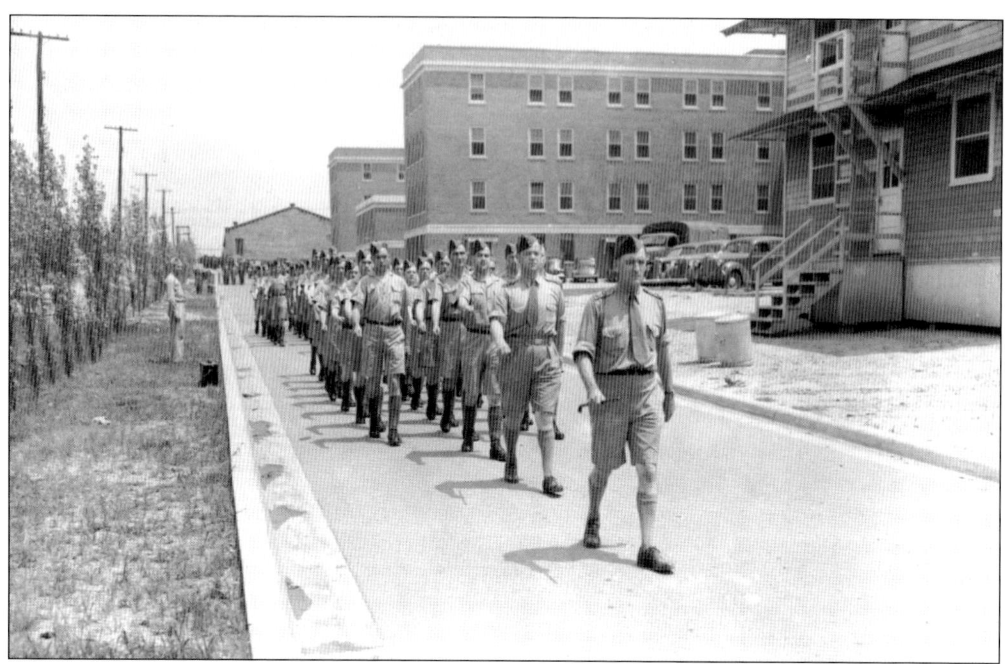

This July 16, 1941, photograph shows a unit from the Royal Canadian Ordnance Corps. They are marching from noon mess after a morning of mechanic and driver training. These are officers and soldiers. The officer is easy to spot; he is the one out in front carrying an officer's swagger stick. (Courtesy NARA.)

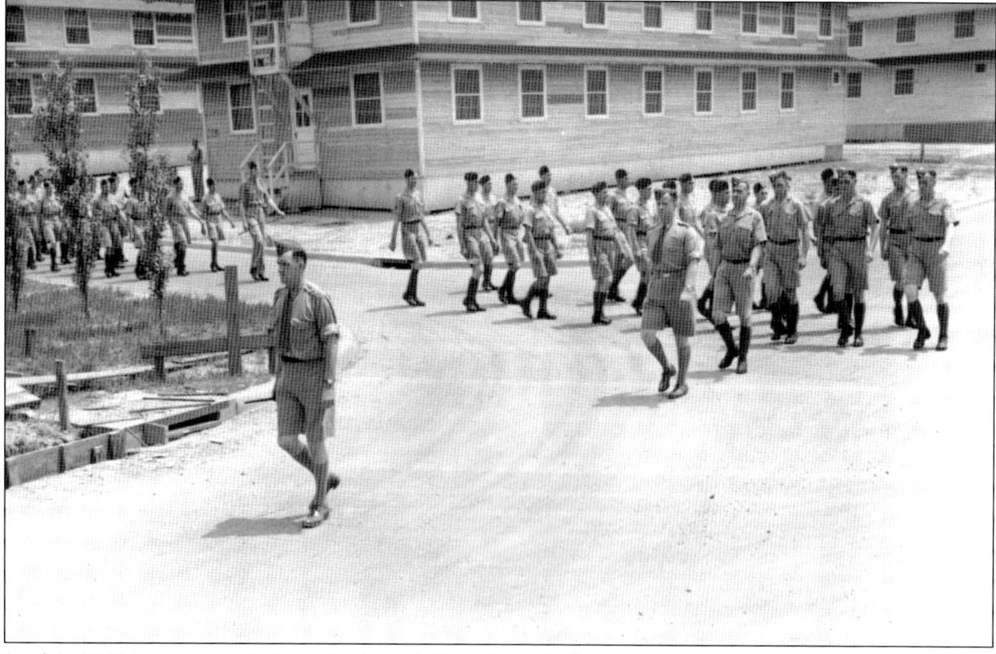

In this 1941 image, a unit from the Royal Canadian Ordnance Corps executing a column right is shown. This appears to be a large movement because there are several sub-units evidenced by the number of officers, swagger sticks in hand, which are present. In the background are the classic World War II barracks that were built on military facilities all over the United States. (Courtesy NARA.)

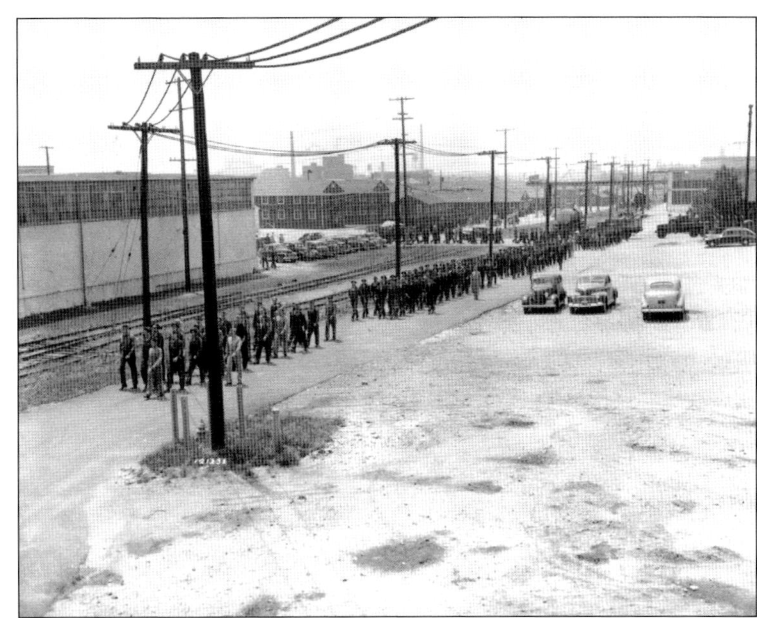

This 1941 photograph shows the movement of a large group of student soldiers on Camp Holabird. Something important is happening to call out what appears to be the entire class of Motor Transport School students. In the background, there are various industrial buildings that would be called into the war effort. (Courtesy NARA.)

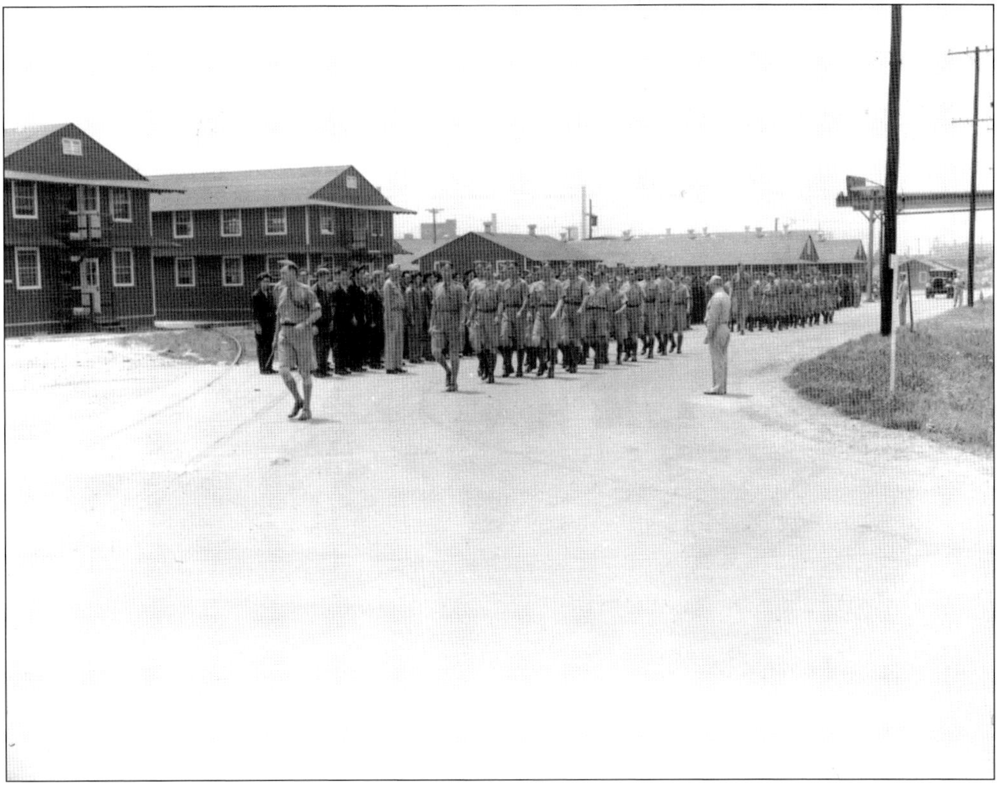

Canadian Ordnance Corps students marching at Camp Holabird. The United States supplied many allied countries with vehicles including the Sherman tank, the MC Scout Car, and the legendary Jeep. It stands to reason soldiers from foreign countries would train at Camp Holabird. American soldiers were probably envious of their short-legged trousers in the Maryland summers. (Courtesy NARA.)

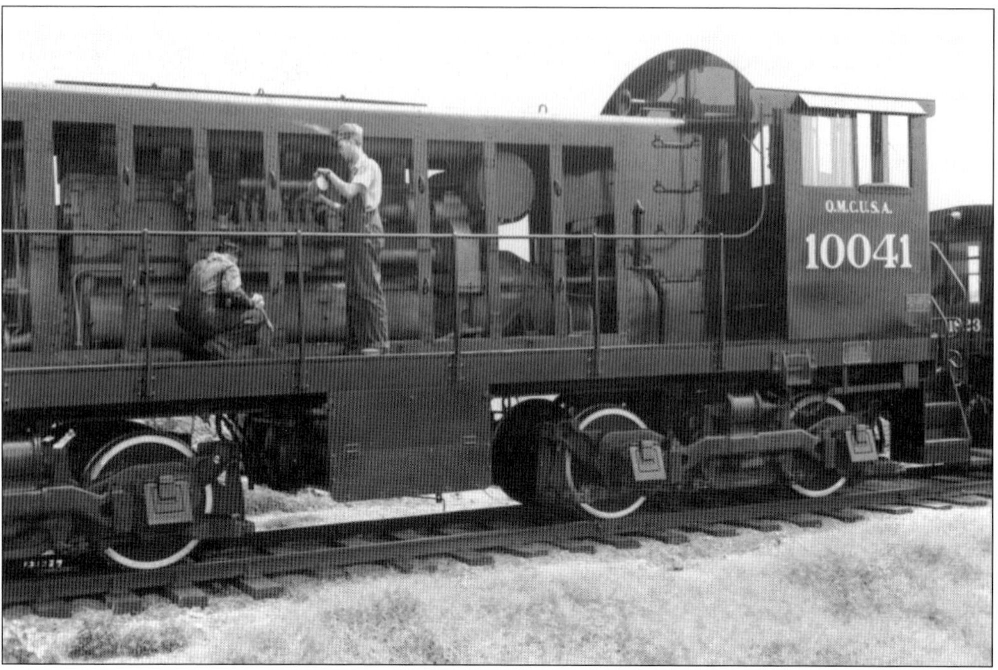

In this image dated July 16, 1941, there are two soldiers "oiling up" a Quartermaster Corps locomotive. The locomotive is a 100-ton diesel engine that is part of the rolling stock serving the Motor Transport School at Holabird Quartermaster Depot. It is a dirty job, but it had to be done. (Courtesy NARA.)

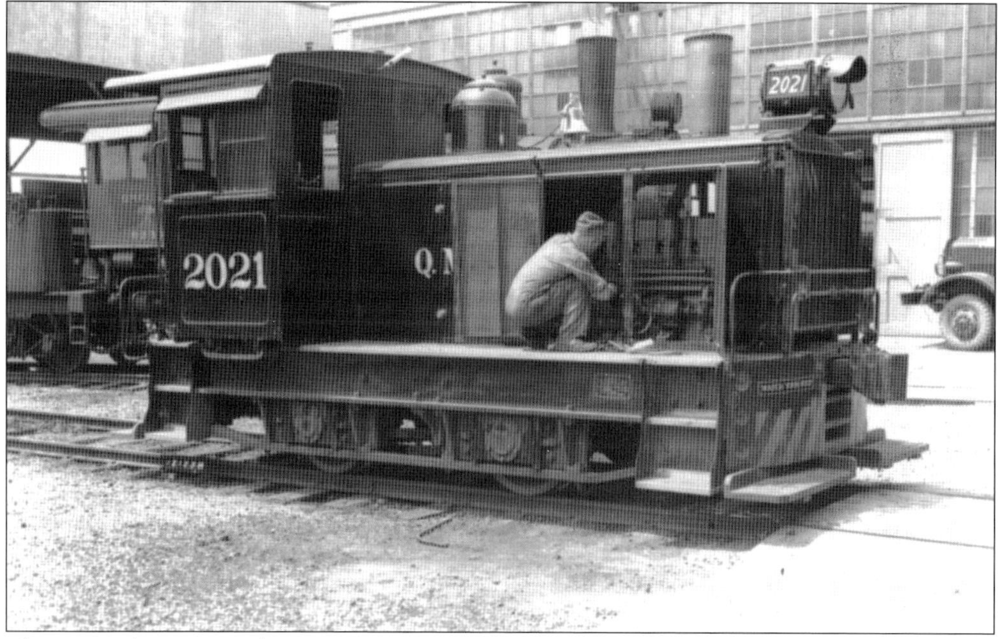

This image depicts a single crewman servicing a 20-ton gasoline locomotive undergoing testing at the Motor Transport School at Holabird Quartermaster Depot. This 1941 photograph was taken just five months before Pearl Harbor, and these machines would soon be called upon to move an endless line of war goods. (Courtesy NARA.)

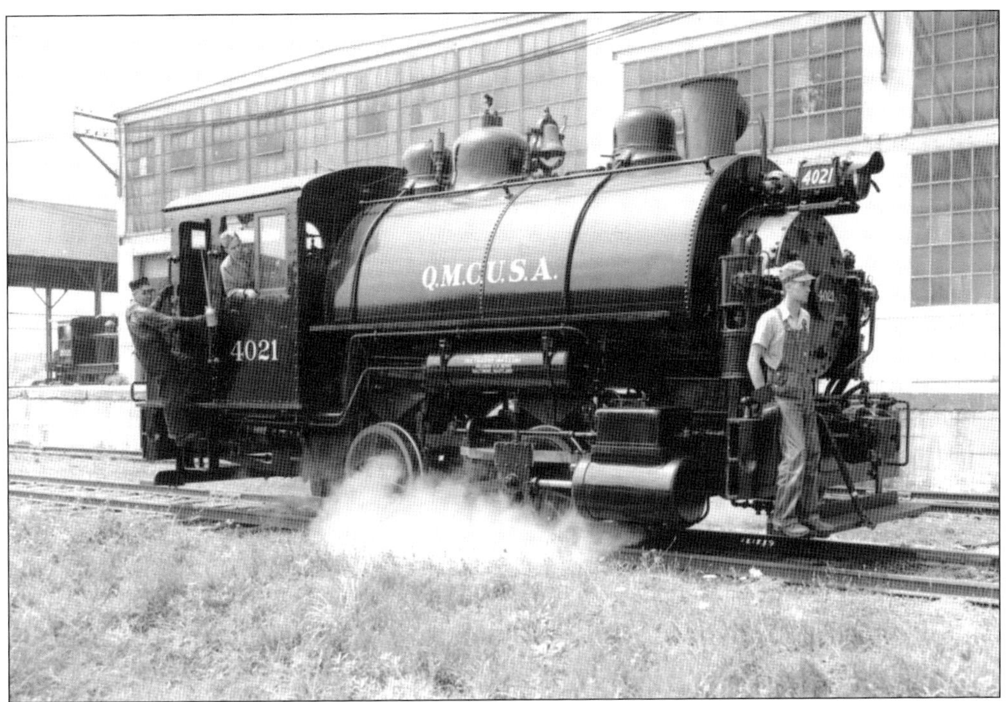

This photograph dated July 16, 1941, shows a 40-ton "baby steam locomotive." She is being operated by a three-man crew at the locomotive shops at Holabird Quartermaster Depot Motor Transport School. The name "baby" is quite interesting because she appears to be a mighty machine with a proud crew. (Courtesy NARA.)

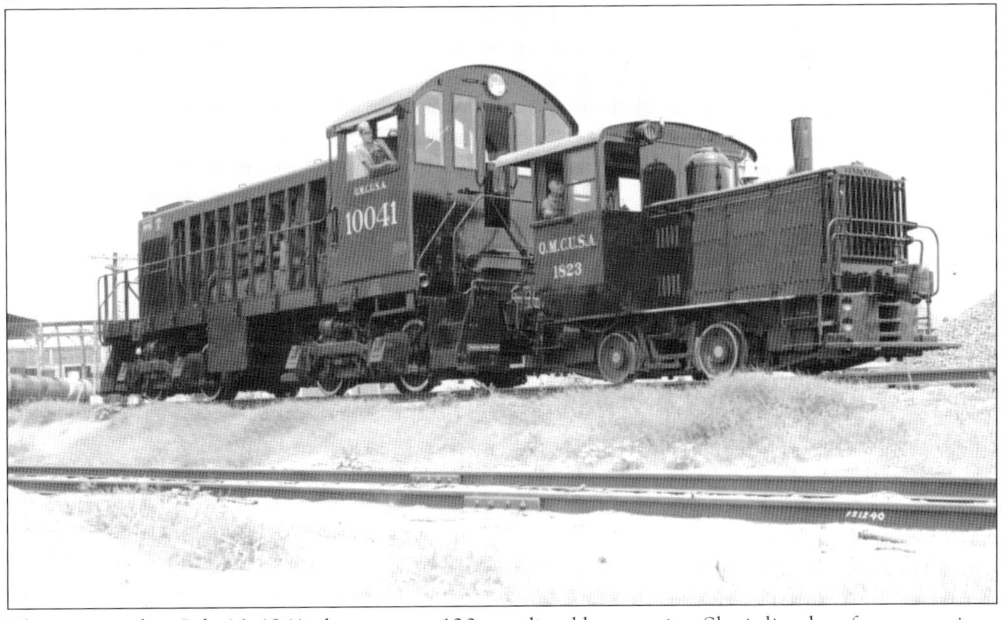

This image taken July 16, 1941, shows a new 100-ton diesel locomotive. She is lined up for comparison with an 18-ton gasoline locomotive. Both engines bear markings of the Quartermaster Corps. Given this image was shot in 1941, it is safe to assume these engines served during World War II. (Courtesy NARA.)

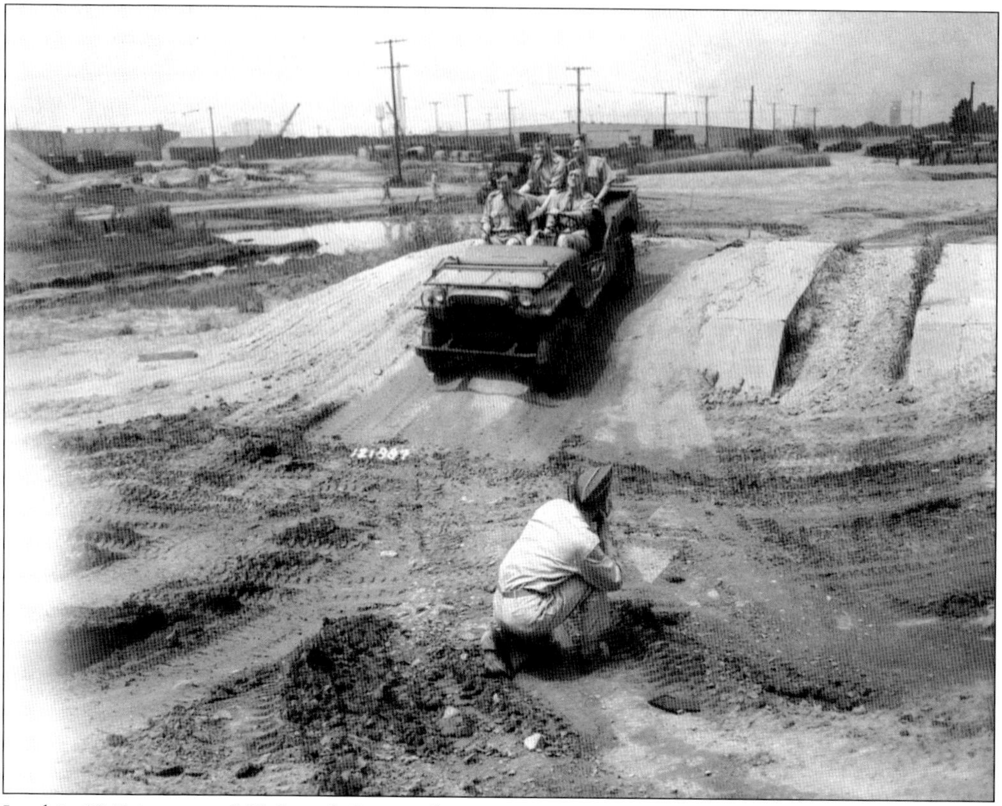

In this 1941 image, a US Signal Corps photographer is shooting an image of a jeep. The jeep appears to be a Willys MA, of which only 1,505 were made. The soldiers appear to be Canadian Ordnance Corps soldiers. They appear to be learning how to handle a jeep in off-road conditions. (Courtesy NARA.)

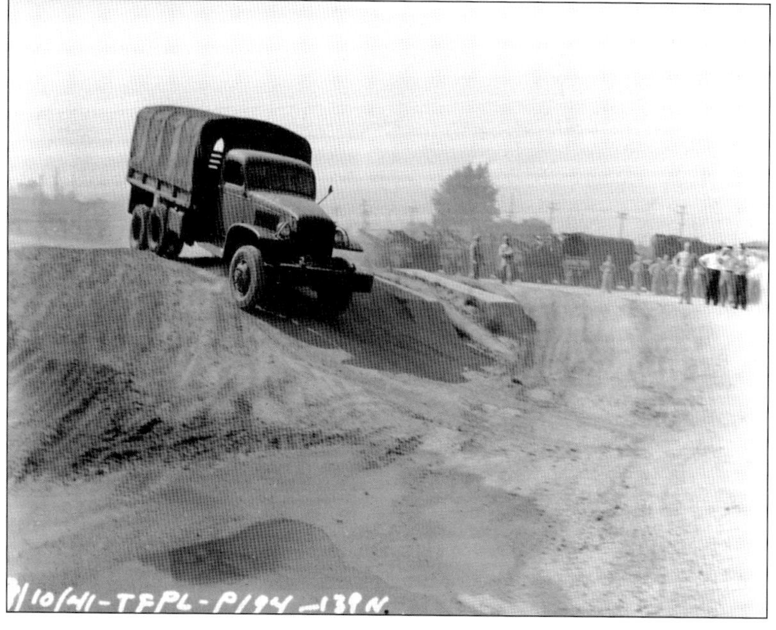

The two-and-a-half-ton cargo truck known lovingly as the Deuce and a Half would be called on to operate in all imaginable conditions. This World War II–era image shows a Deuce and a Half navigating a steep decline on a dirt surface. Several observers are present indicating this was a test of some kind. (Courtesy NARA.)

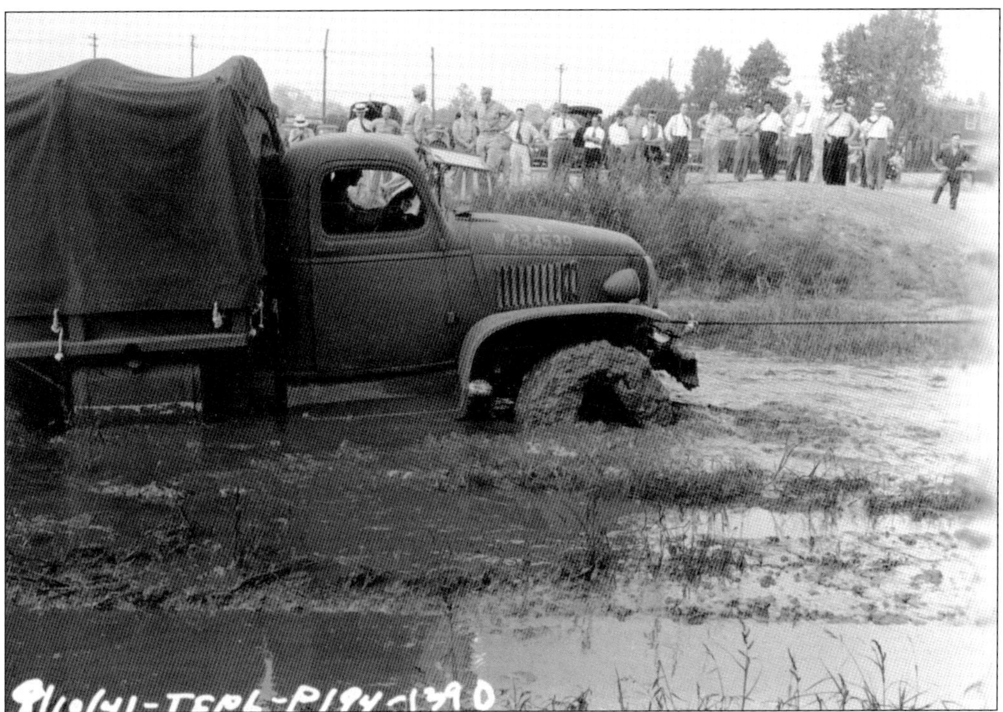

In this 1941 image, another Deuce and a Half is being tested. The truck is operating axle deep in a mud and water obstacle. Several observers are present. It appears tire chains are installed. It also appears the driver is giving it his all. In a few months, this driver might be in North Africa or the South Pacific. (Courtesy NARA.)

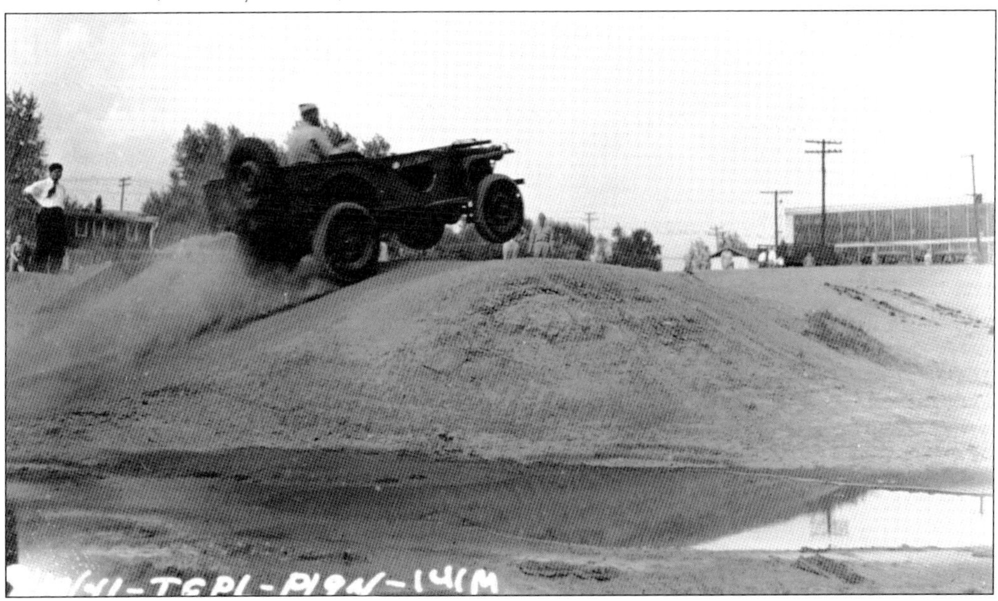

This 1941 photograph shows a jeep being tested hard. She is leaving a cloud of dust as she operates in the dirt. The front wheels are clearly off the ground indicating the driver is operating at a fairly good speed. Several observers are present indicating this is some kind of training or testing. (Courtesy NARA.)

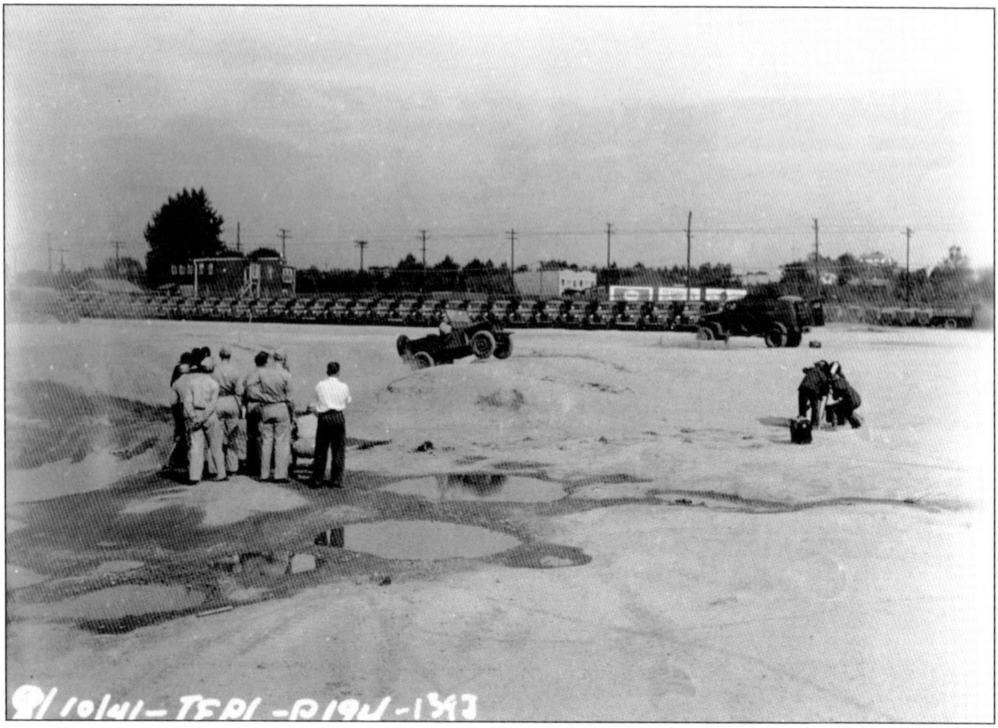

This may be the same intrepid jeep as the previous 1941 photograph but shot from a different angle and by a different camera. The jeep is apparently accelerating up and over the dirt obstacle. A brave cameraman is positioned near the path of the speeding jeep. The observers are also present. (Courtesy NARA.)

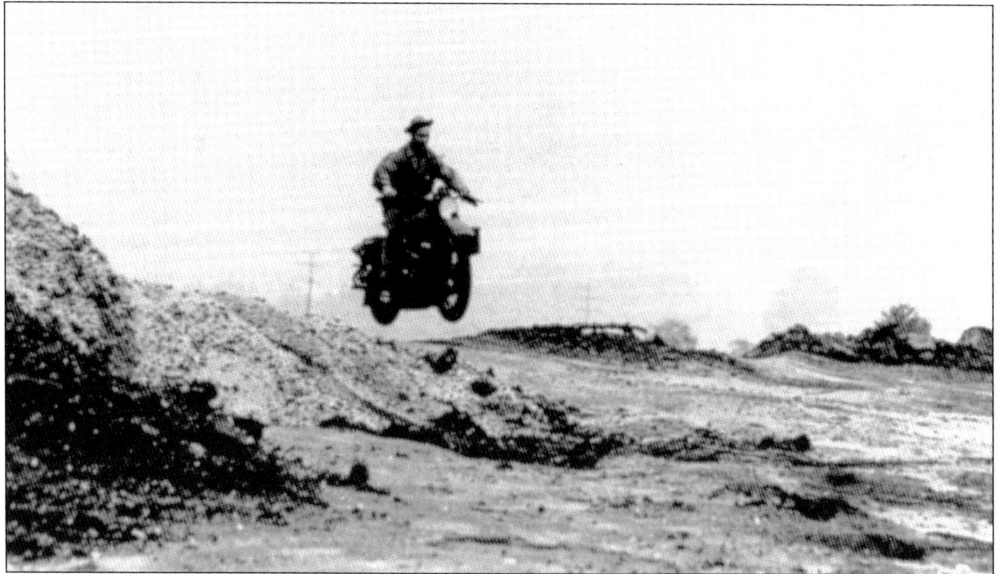

This Army motorcycle has both wheels off the ground on a dirt test track at Camp Holabird. It is either an Indian Scout 640B or a Harley-Davidson WLA, but it is uncertain from this angle. The driver looks quite confident and in control. Perhaps he should have enlisted in the Air Corps. (Courtesy Dundalk-Patapsco Neck Historical Society & Museum.)

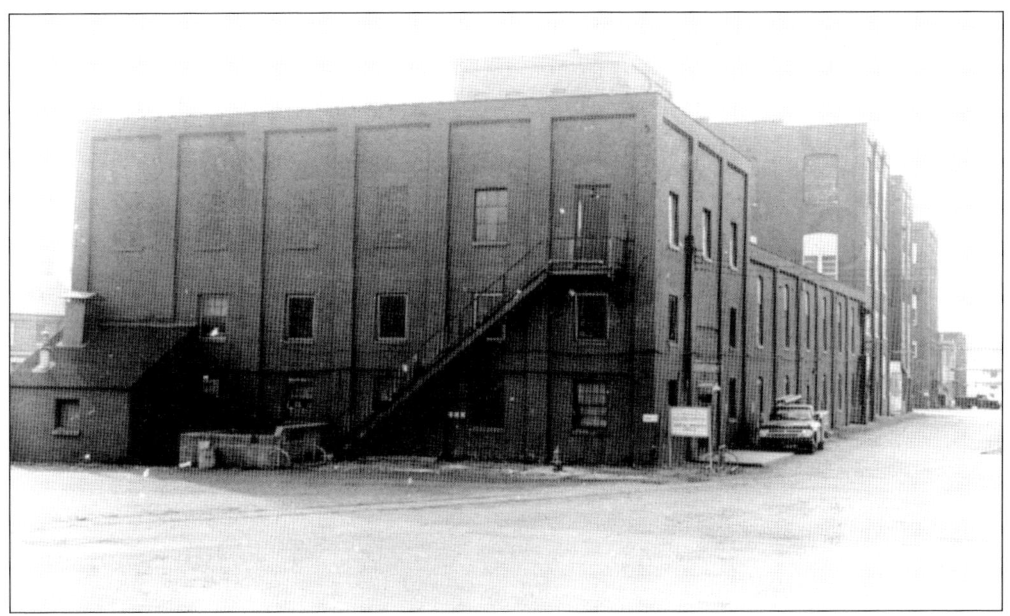

This World War II–era photograph shows one of the few pre–Camp Holabird buildings to survive. It was a distillery on the land that would become Camp Holabird. The Army put the building to good use and converted it into the post gymnasium and the Special Services Office. (Courtesy Dundalk-Patapsco Neck Historical Society & Museum.)

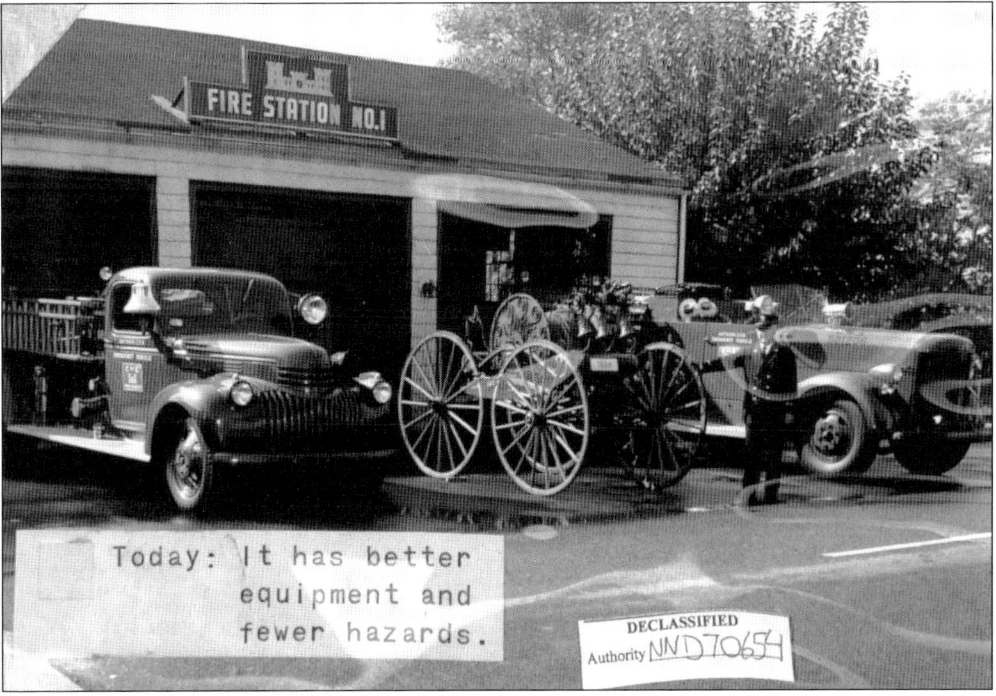

This 1940s-era photograph depicts the Camp Holabird fire station. The engines were operated by the Corps of Engineers. The fire engines appear to be, from left to right, a 1940 Dodge and possibly an Oshkosh. In between the engines is what appears to be some antique firefighting equipment. (Courtesy NARA.)

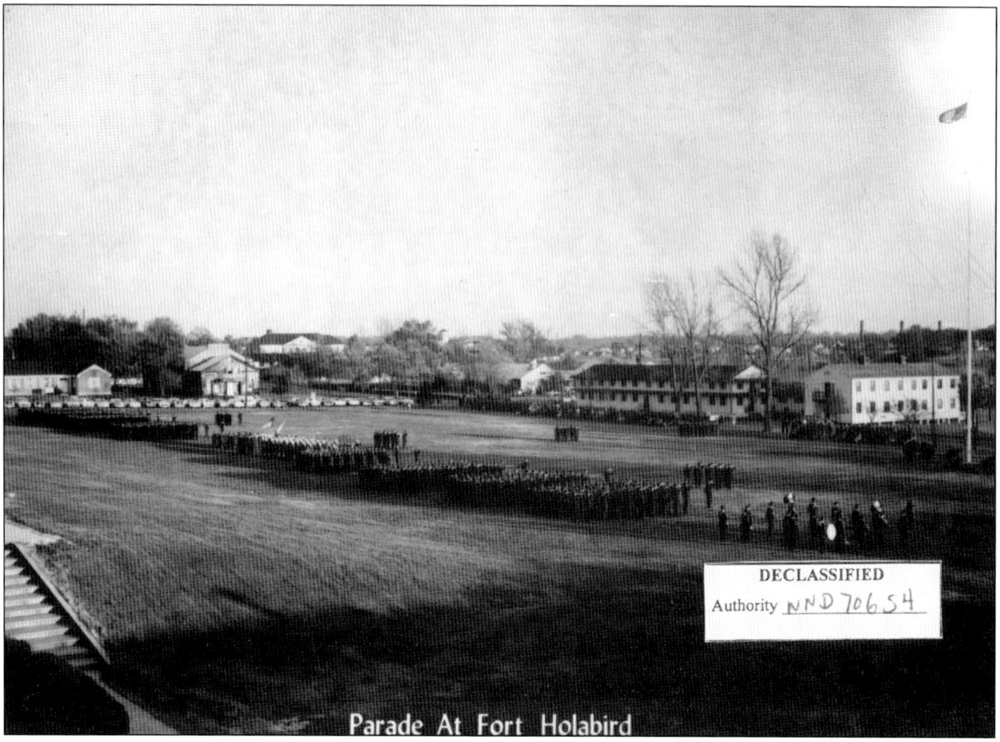

DECLASSIFIED
Authority NND 70654

Parade At Fort Holabird

This photograph depicts a parade at Fort Holabird. Parades are a regular event on an Army post. They may be held for various reasons including inspections, VIP visits, change of command, and retirements. The reason for this parade is unknown, but it appears the entire post came out for the event. (Courtesy NARA.)

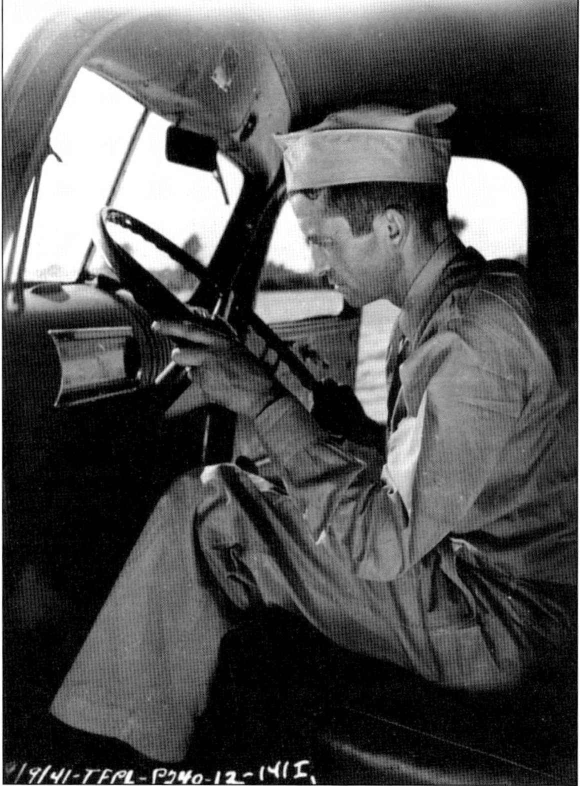

This 1941 photograph shows a soldier seated in the driver's seat. From the look on his face, he appears to be about to say, "How do I start this thing?" In fact, in 1941, many soldiers arrived having never driven a motor vehicle before. Holabird was the place to learn. (Courtesy NARA.)

Three

INTELLIGENCE YEARS

In the 1950s, Holabird became an intelligence post. Holabird had a Counterintelligence Corps training presence since 1945. In 1954, the Counterintelligence Corps Center at Holabird became the Army Intelligence Center. This move centralized intelligence training at Holabird as the US Army Intelligence Center & School. The intelligence school would remain at Holabird until 1971, when it moved to Fort Huachuca in Arizona.

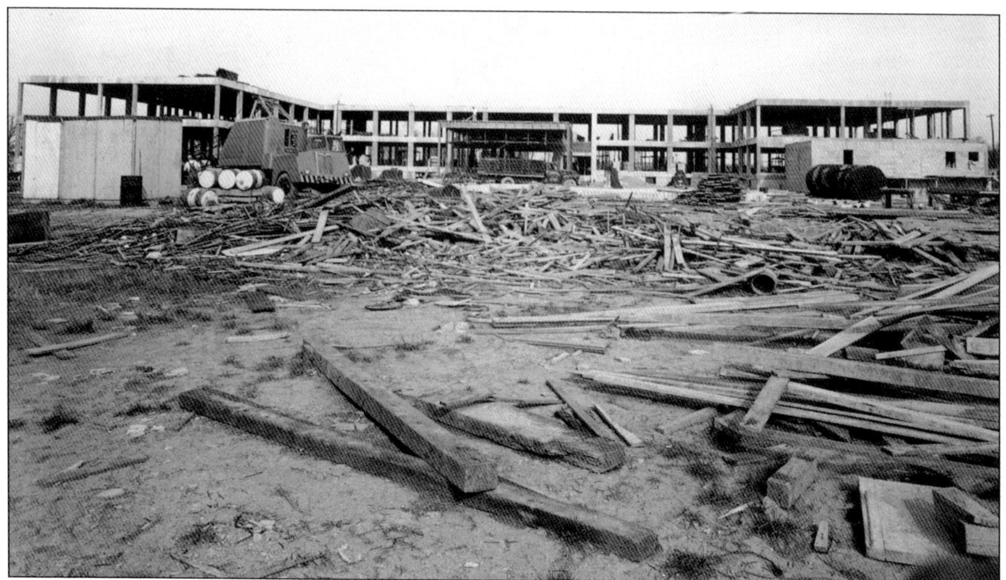

In the early 1950s, construction began on converting Holabird from a dusty vehicle maintenance post to a state-of-the-art intelligence training facility. It was a big job, and many contractors were brought in to accomplish the mission. It is difficult to tell at this stage, but this project could be post headquarters or the enlisted barracks. (Courtesy Dundalk-Patapsco Neck Historical Society & Museum.)

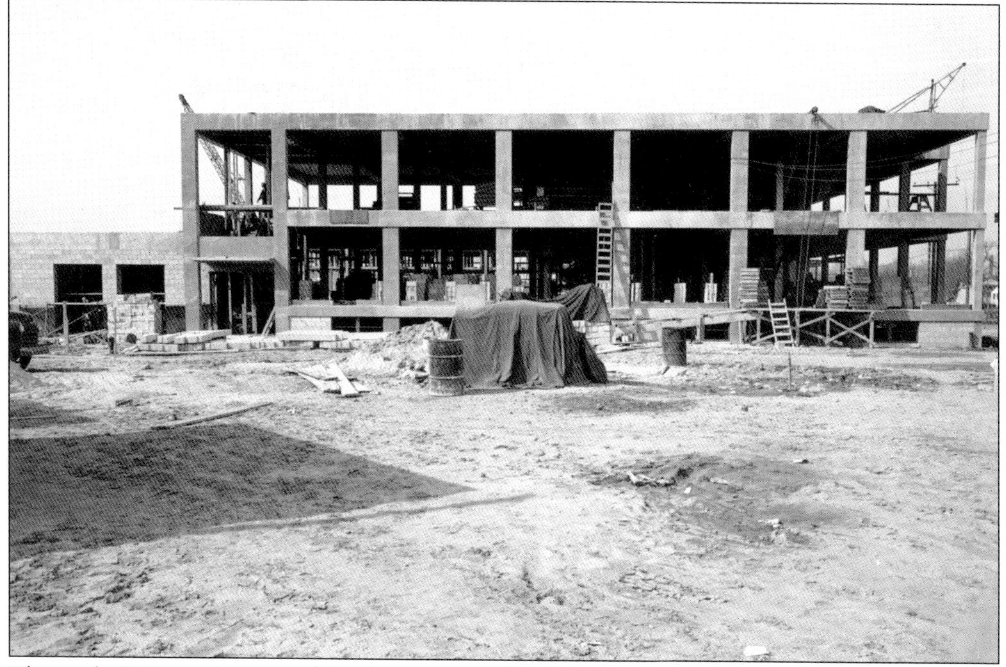

This early-1950s project resembles the US Army Intelligence Center. It is a humble beginning for a building that will house and staff a mission of vital national security. The facility would not be open for business until 1954, but the Army was getting a good start. The decision to centralize intelligence training was made during the Korean War. (Courtesy Dundalk-Patapsco Neck Historical Society & Museum.)

Here is an aerial view of the US Army Intelligence Center Headquarters. This was a highly secure facility where security clearances were as common as epaulets. In the foreground, the Sphinx status is mounted out in front. More on this later, but this gives us a reference as to its location. (Courtesy NARA.)

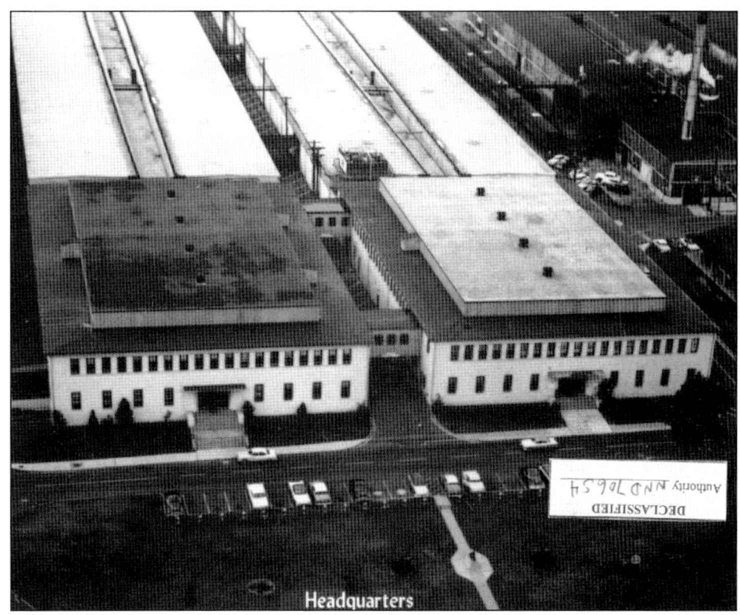

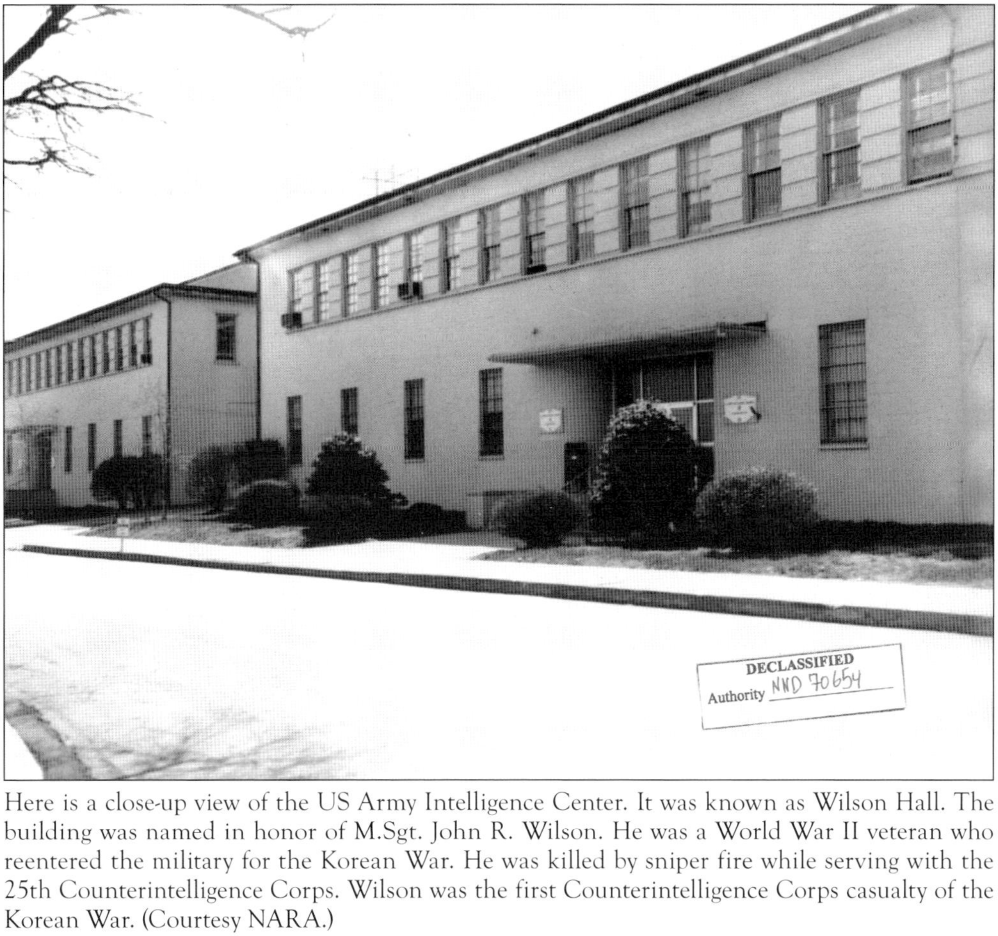

Here is a close-up view of the US Army Intelligence Center. It was known as Wilson Hall. The building was named in honor of M.Sgt. John R. Wilson. He was a World War II veteran who reentered the military for the Korean War. He was killed by sniper fire while serving with the 25th Counterintelligence Corps. Wilson was the first Counterintelligence Corps casualty of the Korean War. (Courtesy NARA.)

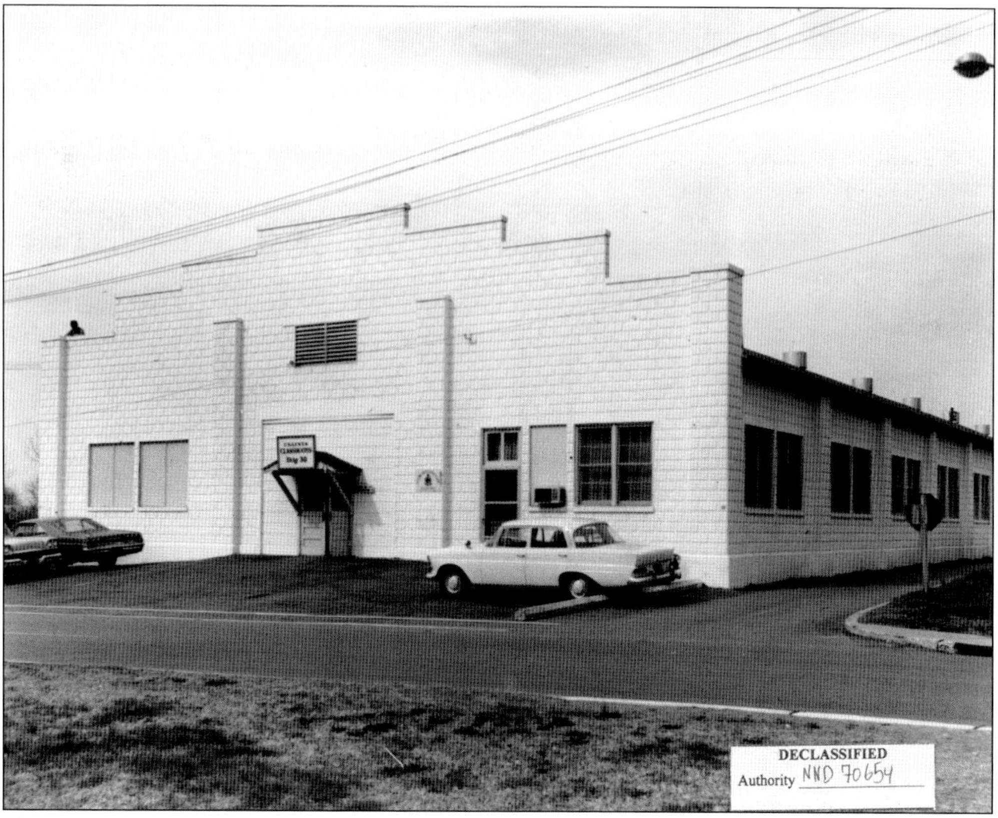

The sign outside this building reads, "USAINTS Classrooms." In this nondescript building, the hard work of becoming a US Army Military Intelligence Specialist took place. It was also known as Allen Hall or "Building 30." It was named Allen Hall in honor of 1st Lt. Eldon L. Allen, who was killed in action in 1945 while serving as an intelligence officer with the 82nd Airborne. (Courtesy NARA.)

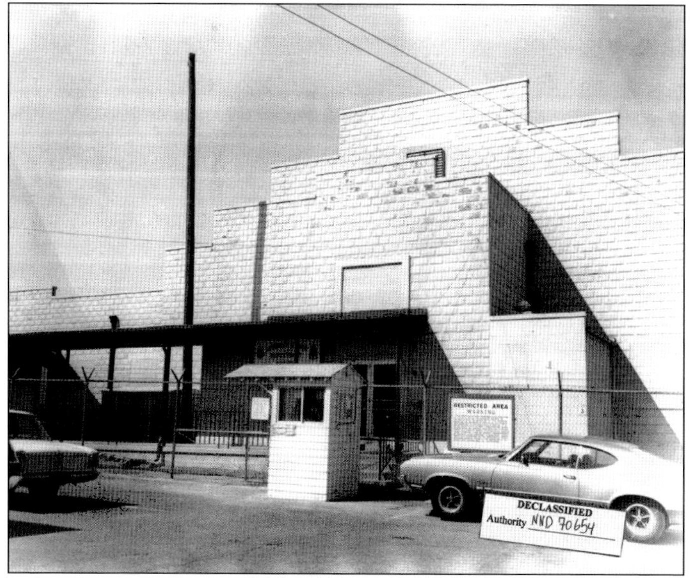

The sign on this building reads, "Advanced Course Department." It looks like serious business. The building has a guard shack, a fence with barbed wire, and a sign that reads "Restricted Area." It was known as Hunter Hall, and it was named for Sgt. Woodrow G. Hunter. Sergeant Hunter was killed in action while serving with the Counterintelligence Corps in Papua New Guinea in 1944. (Courtesy NARA.)

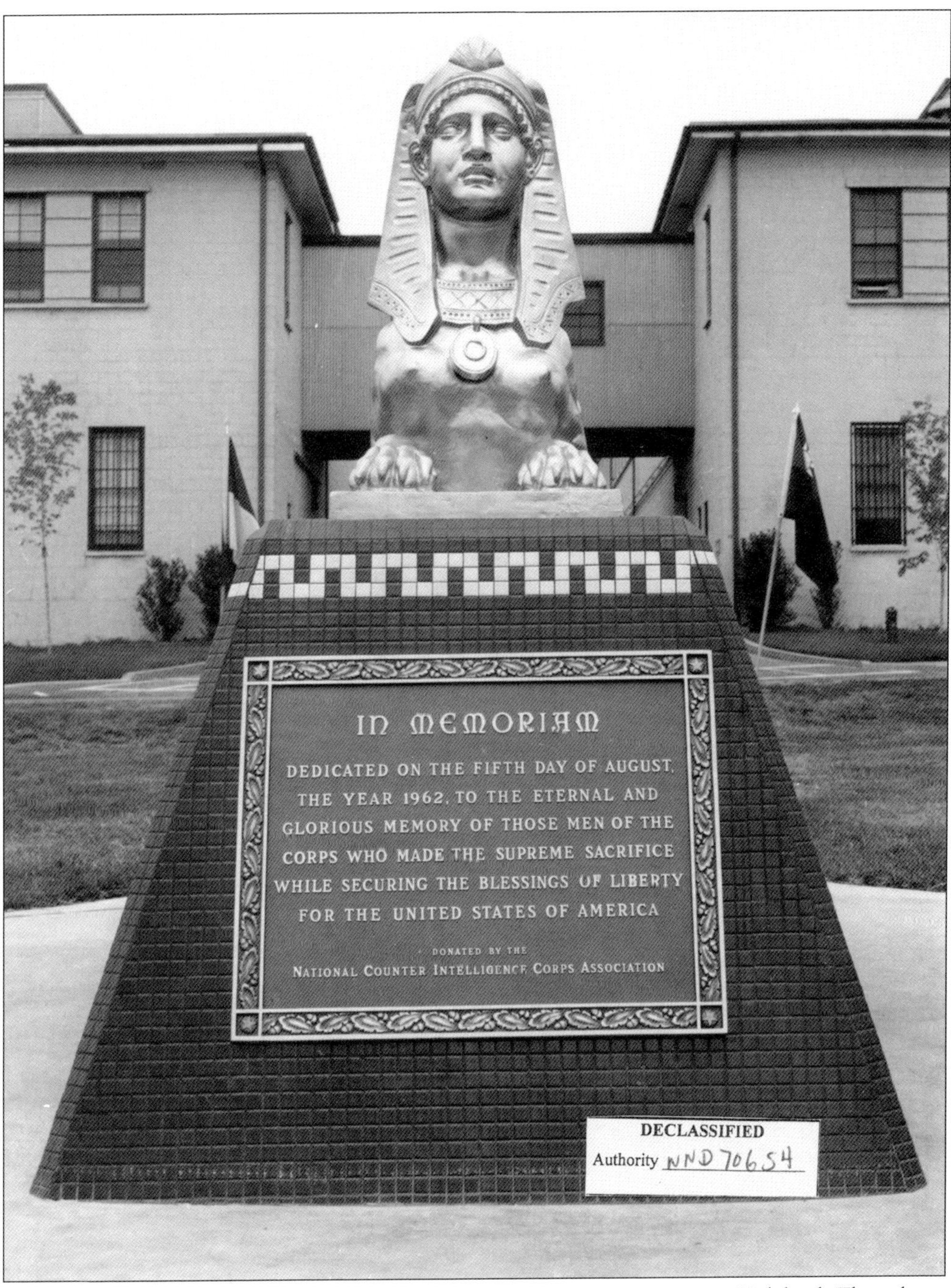

This Sphinx statue stood outside the US Army Intelligence Center at Fort Holabird. The sphinx was chosen to represent military intelligence because it was a symbol of wisdom and mystery. The statue was dedicated to the "Eternal and Glorious Memory of Those Men of the Corps Who Made the Supreme Sacrifice." The sphinx stood guard at Holabird until the intelligence center was moved to Fort Huachuca, Arizona, in 1971, where it resides today. (Courtesy NARA)

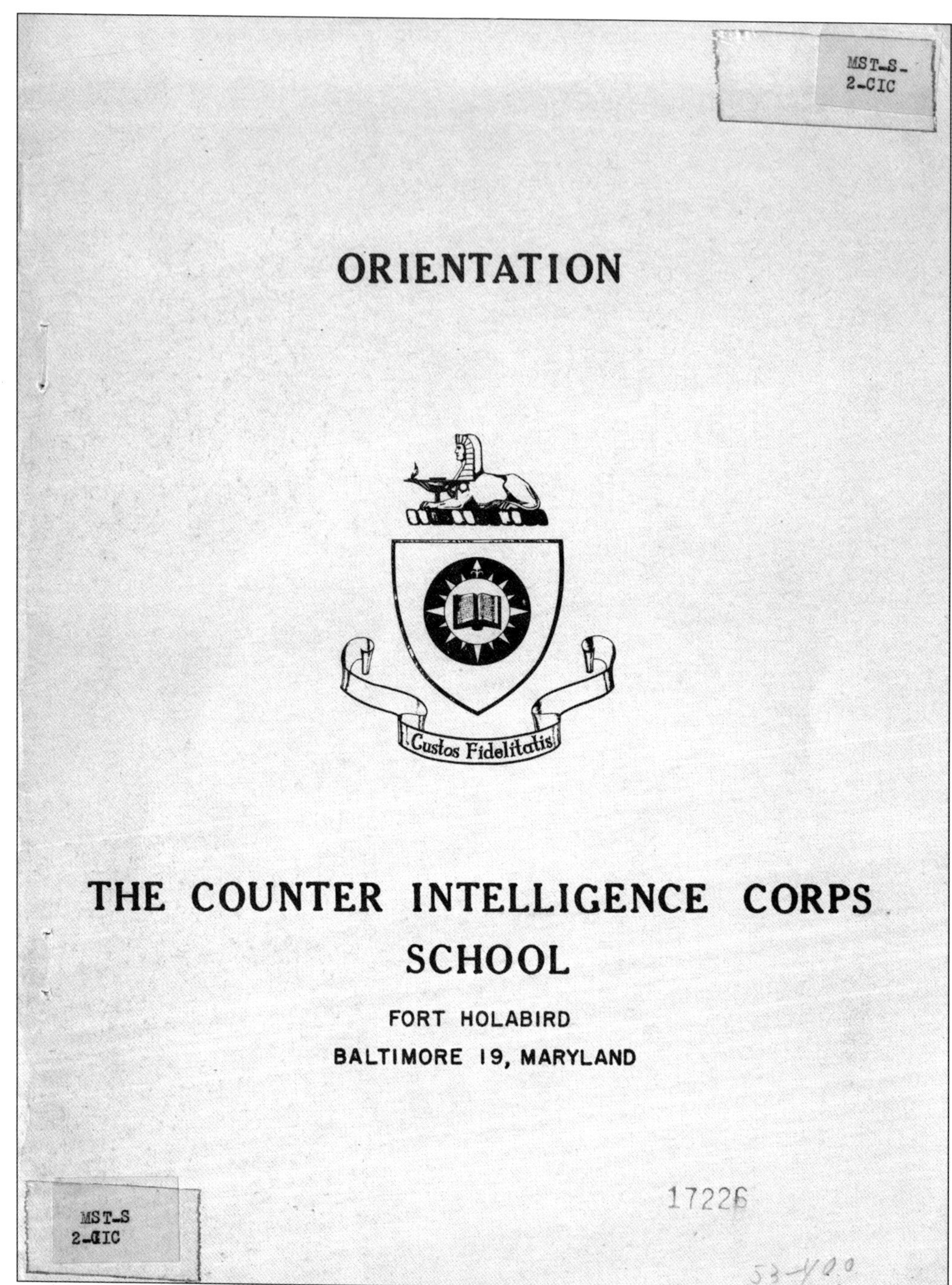

This image is an orientation booklet cover for newly arriving students at the Counter Intelligence Corps School. The booklet was very likely classified. The date of the booklet is uncertain, but the address lacks a zip code. This would date it sometime before 1963. (Courtesy US Army Heritage and Education Center.)

IF
67050
67060 (D/NRI)
Oct 58

U.S. ARMY INTELLIGENCE SCHOOL

FORT HOLABIRD · MARYLAND

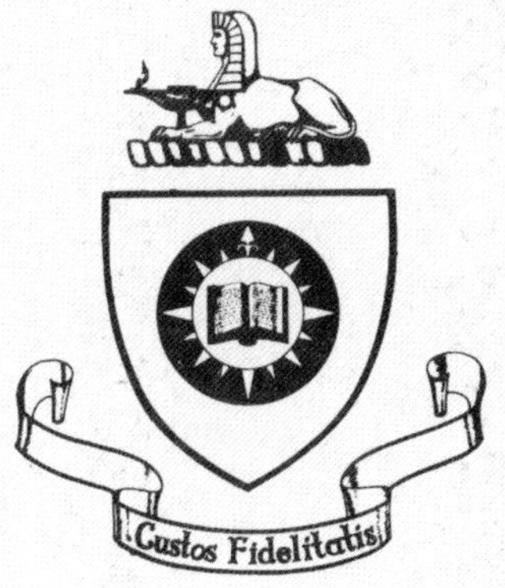

INSTRUCTOR FOLDER

SUBJECT DEVELOPMENT OF ORDER OF BATTLE INTELLIGENCE

LIST OF COMPONENT PARTS

1. Instructor Data Sheet
2. Instructor Manuscript
3. Practical Exercise

(Same as IF I-6317/B, Mar 57)

This "Instructor Folder" cover is from October 1958. It is from the U.S. Army Intelligence School, and the subject is "Development of Order of Battle Intelligence." Like the previous orientation booklet, it is not known what was inside, but 1958 was at the height of the Cold War, so surely it was sensitive information. (Courtesy US Army Heritage and Education Center.)

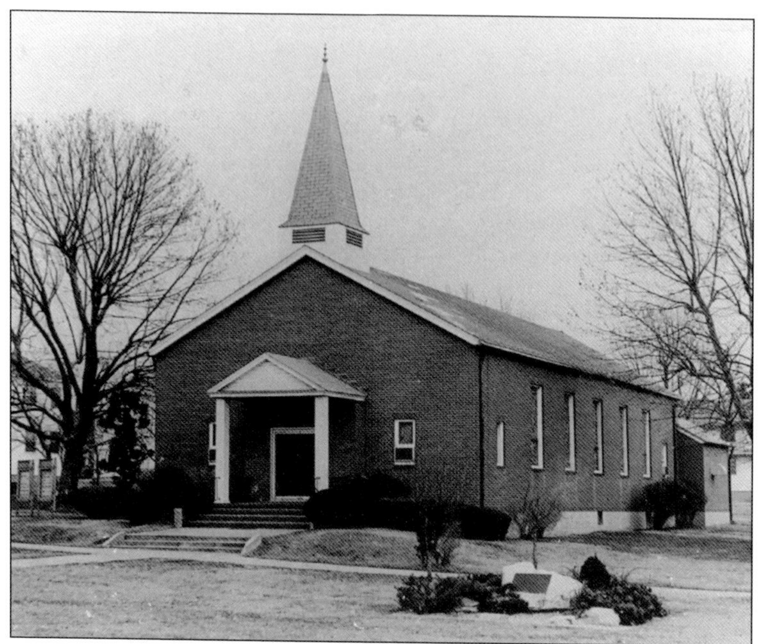

Pictured here is the post chapel at Fort Holabird. It was located on East Main Street near the theater. It was a serene location on a manicured wooded lot. The chapel was open to soldiers and families of all faiths, and it bears no inscription or symbol specific to any particular religion. (Courtesy Dundalk-Patapsco Neck Historical Society & Museum.)

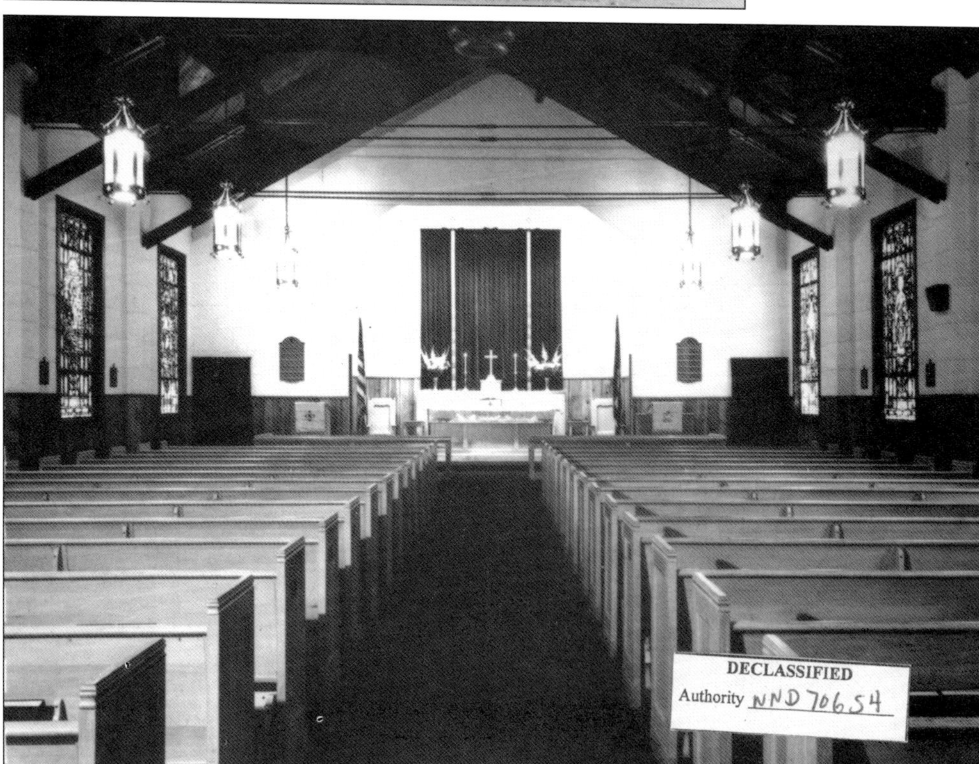

This image shows the interior of the post chapel at Fort Holabird. A stately and serene building, it was here that soldiers of all faiths worshipped and found solace. Many faith-related functions, took place in this chapel including weddings, baptisms, and funerals. Like most of the Holabird structures, the chapel was demolished when the post closed. (Courtesy NARA.)

Along with the gym, the theater, and the chapel, the post library was a popular diversion for soldiers at Fort Holabird. It was located on Van Deman Drive, which bisected the post starting at the main gate. The library was located on the same block as the chapel and the theater. (Courtesy NARA.)

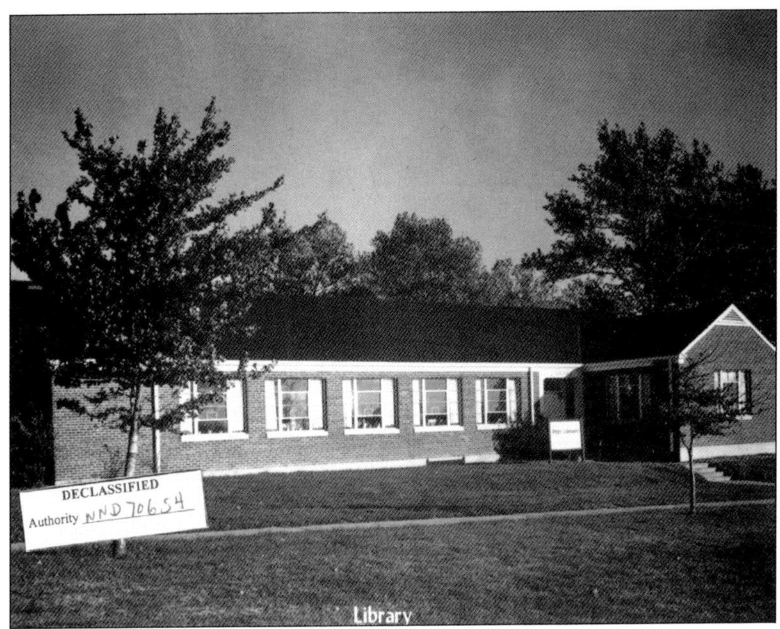

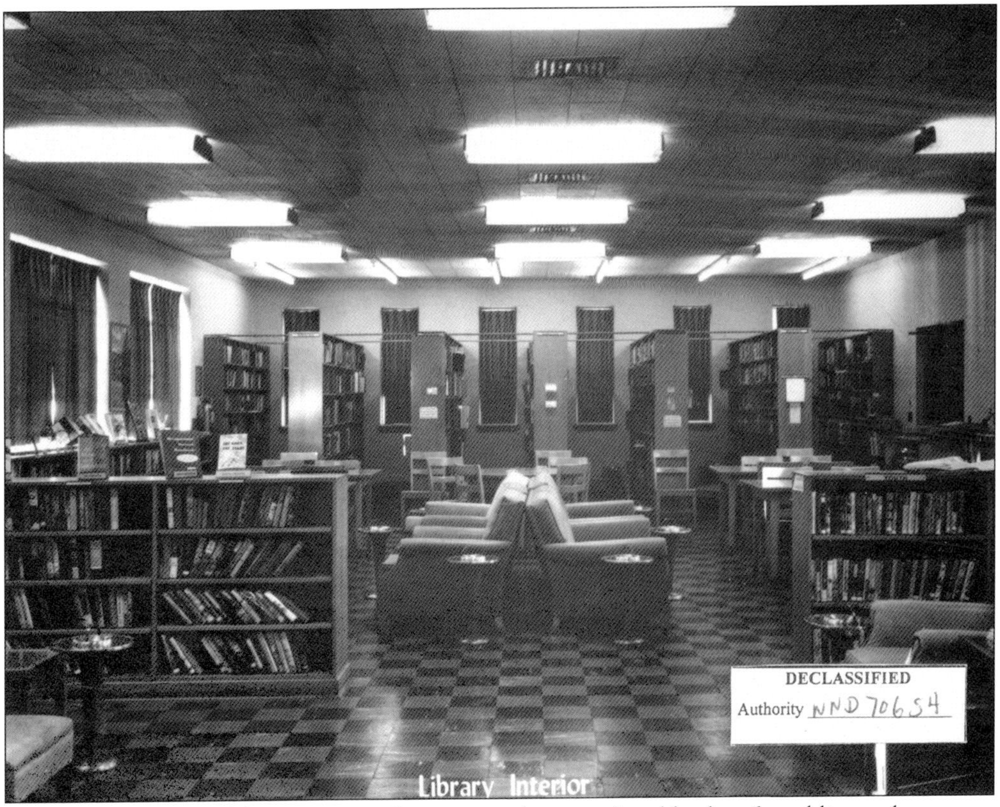

This image is the post library Interior. It appears to be a comfortable place for soldiers to have some R&R (rest and relaxation). In addition to books and encyclopedias, the library was well-stocked with popular periodicals. A favorite among soldiers was the collection of out-of-town newspapers where soldiers could hope for hometown news. (Courtesy NARA.)

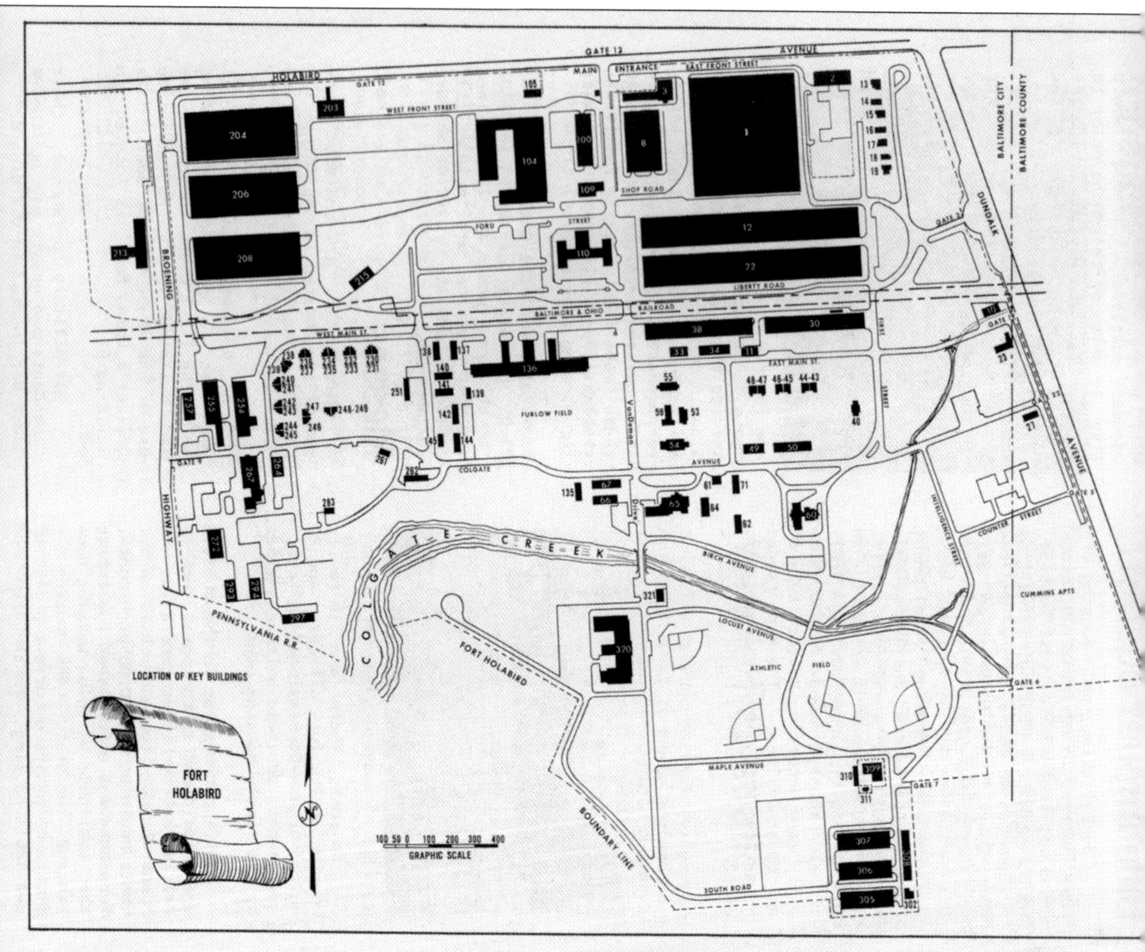

This is a map of Fort Holabird during the intelligence post years. The map was included in the welcome booklet issued to every arriving soldier. The map also shows how the post interacted with the local community including Dundalk Avenue, Holabird Avenue, and Broening Highway. In a few weeks, most soldiers could find their way around post blindfolded. (Courtesy US Army Heritage and Education Center.)

KEY TO FORT HOLABIRD MAP

#1 Post Signal
USA Claims Svc
AG, Printing Plant
USAINTS, P&VA, DNRI
Det 402, 4th Dist OSI-IG, USAF
MARS Station
Area Supply, USAR Activities
#2 USAIIC
F&AO
P&C
Post Motor Pool
#3 Hunter Hall
#8 USACDCINTA
USAIMDO
Post Exchange
Post Barber Shop
Post Cafeteria
#10 Auto Craft Shop
#12 Headquarters USAINTC
USAPSG
#13 to 19 Officer Family Housing
#22 Headquarters Fort Holabird
Family Housing Storage Area
Railway Express
TC Warehouse
Supply Office
Post Transportation
Baltimore Dist. DCASR
Admin Survey Det.
#23 Pre-School Nursery
#27 USA Recruiting Main Station
#30 Allen Hall
#33 - 34 BOQs
#38 Hubbard Hall
#40 Commanding General's Quarters
#43 - 48 Officer Family Quarters
#49 BOQ (WAC Officers)
#50 Guest House
#53 Officer Family Quarters
#54 Post Theater
#55 Post Chapel
#59 Post Library
#60 Dispensary and Dental Clinic
#62 BOQ
#64 Officers' Swimming Pool
#65 Officers' Open Mess
#66 Officers' Field Ration Mess
#67 - 71 BOQs

#100 Service Club
#104 Property Disposal Office
#105 Provost Marshal
#109 Family Housing & Billeting Office
#110 Hq & Hq Co. USAG (2111)
Hq & Hq Co. USAINTC
Barracks & Mess Hall
#135 BOQ
#136 Hq & Hq Co, Troop Command
Barracks & Mess Hall
Post Office
Commercial Cleaners & Tailors
#137 - 138 BEQs
#139 Orderly Room OSD
#140 - 141 BEQs
#142 - 144 BOQs
#145 Colgate Federal Credit Union
#208 Commissary
Post Quartermaster
Self-Service Supply Center
Clothing Sales Store
Furniture Repair Shop
Clothing & Textile FM Shop
#213 Jecelin Army Reserve Center
#230 - 249 Enlisted Family Quarters
#254 Post Gymnasium
#255 Post Laundry
#261 Orderly Room WAC Det
#262 Post Education Center
Beauty Shop
#267 NCO Open Mess
1-2-3 Club
USAINTS Classroom (Upstairs)
#272 Post Engineer
#286 Thrift Shop
#297 Post Indoor Range
#302 Officers' Family Quarters
#307 Post Bowling Lanes
Boy and Girl Scout Activities
#309 - 311 Enlisted Swimming Pool
Bathhouse & Wading Pool
#320 Headquarters USAINTS
School Administrative Offices
#321 PX Gas Station

Gate 13 - Main Exit and Entrance to
Fort Holabird

5

The map would be of little use with the key, which coordinated with numbered locations on the map. The key serves as a list of what was on post during this historic time. The map included places of interest to soldiers including barracks, post exchange, barbershop, chapel, theater, library, and dispensary. (Courtesy US Army Heritage and Education Center.)

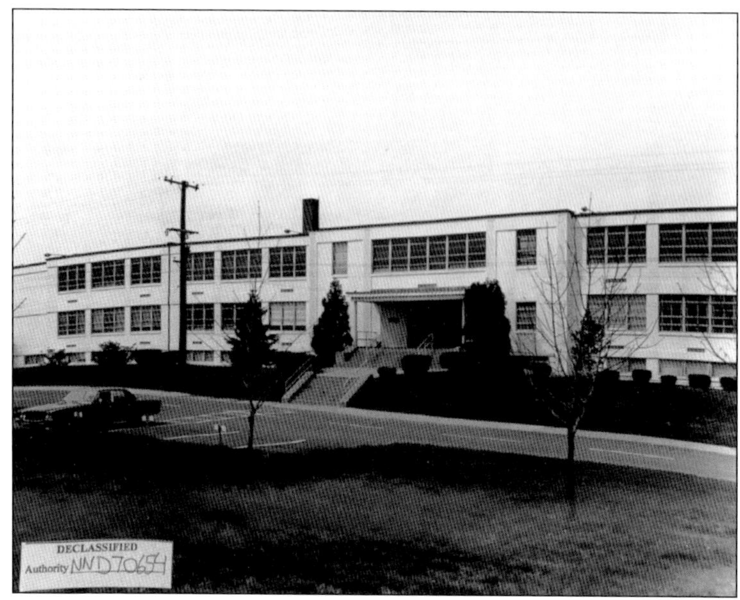

This photograph is of the US Army Intelligence School at Fort Holabird. This is where the training took place for the military intelligence specialists. It was a tough school to gain acceptance to and even tougher to graduate from. But it was a vitally important mission these graduates would carry out. (Courtesy NARA.)

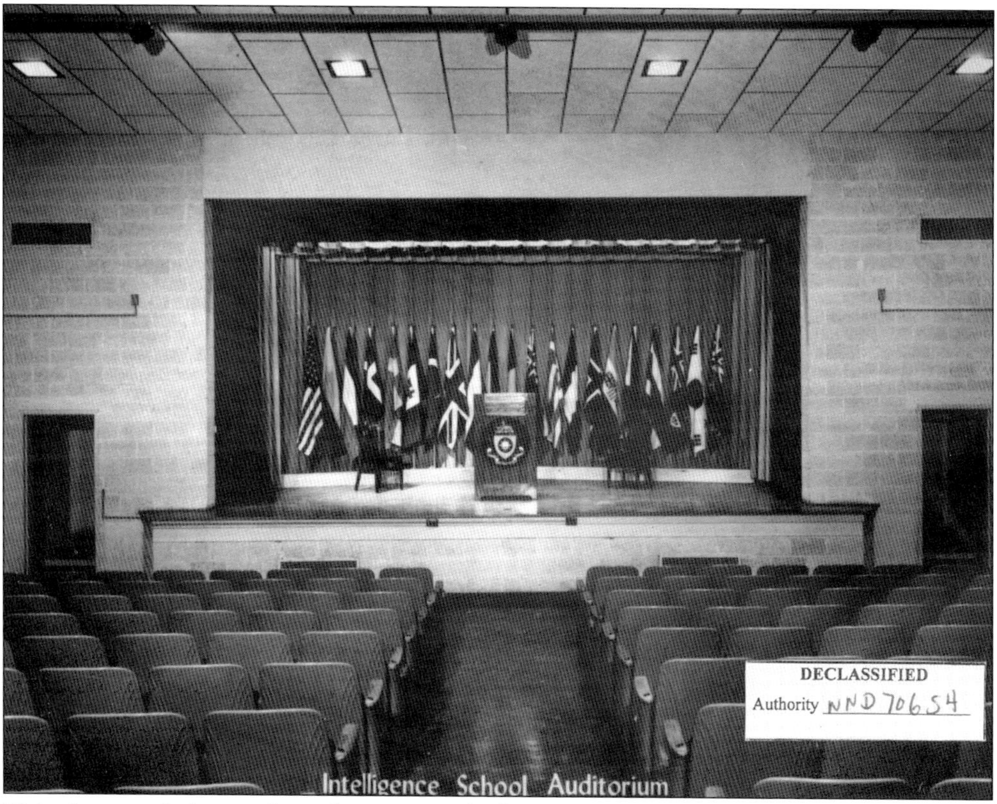

This photograph depicts the auditorium inside the US Army Intelligence School. Here is where general meetings and large classes were held. The stage is decked with flags of allied nations illustrating the international role of the military intelligence specialist. The podium is decorated with a sphinx, the symbol of military intelligence. (Courtesy NARA.)

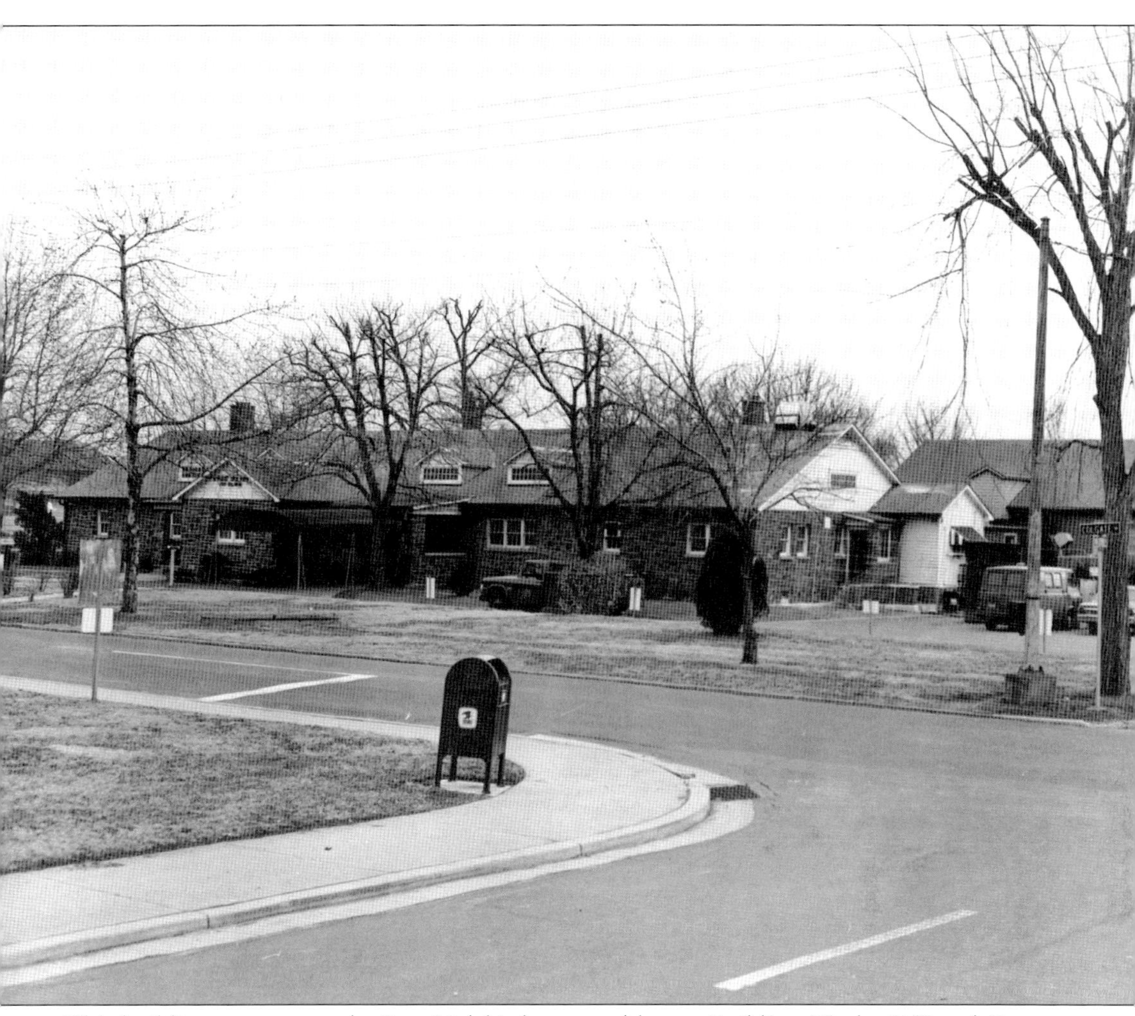

This building appears on the Fort Holabird map and key as Building 65, the Officers' Open Mess. It was more commonly just called the "Officers' Club." It was here Holabird's officers could unwind with a drink, a casual meal, or a game of pool. Its stately design of stone and timber gave it a welcoming appearance. (Courtesy NARA.)

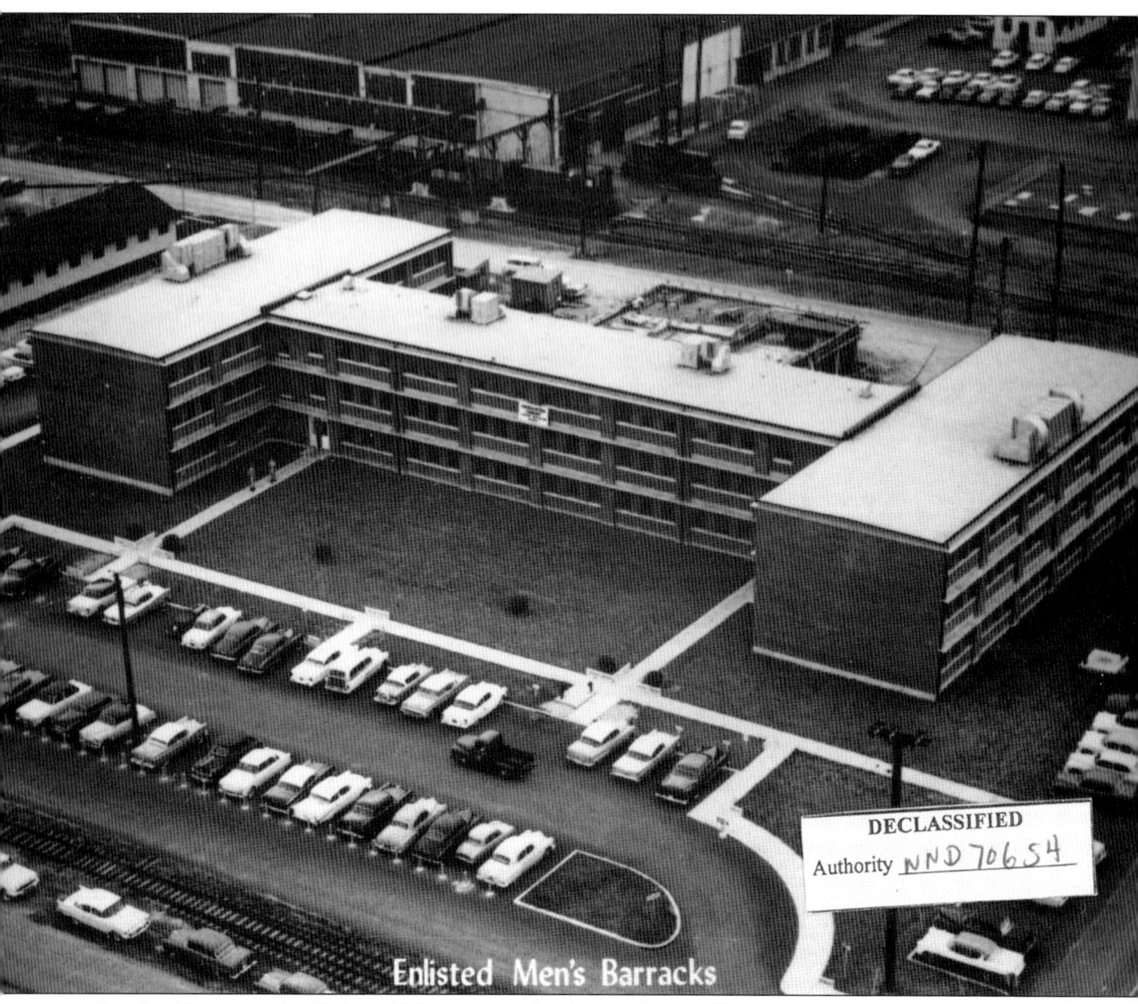

This building was the Enlisted Men's Barracks during the intelligence post years at Fort Holabird. Compared to the wooden barracks of the World War I and World War II years these accommodations are quite nice. The parking lots indicate that some of the enlisted soldiers had cars—a luxury that was unheard of in the early years at Holabird. (Courtesy NARA.)

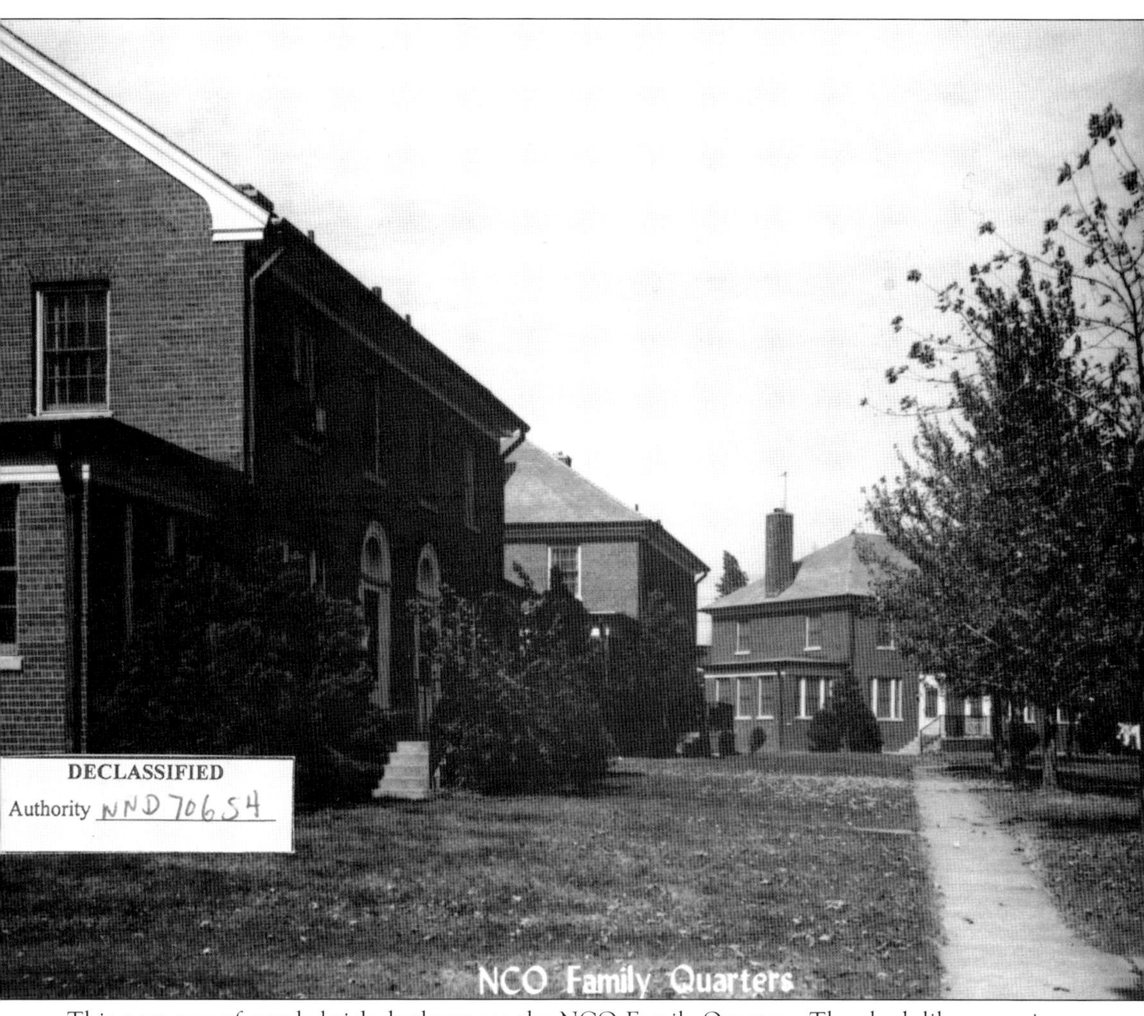

This neat row of stately brick duplexes are the NCO Family Quarters. They look like very nice homes for the sergeants and their families to reside in. For the sergeant, they are a big step from barracks life and the wooden duplexes that preceded them. (Courtesy NARA.)

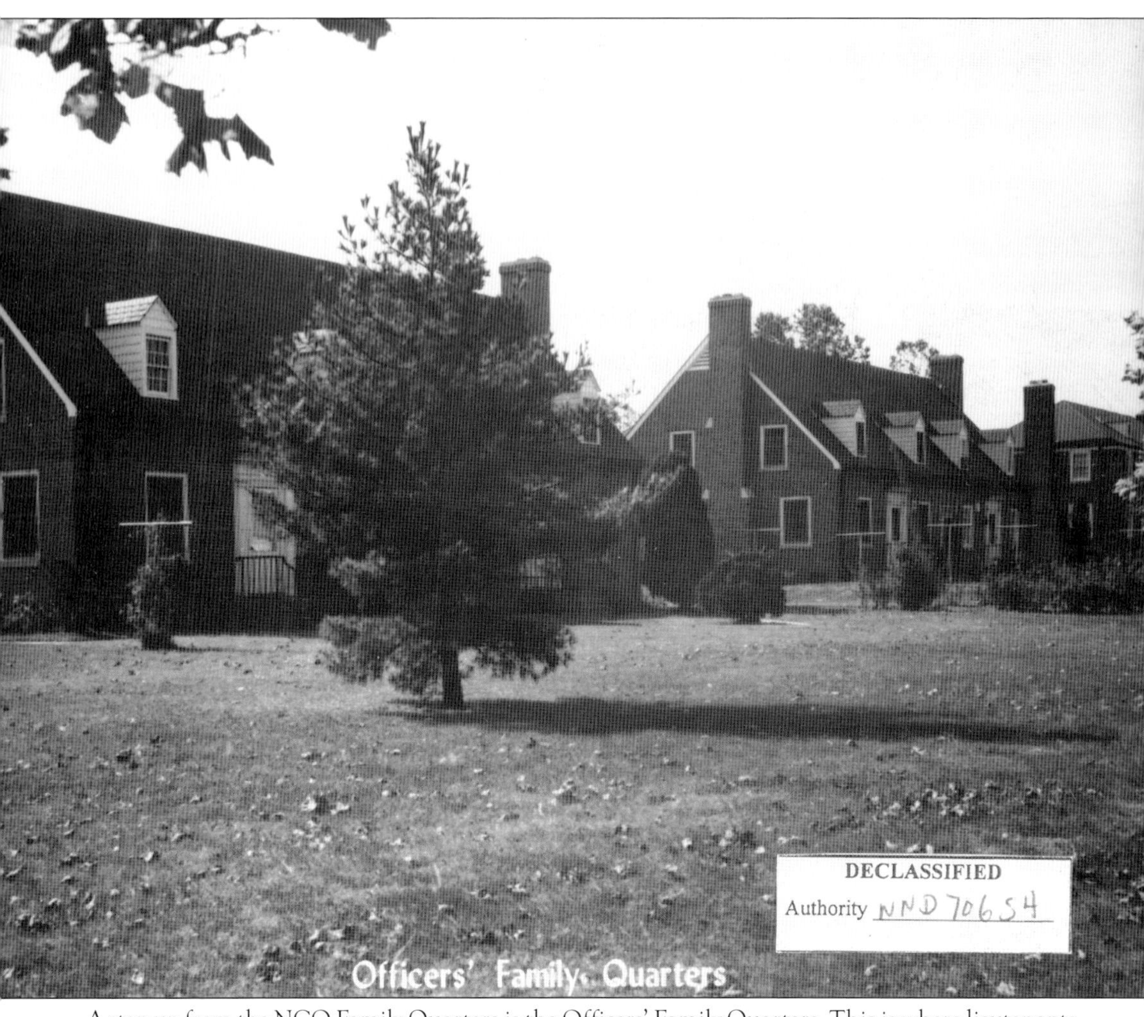

A step up from the NCO Family Quarters is the Officers' Family Quarters. This is where lieutenants and above would reside with their families. The houses are charming and resemble upscale tract housing in any suburb. Officers without families resided in Bachelor Officer Quarters, which were a kind of barracks but nicer than the enlisted barracks. (Courtesy NARA.)

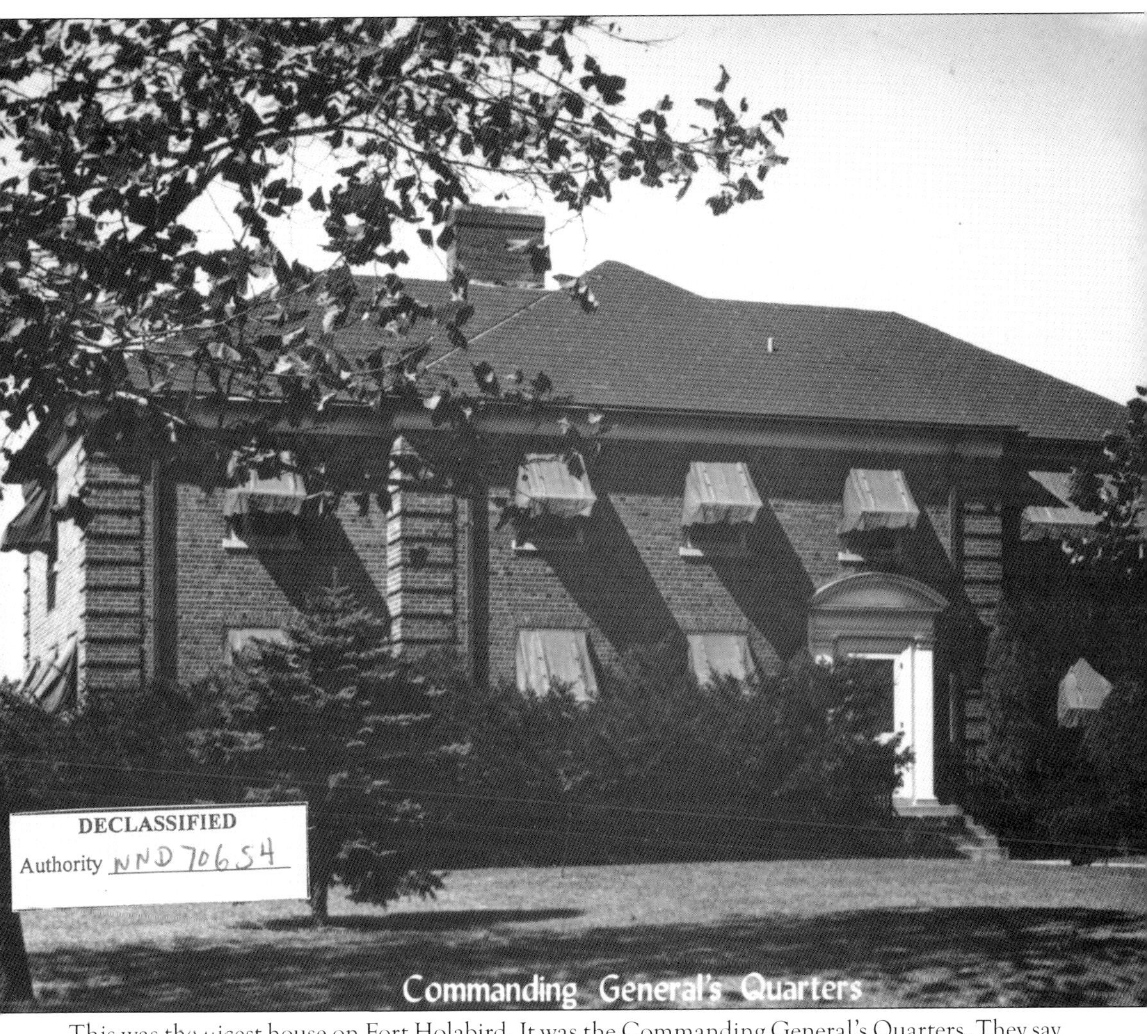

This was the nicest house on Fort Holabird. It was the Commanding General's Quarters. They say rank has its privileges, and judging by these accommodations, it would appear so. A succession of general officers and their families would pass through this home during Fort Holabird's history. Sadly, it was demolished when Holabird was shut down. (Courtesy NARA.)

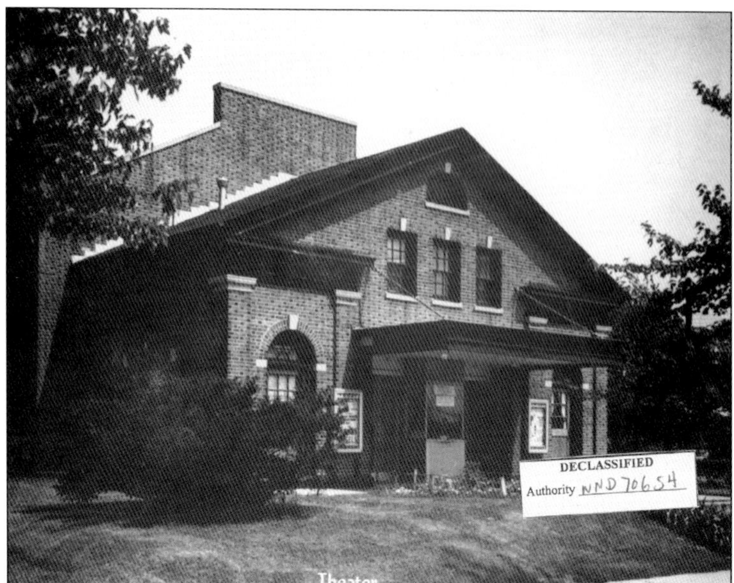

This photograph is of the Fort Holabird post theater. It was located on Colgate Avenue just inside one of the Dundalk Avenue gates. This placed the theater on the same block as the chapel and the library. If a soldier had some time on his hands and needed some relaxation, this block was the place to go. (Courtesy NARA.)

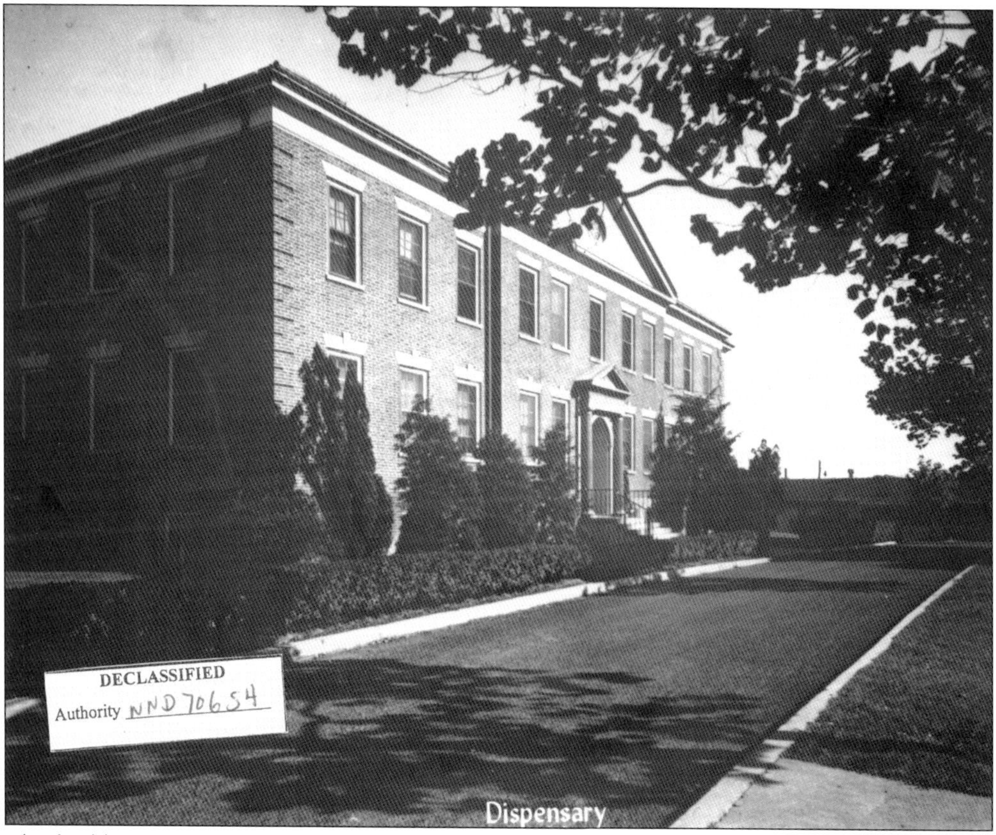

This building was the dispensary. Staffed by medical corpsmen, nurses, physicians, and dentists all of a soldier's health care needs were provided for here. Daily "sick call" was a morning ritual where soldiers were screened for acute illnesses. Soldiers' long-term health needs were also handled here, including vaccinations for current duty as well as deploying soldiers. (Courtesy NARA.)

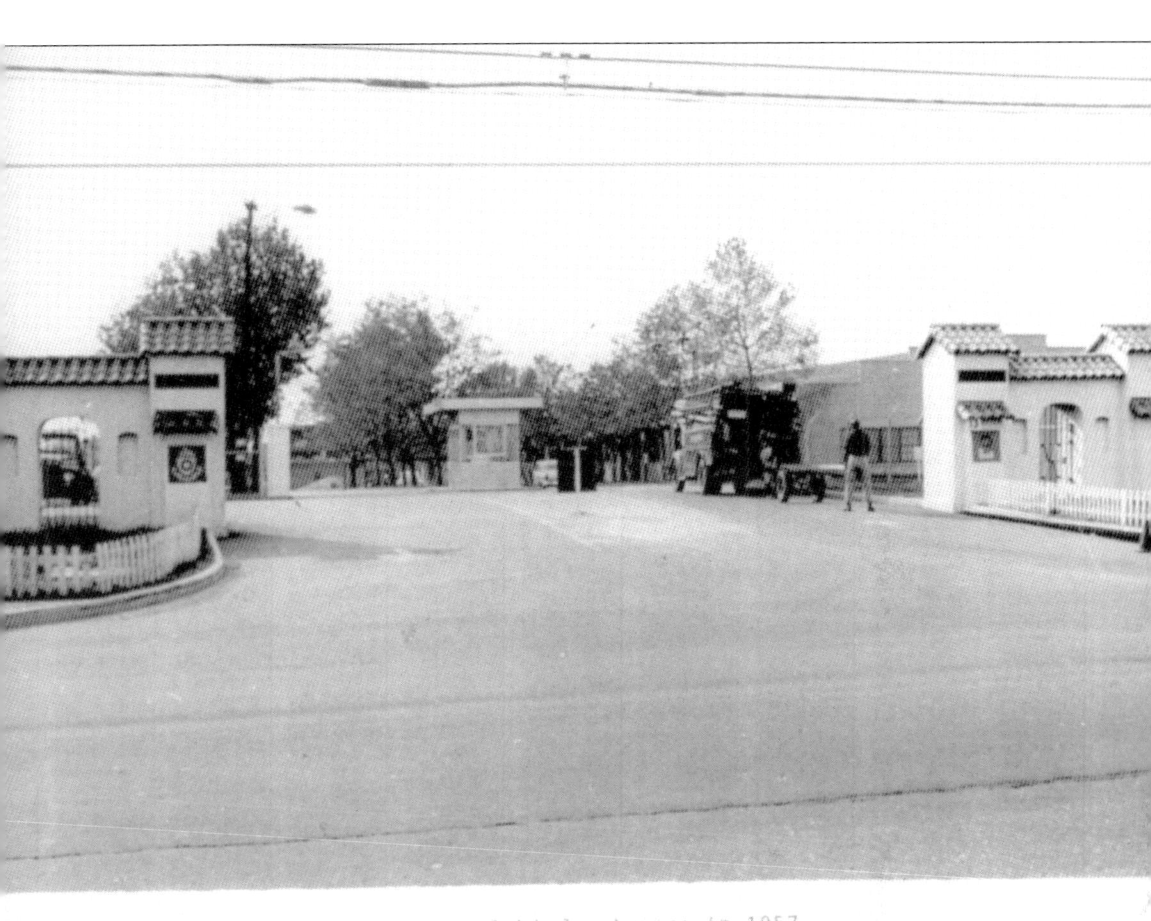

48- Fort Holabird entrance in 1957.

This 1957 photograph looks like the main gate on Holabird Avenue. MPs (military police) are on duty to check IDs for staff and visitors to Fort Holabird. As an intelligence facility, access to the post was restricted. On the left, the gate is marked with the symbol of a sphinx, indicating Holabird's role as an intelligence post. (Courtesy Dundalk-Patapsco Neck Historical Society & Museum.)

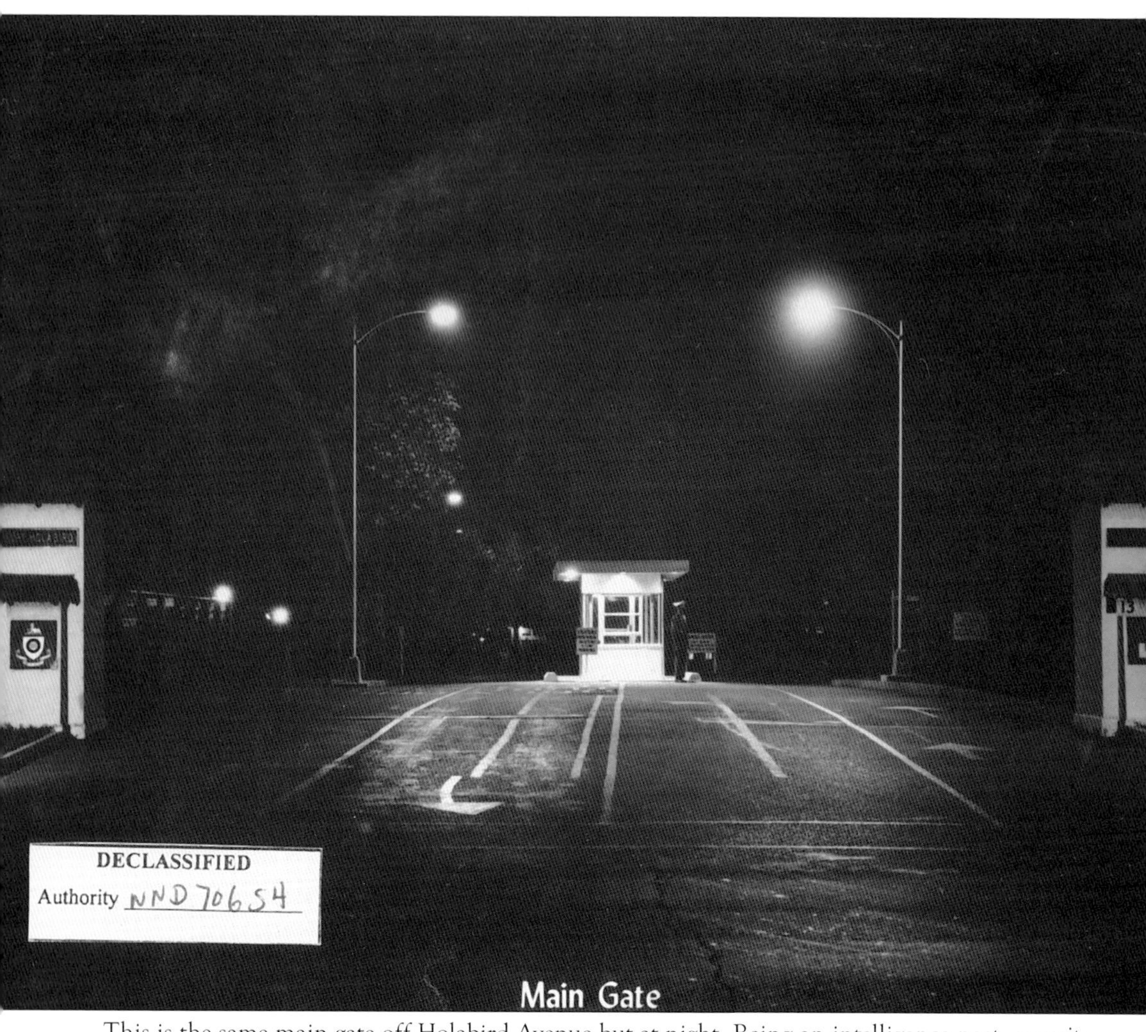

This is the same main gate off Holabird Avenue but at night. Being an intelligence post, security was a 24-hours-a-day, seven-days-a-week mission, and the MP at the guard house appears alert and ready. ID and visitor passes had to be presented to gain access to Fort Holabird during this historic period. (Courtesy NARA.)

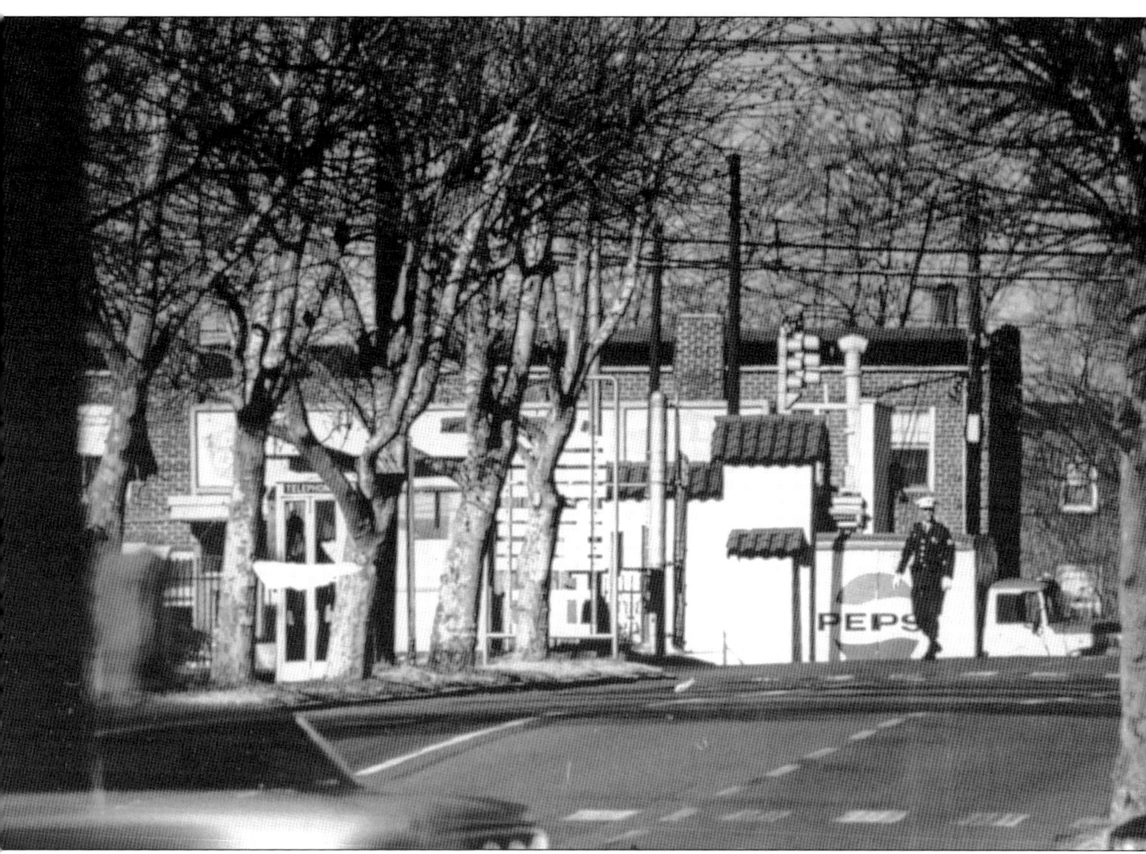

This photograph shows an alert MP on duty at a busy Dundalk Avenue gate. The MP had his hands full screening entrants to Fort Holabird. There were numerous people with legitimate access to the post. They include soldiers, civilian employees, contractors, and vendors. It was the MP's job to make sure no unauthorized people entered. (Courtesy Dundalk-Patapsco Neck Historical Society & Museum.)

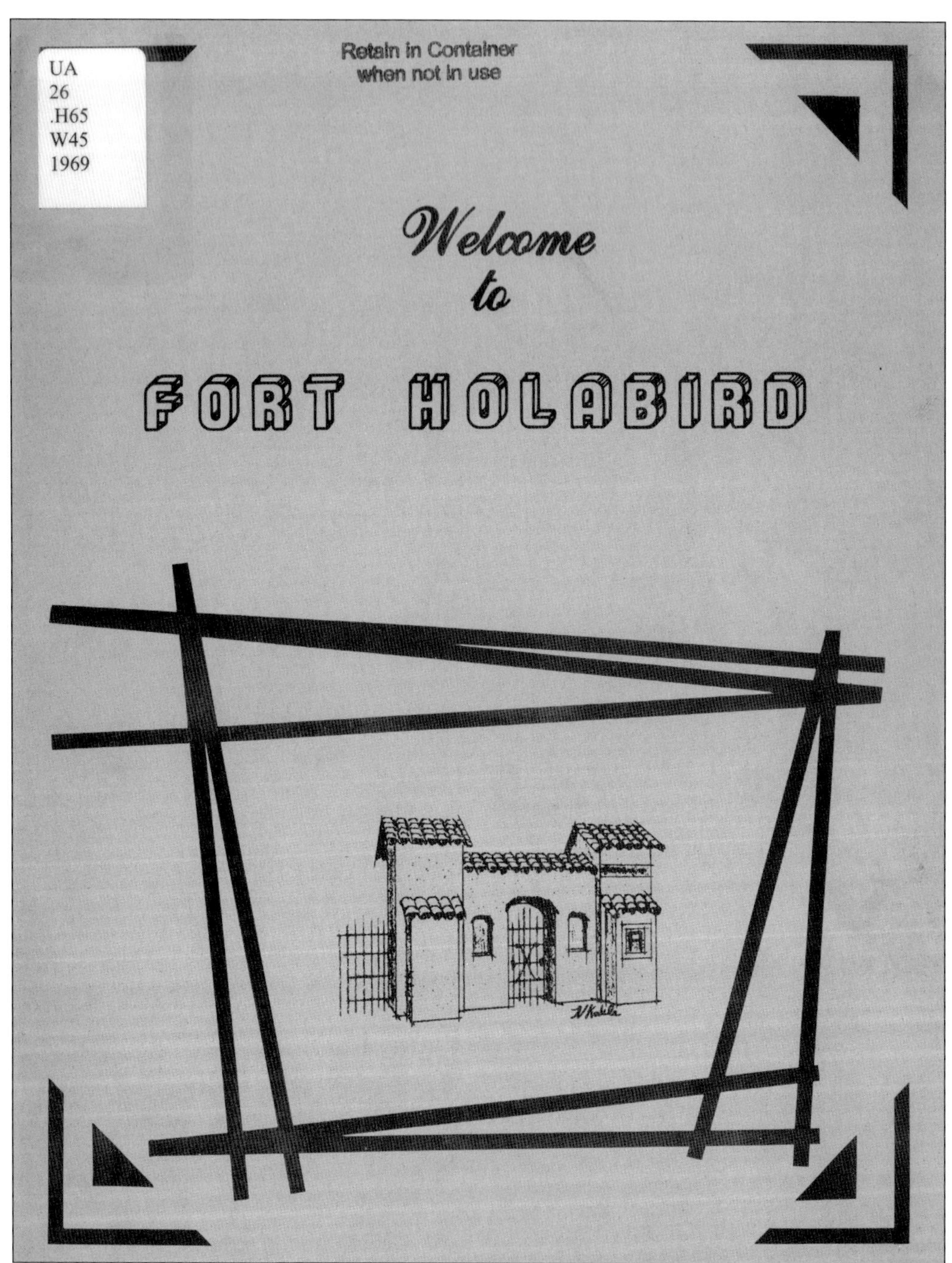

This booklet is dated 1969. It was issued to all newly arriving soldiers and officers. Inside was a map of Holabird as well as a map of the general area. The booklet also includes where to find necessary services both on and off post and history of the area and Holabird. (Courtesy US Army Heritage and Education Center.)

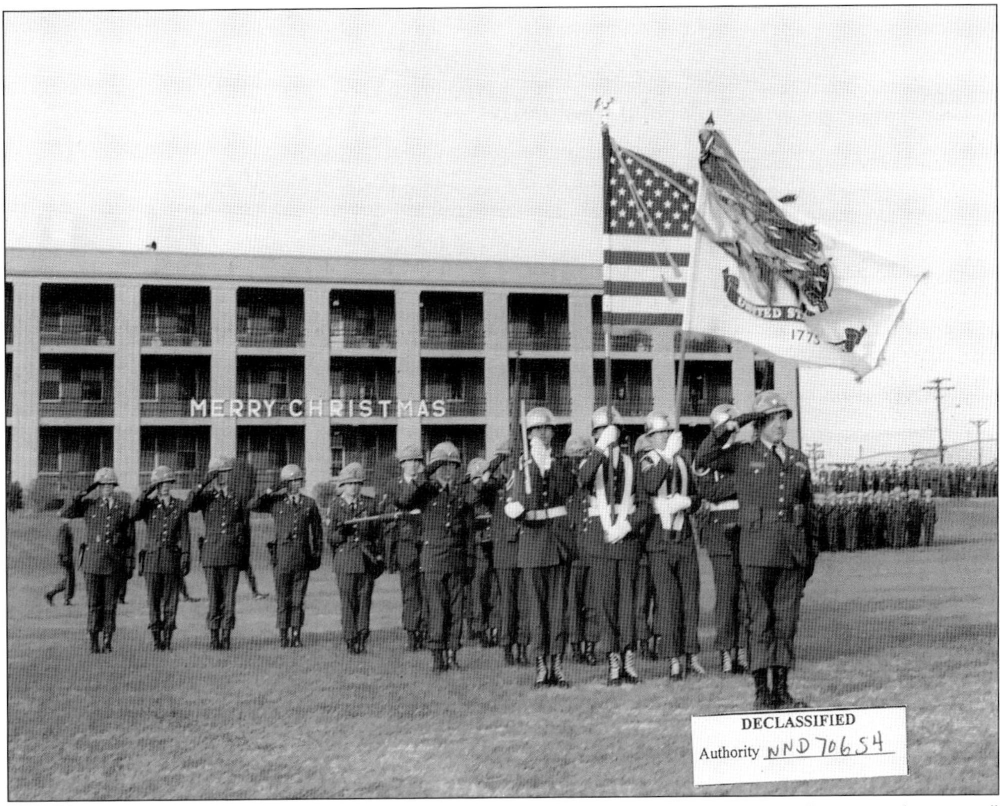

Holidays were incorporated into the daily routine at Fort Holabird. Given the "Merry Christmas" on the building indicates this photograph might be from Christmastime. This full-dress formation complete with a drill team may be part of a holiday celebration. The colors are unfurled, and the uniforms are sharp. Whatever is happening here, it is something important. (Courtesy NARA.)

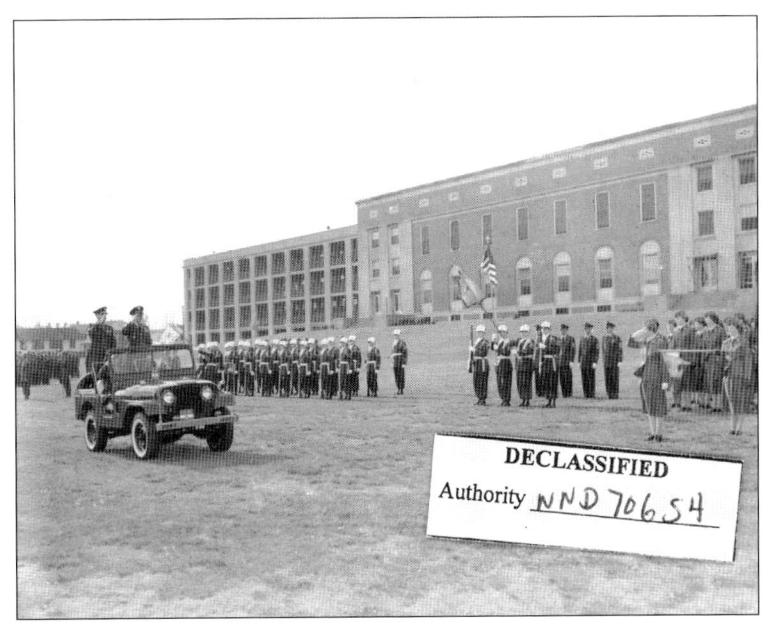

This appears to be a general officer reviewing the troops in front of post headquarters. They are wearing dress uniforms, and the colors are unfurled indicating this is a serious inspection. In this photograph, the female troops are still segregated from the male troops. That is not the case in today's Army. (Courtesy NARA.)

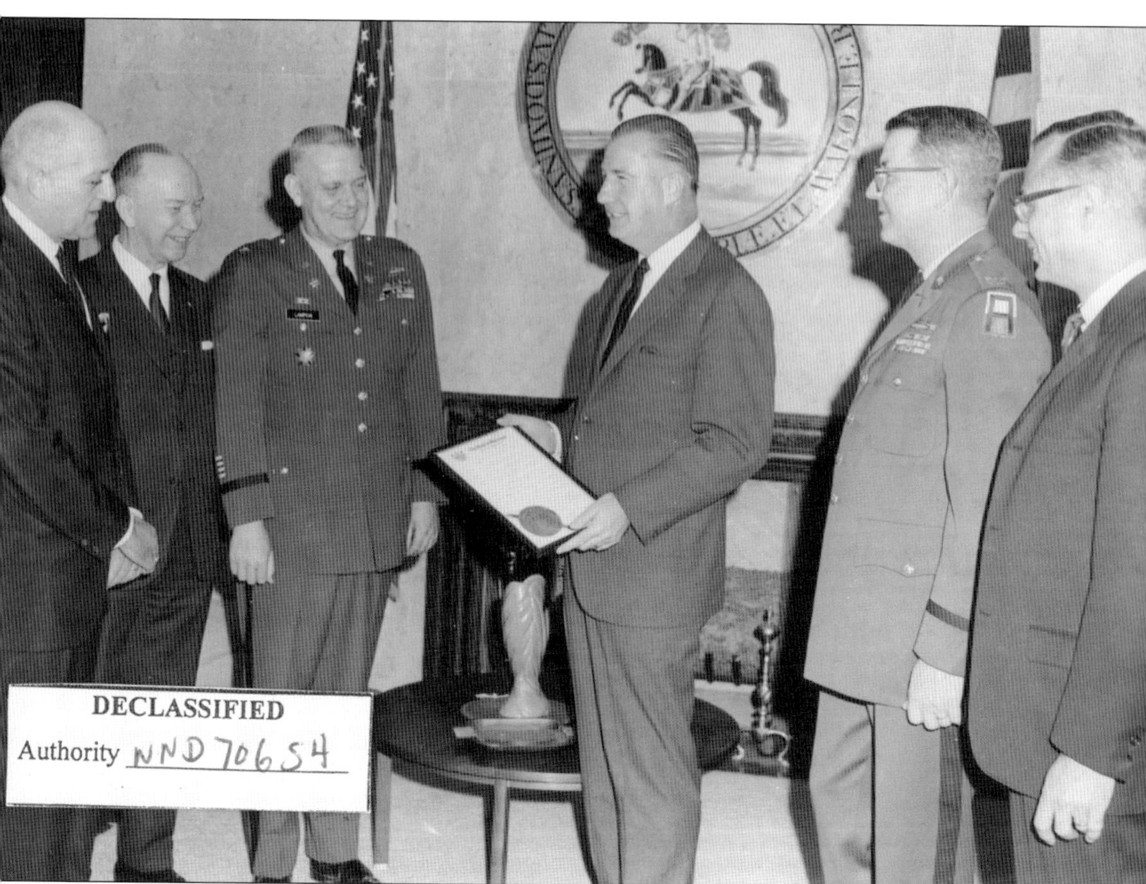

In this photograph, Maryland governor Spiro T. Agnew is with several high-ranking officers at Fort Holabird. This meeting was one of many in the long process of closing Fort Holabird. When it finally shut down the land was turned over to local governments. Governor Agnew was there to represent the State of Maryland. (Courtesy NARA.)

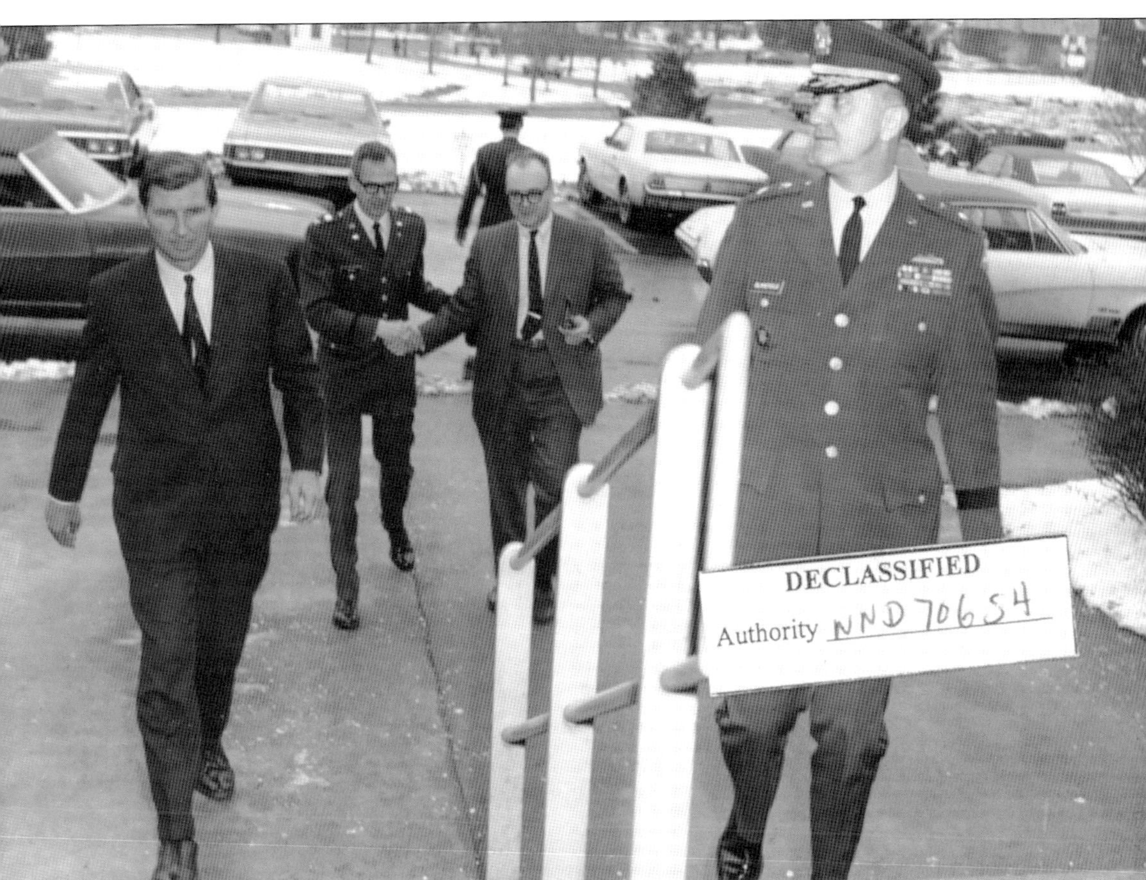

This 1970 photograph shows Maj. Gen. William H. Blakefield welcoming Maryland senator Joseph D. Tydings. Major General Blakefield was the commanding general of the US Army Intelligence Command at Fort Holabird from 1967 to 1970. The general was welcoming the senator for an orientation visit. General Blakefield was a World War II veteran who served during the Battle of the Bulge. (Courtesy NARA.)

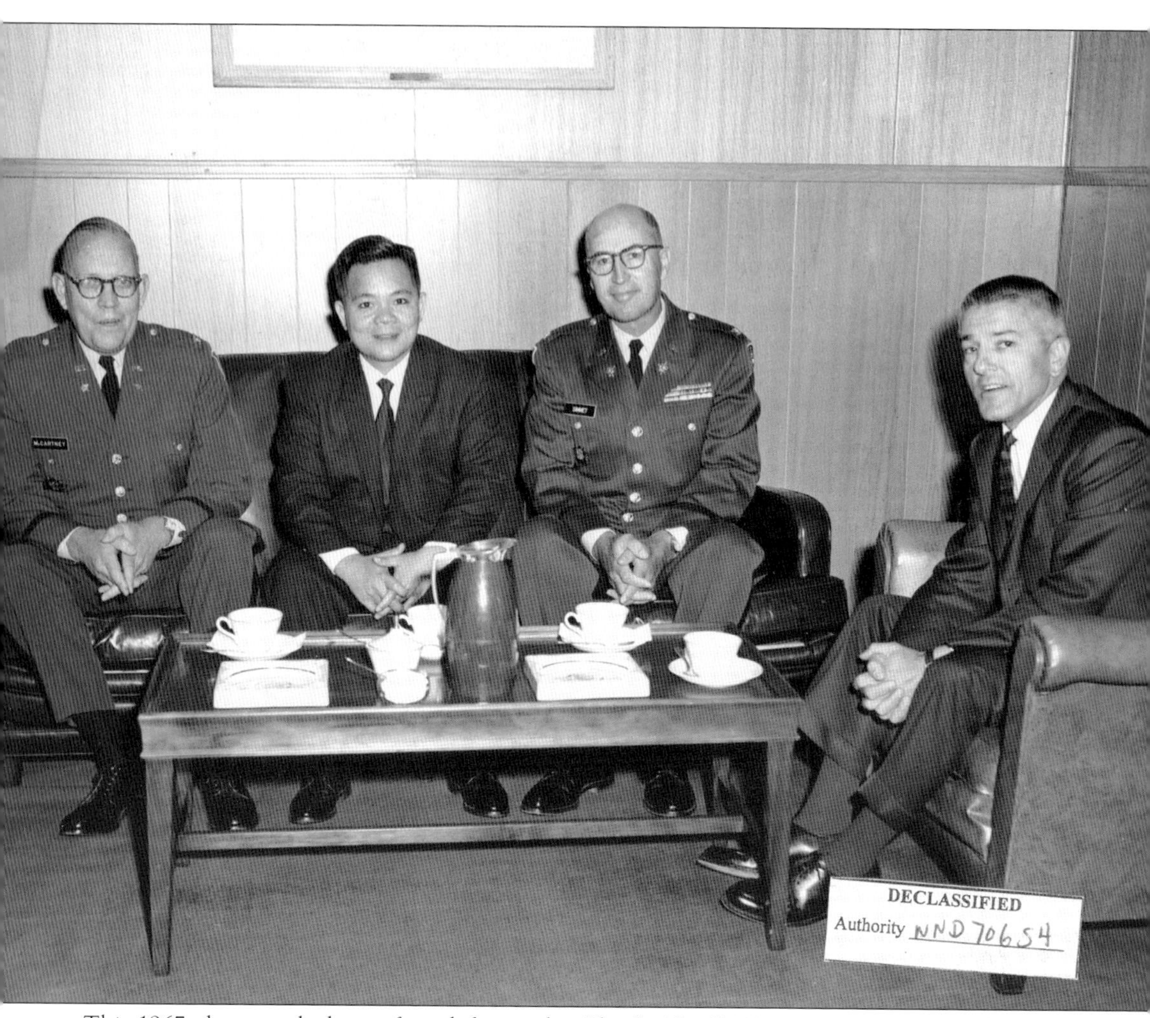

This 1967 photograph shows, from left to right, Chief of Staff US Army Intelligence Command Col. Robert W. McCartney, Republic of Vietnam Col. Pham Huu Nhon, Col. Kenneth D. Simmet, and Mr. Richard Chillemi. The war in Vietnam was raging, and the two nations were cooperating in the intelligence sphere. (Courtesy NARA.)

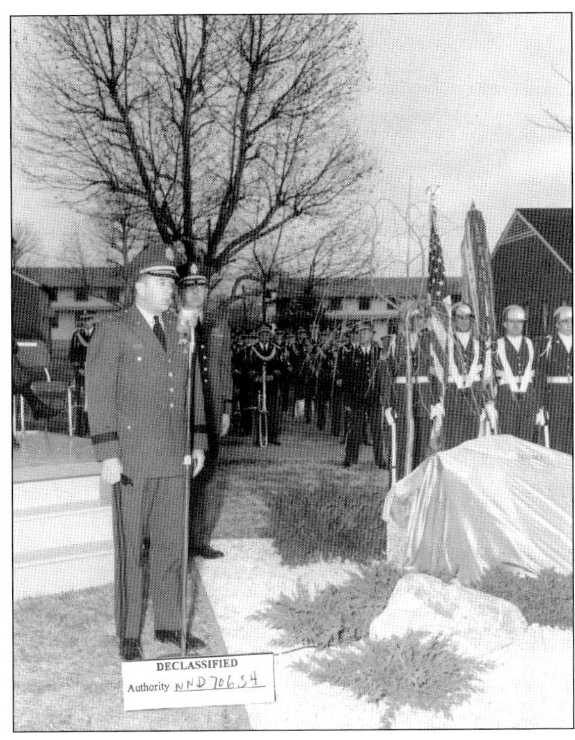

In this 1967 image, a monument is being dedicated. Dedication of a monument is a solemn occasion. A military band is present. Also present is a drill team with colors unfurled. The officer at the microphone is unidentified, but he is most likely the post commander or a high-ranking officer in the intelligence command. (Courtesy NARA.)

The monument being dedicated is to Maj. Gen. Ralph H. Van Deman. He was called the "Father of Modern Military Intelligence." In 1897. Major General Van Deman joined the War Department Military Information Division. He served in an intelligence capacity during the Spanish-American War and World War I. During World War II. He served in the War Department as a consultant. (Courtesy NARA.)

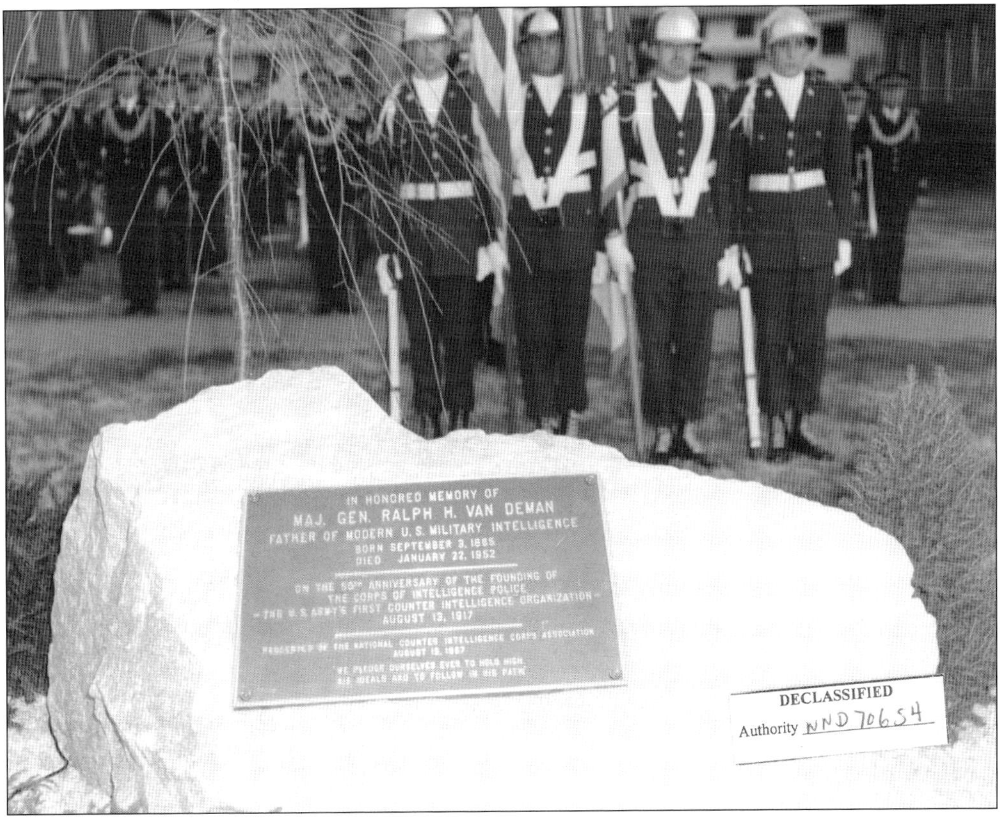

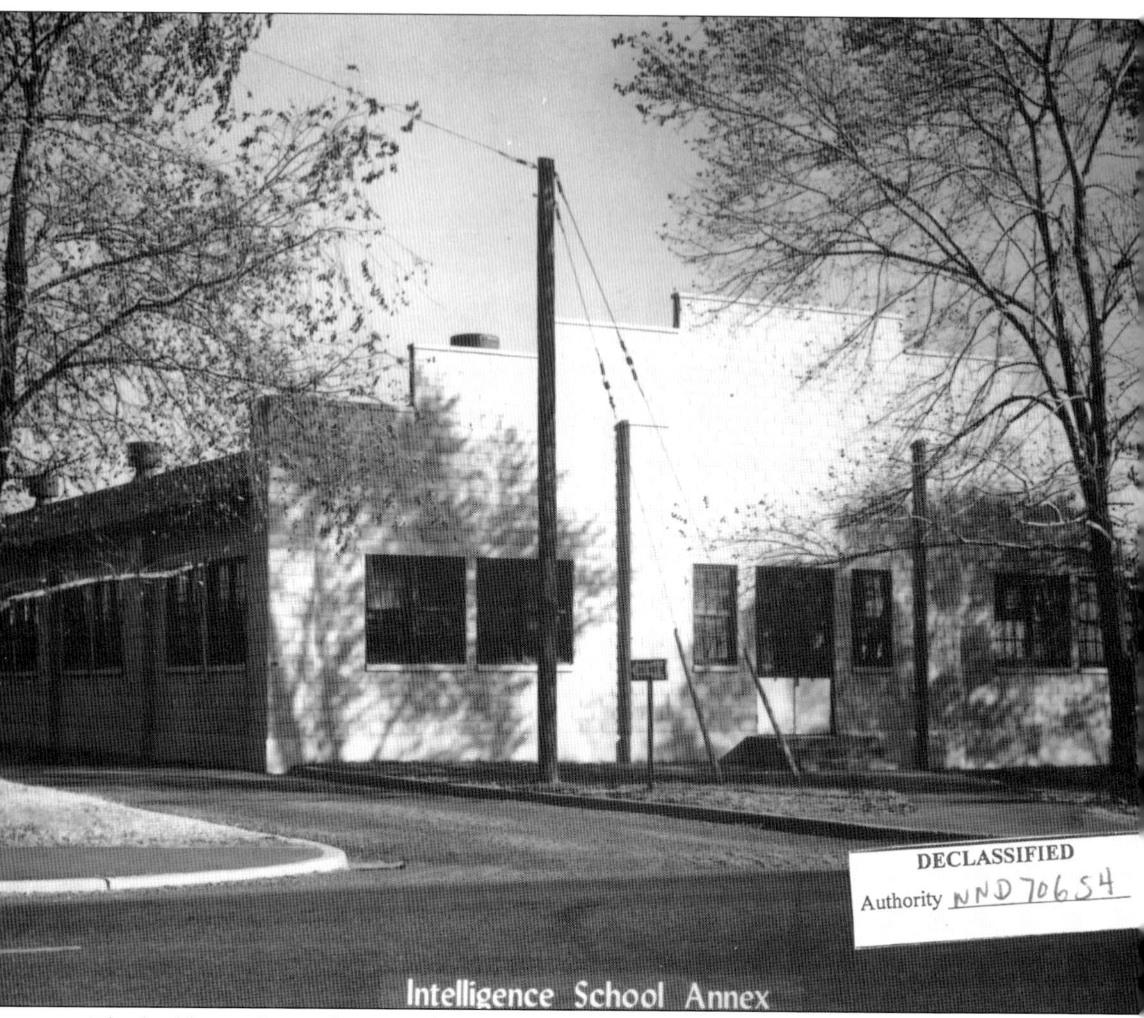

This building is the Intelligence School Annex. Given the secretive nature of the mission, what took place in these walls is not known. It may have been used for training or something as mundane as storage. In any event, it was also known as Hubbard Hall or simply "Building 38." (Courtesy NARA.)

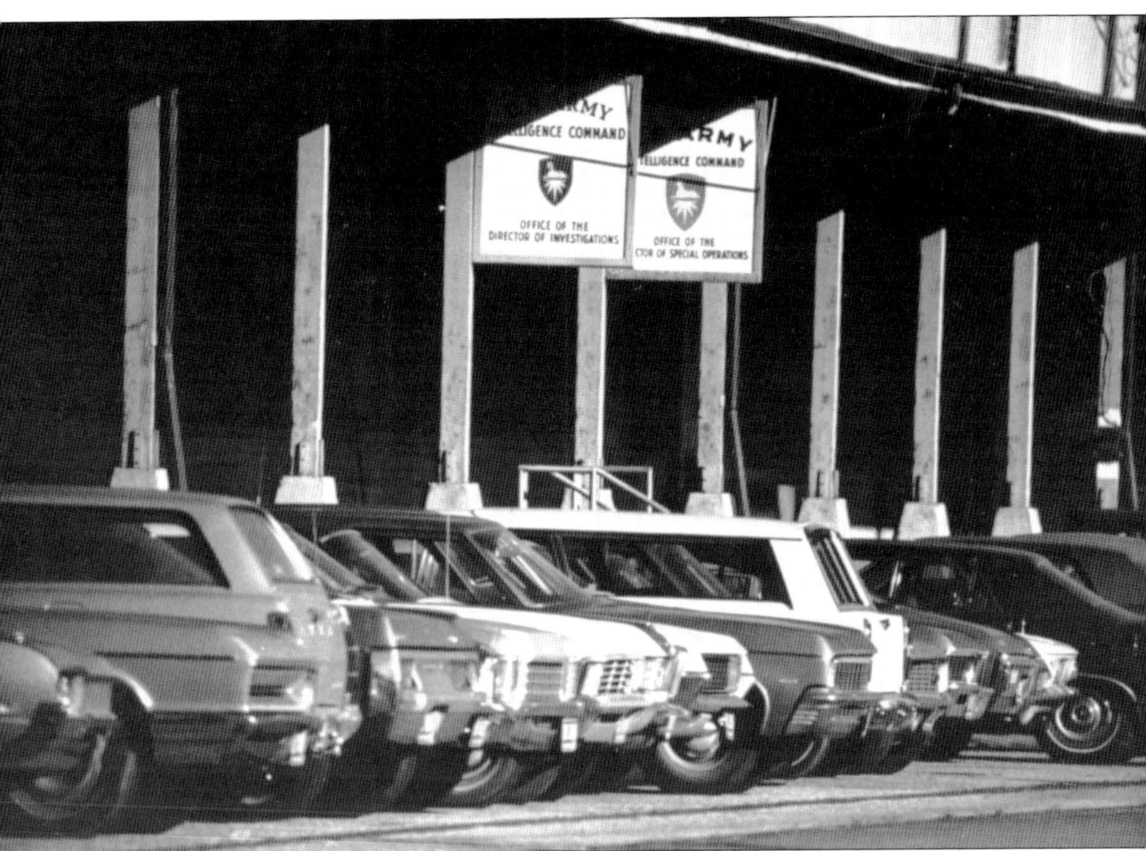

This photograph appears to be the parking area for the US Army Intelligence Command. The specific mission taking place in this building is that of the Office of the Director of Investigations. Quite an unassuming building for what sounds like real spy craft work. That was the nature of Holabird—plain looking on the outside while vital missions and training take place inside. (Courtesy NARA.)

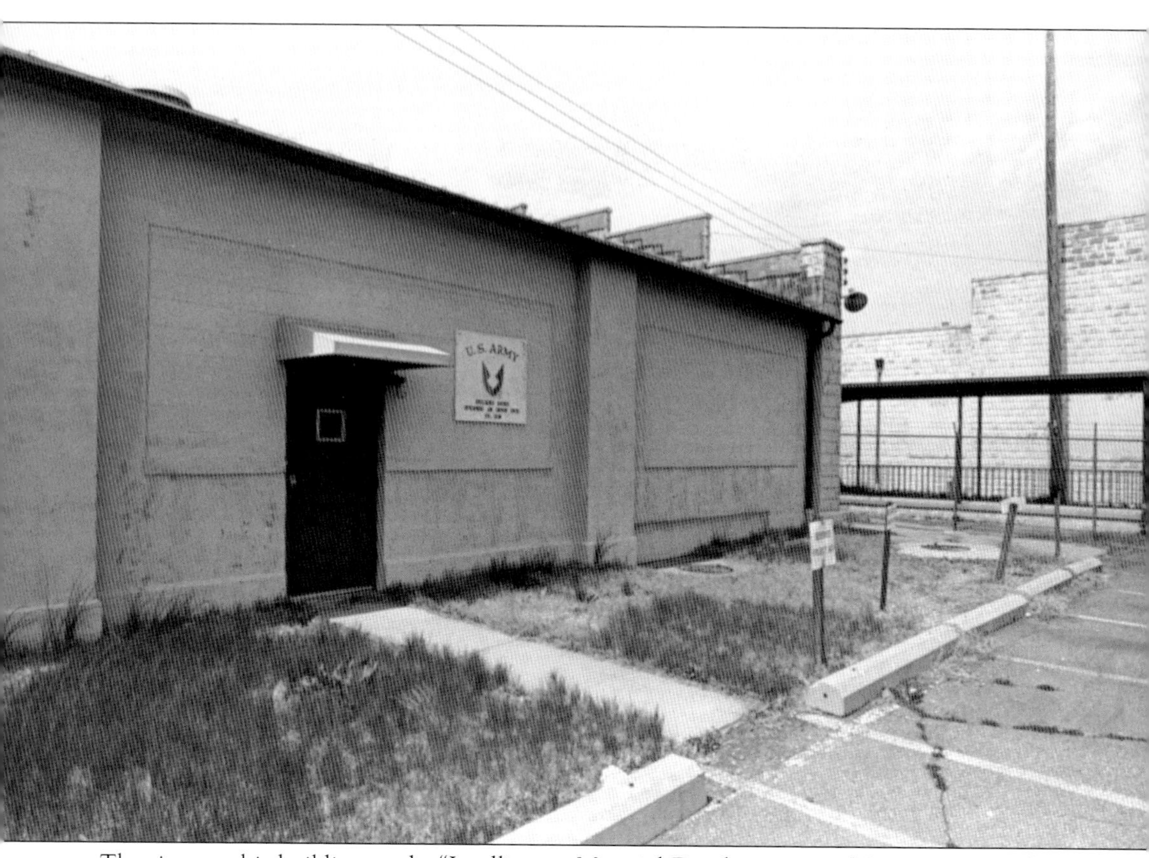

The sign on this building reads, "Intelligence Material Development and Support Office." This could be as mundane as a storehouse for the training booklets. It could also be a much higher military intelligence function. There is no way to tell, and Holabird had a tendency to present a plain appearance. The sign also reads "Evl. Econ." What that means is anyone's guess. (Courtesy NARA.)

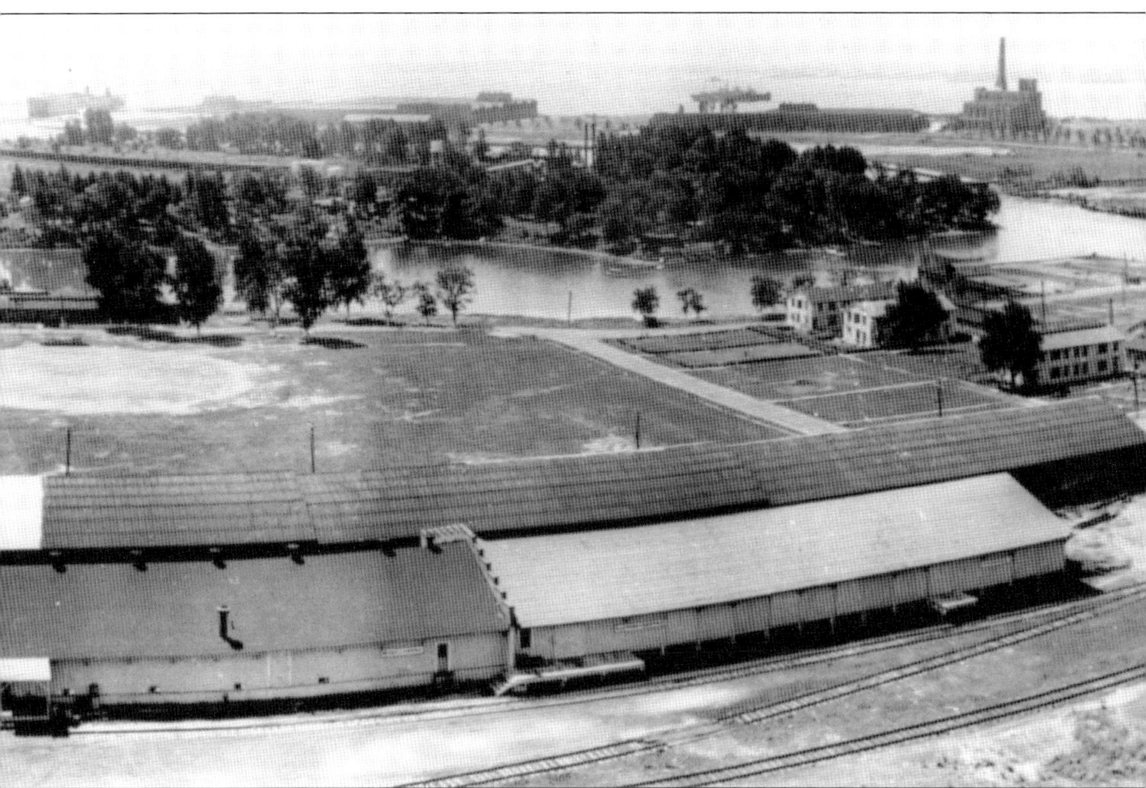

Railroads still serviced Fort Holabird during the intelligence years. Though far less frequently than during the Quartermaster Corps years. This aerial shot shows a serene view with the tranquil waters of Colgate Creek bisecting the post. Some World War II buildings are still present; some would stand until Holabird's final days. (Courtesy NARA.)

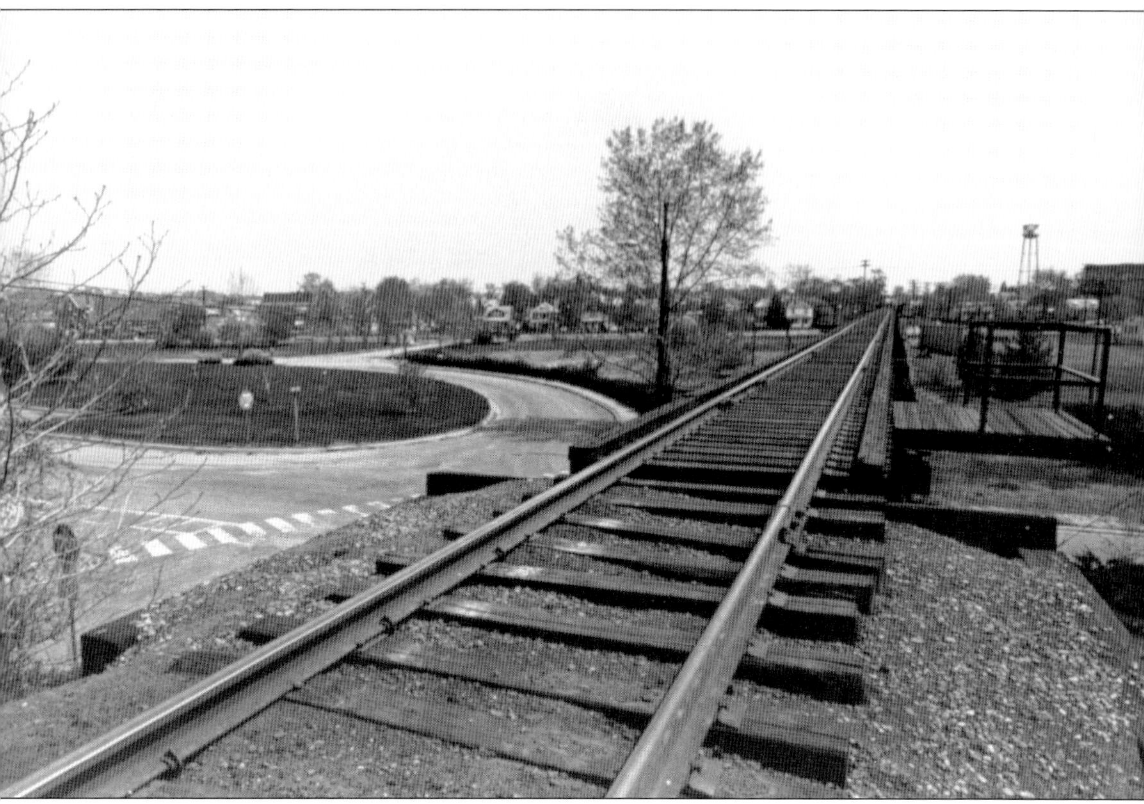

The tracks of the Baltimore & Ohio Railroad cut across Fort Holabird. In the distance is Dundalk Avenue, which bounded Fort Holabird on the north side. The traffic circle in the foreground is a new addition. This indicates this photograph is from the transition years between the military post and the civilian industrial park. (Courtesy Dundalk-Patapsco Neck Historical Society & Museum.)

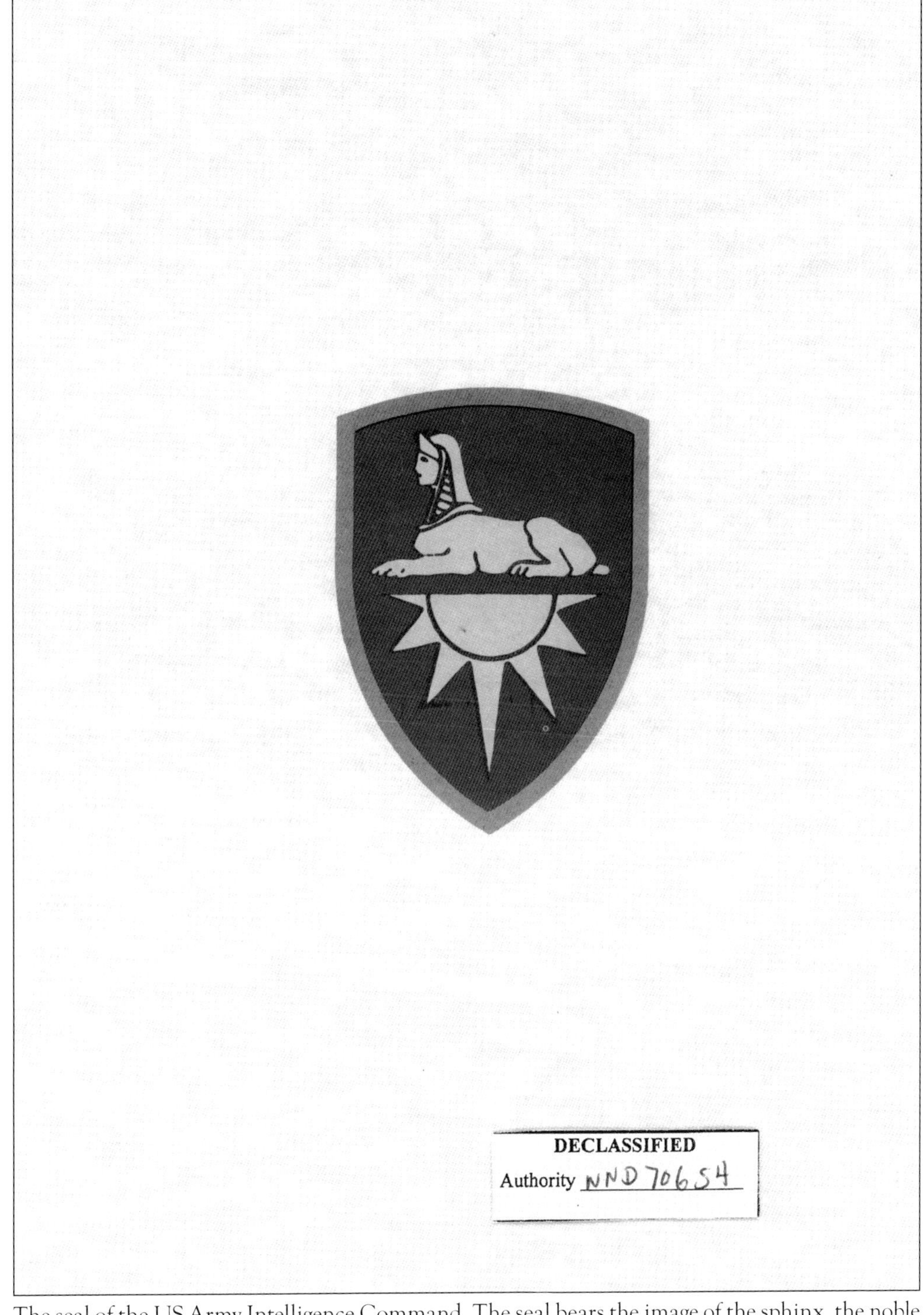

The seal of the US Army Intelligence Command. The seal bears the image of the sphinx, the noble symbol of military intelligence. The sphinx was chosen as a symbol because it represents wisdom and mystery. This seal was on heavy stock paper, and it may have been a cover sheet. (Courtesy NARA.)

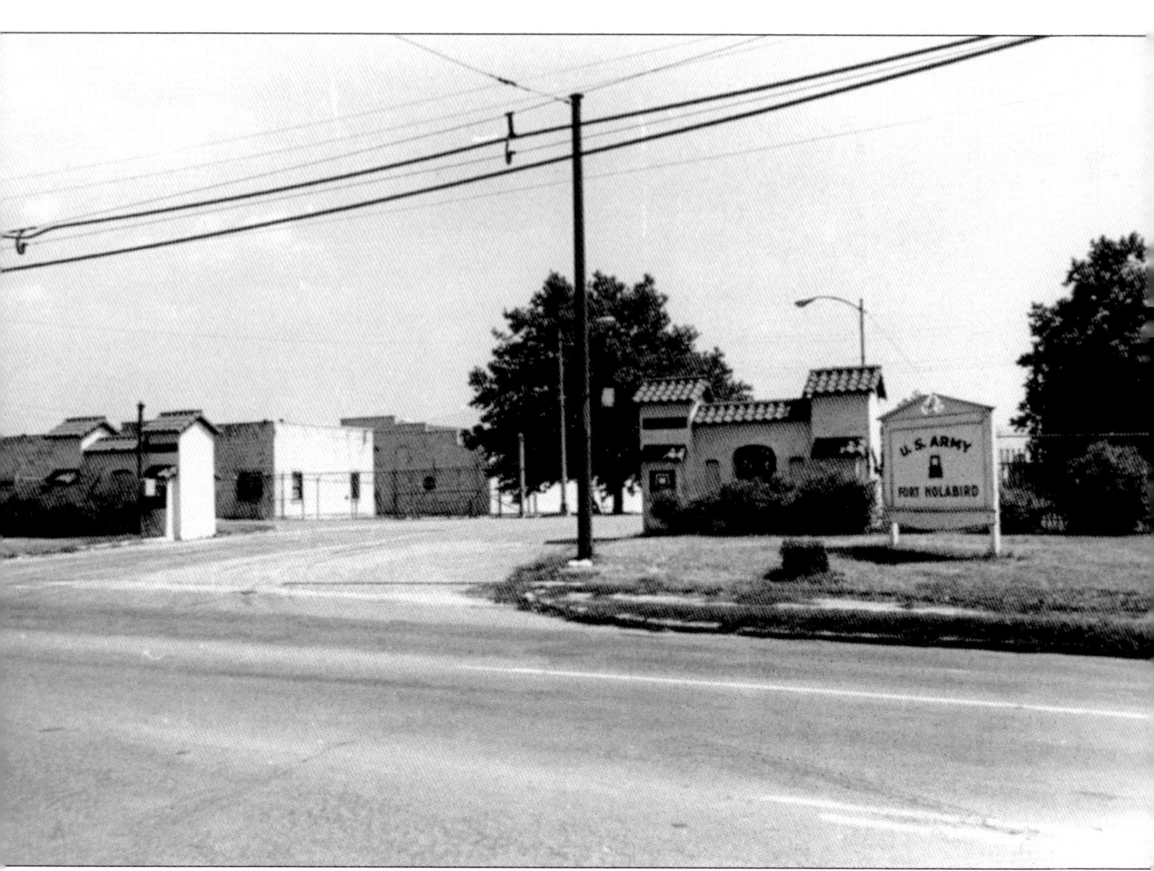

This photograph shows Fort Holabird's main gate as it looked in its final days. This gate was on Holabird Avenue, and it remained active until Holabird was shut down and the post was handed over to the local government. The gate is quiet today, indicating this image was shot in Holabird's waning days. (Courtesy Dundalk-Patapsco Neck Historical Society & Museum.)

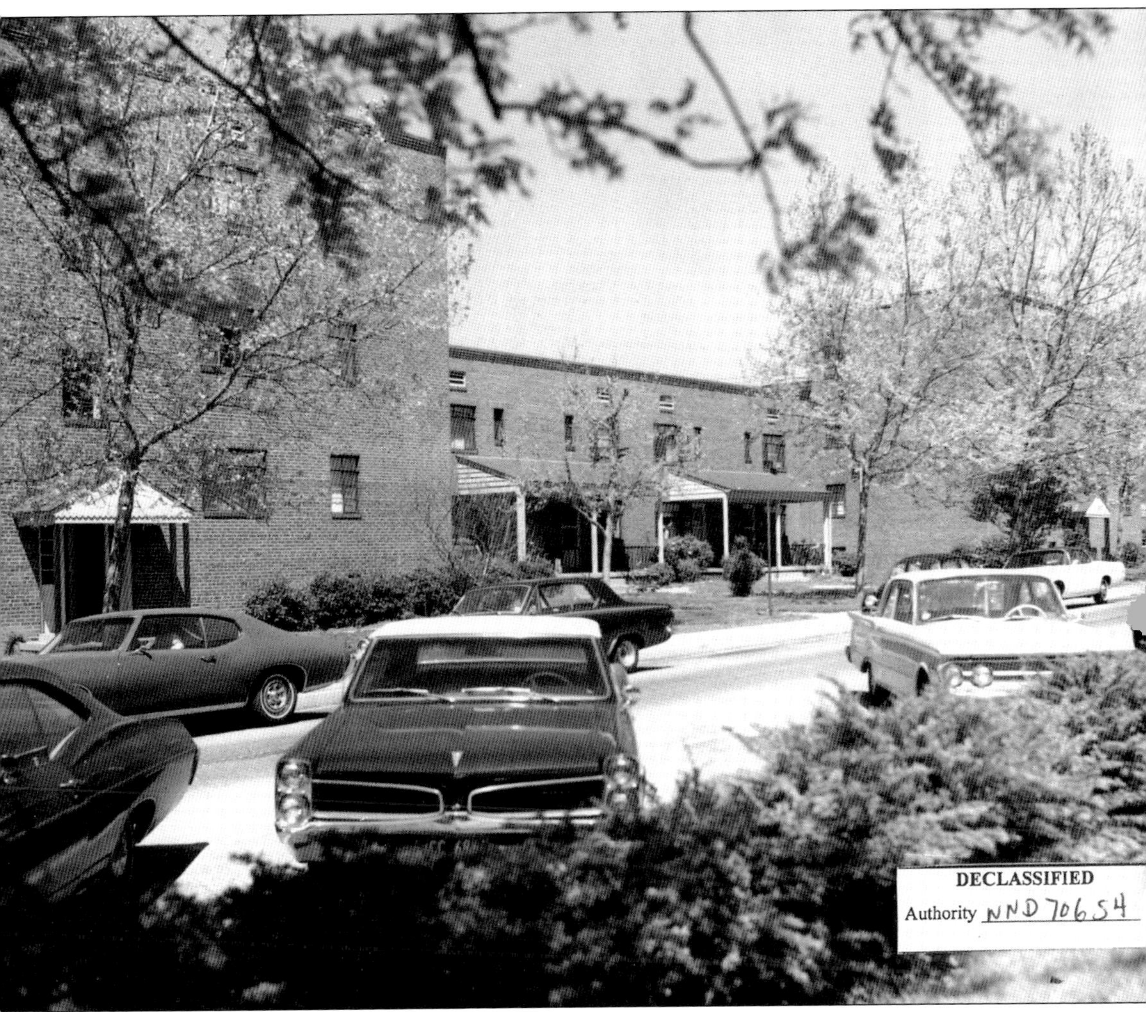

Here is a 1960s-era image of the Cummings apartments. These apartments provided housing for soldiers with families. For many young couples just starting out, Cummings was their first home. The exact date of the photograph is not known, but the cars appear to be mid-to-late-1960s models. (Courtesy NARA.)

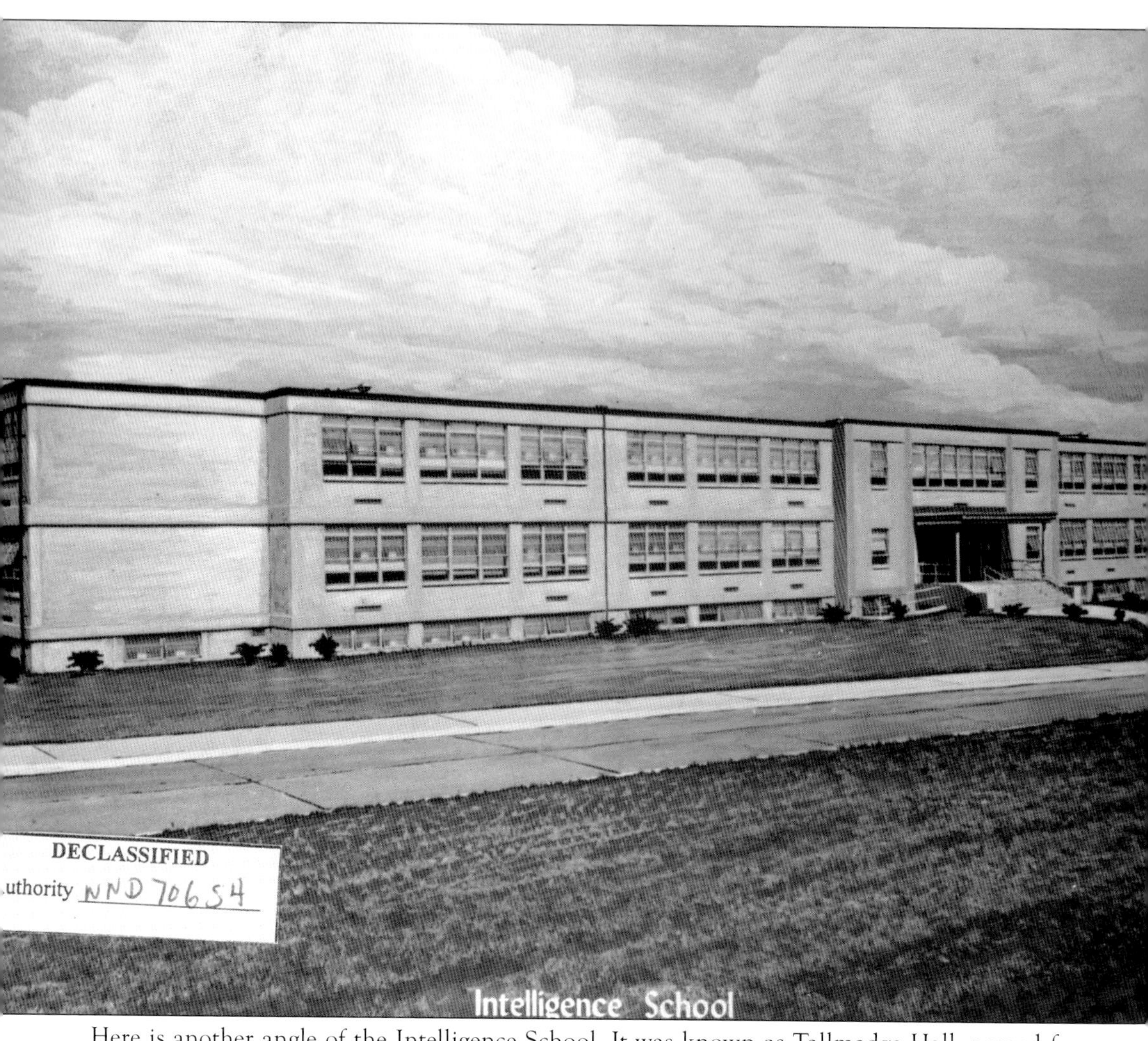

Here is another angle of the Intelligence School. It was known as Tallmadge Hall, named for Benjamin Tallmadge, who was a Revolutionary War spymaster. Tallmadge was appointed as head of military intelligence by George Washington. He operated a ring of spies in New York known as the Culper Ring. He was successful in providing military intelligence to the Continental Army. (Courtesy NARA.)

Four

African American Troops at Holabird

African Americans have served in the US military from its inception. In World Wars I and II alone, two million African Americans served with distinction. For most of the country's history, they served in a segregated military. The US military began desegregating in 1948 when President Truman issued an executive order.

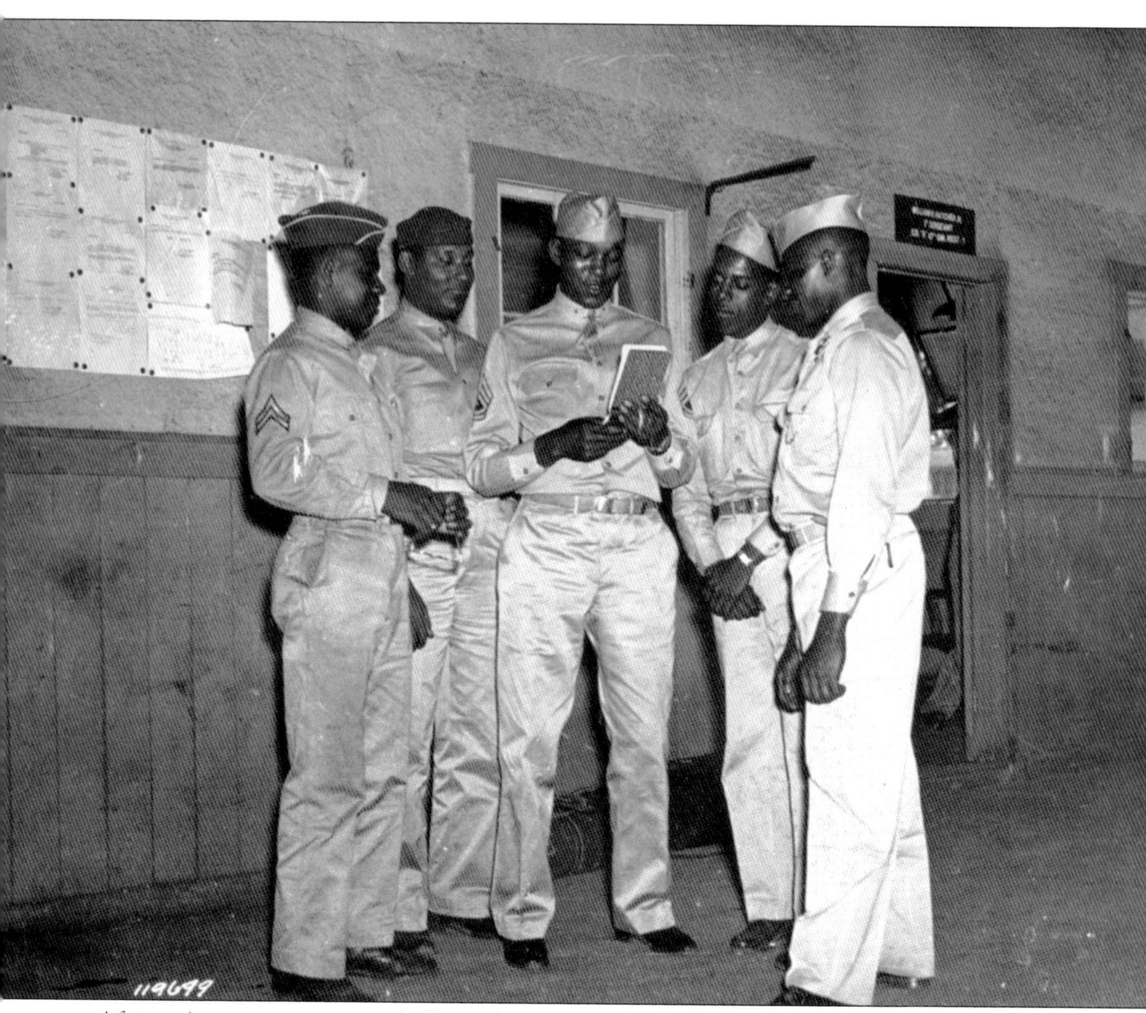

African American troops in a hallway photographed on May 19, 1941. The taller man in the center is 1st Sgt. William H. Hatcher Jr. of Richmond, Virginia. He had been in the Army for 27 years and is passing out assignments to the soldiers. The other members of the group are, from left to right, Corporal Gilbert Mays of Dolphin, Virginia; PFC Wilburn Hawkins of McKeesport, Pennsylvania; Sgt. Arthur B. Fletcher of Alexandria, Virginia; and Cpl. James T. Beach of Omaha, Nebraska. Private First-Class Hawkins wears what has been called a "Jeep Driver" cap, and he has wrinkles in the upper legs of his pants. One could assume his MOS (military occupational specialty) was that of a driver. (Courtesy NARA.)

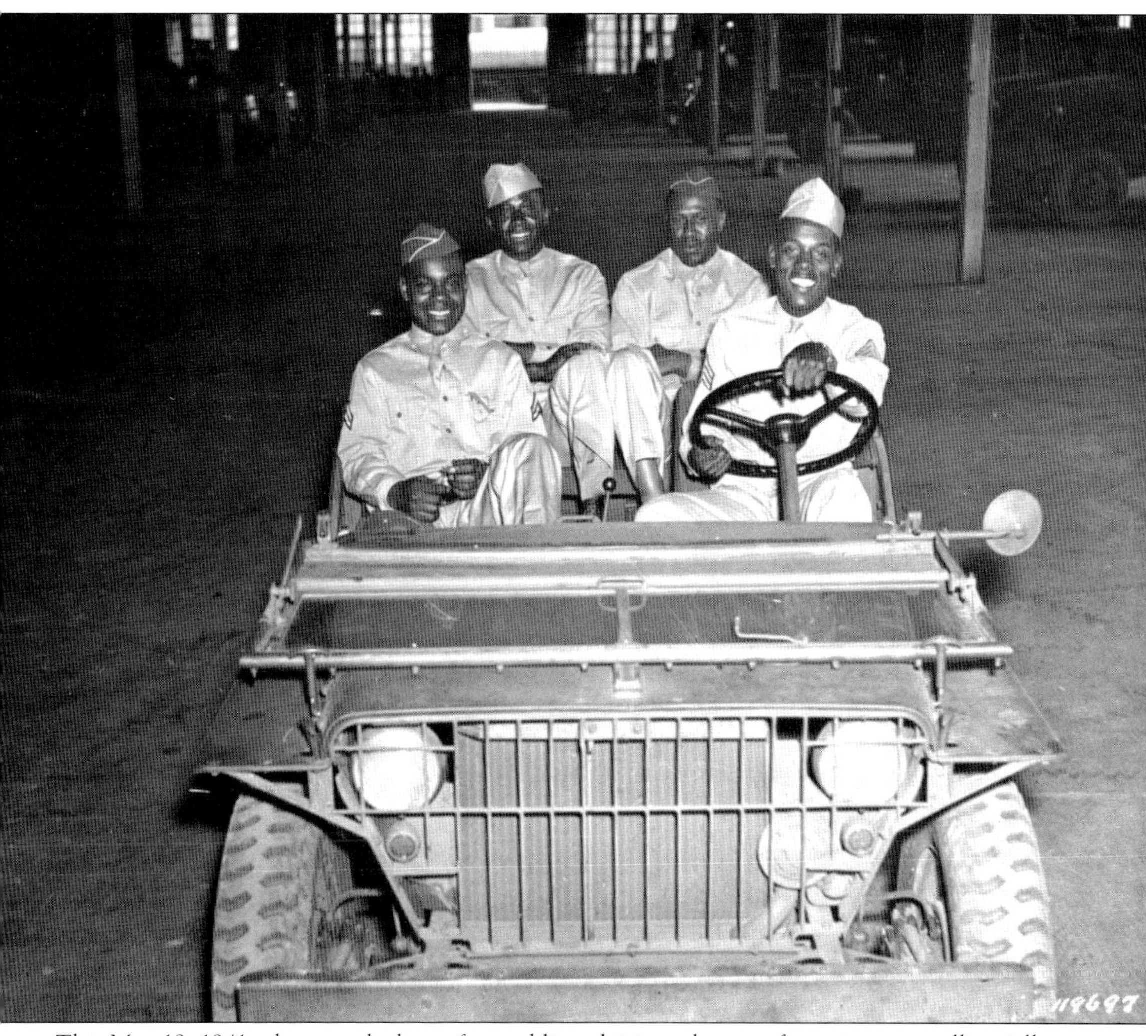

This May 19, 1941, photograph shows four soldiers driving what was for a time was colloquially known as a "midget jump wagon." The soldiers are, from left to right, (first row) Cpl. Gilbert Mays of Dolphin, Virginia, and Sgt. Arthur B. Fletcher of Alexandria, Virginia; (second row) Cpl. James T. Beach of Omaha, Nebraska, and Cpl. John R. Stancil of Newport News, Virginia. (Courtesy NARA.)

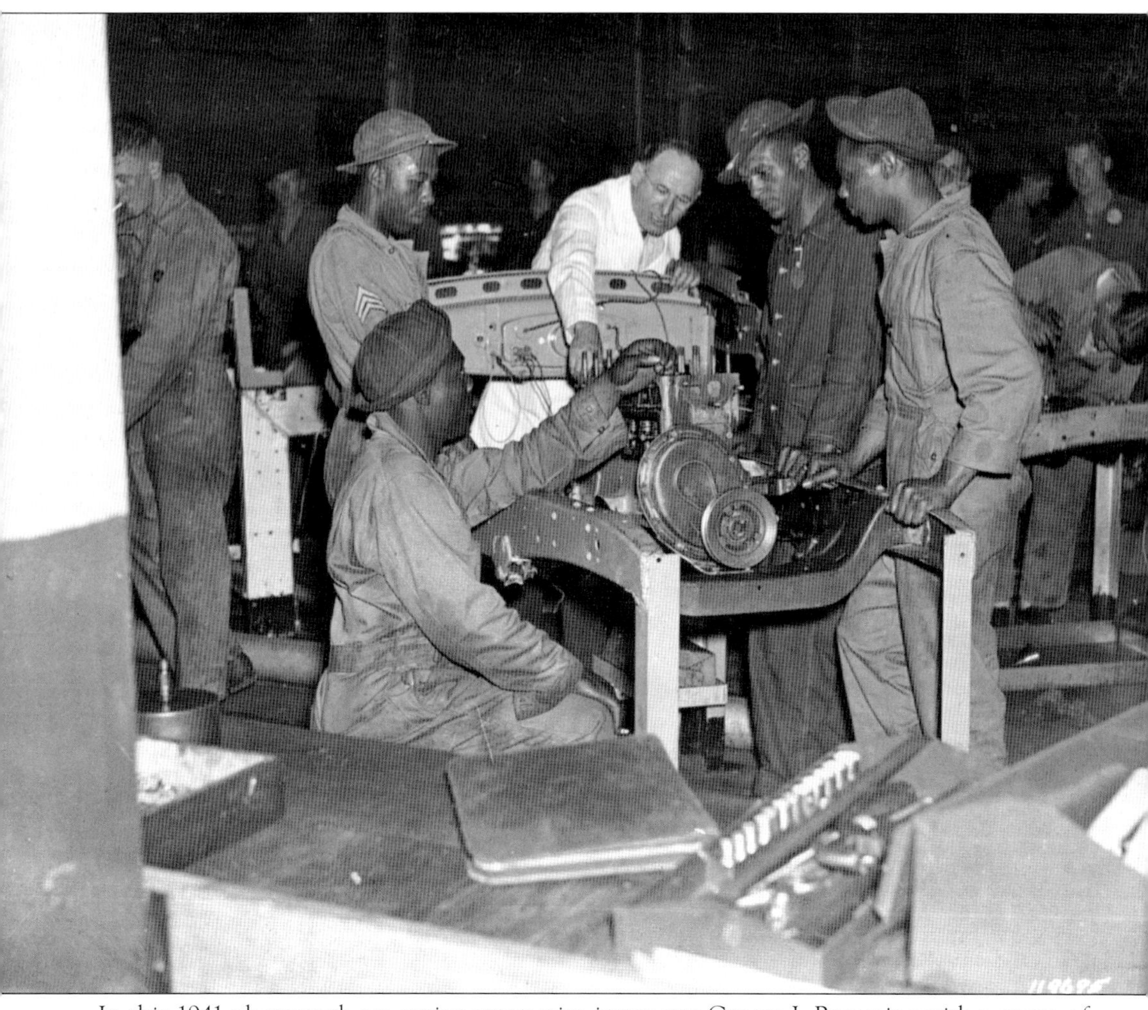

In this 1941 photograph are senior automotive instructor George J. Ramming with a group of African American student mechanics. These students are receiving expert instruction in basic engine operation at the Motor Transport School at Holabird Quartermaster Depot. There are white students at other benches indicating the class was segregated. (Courtesy NARA.)

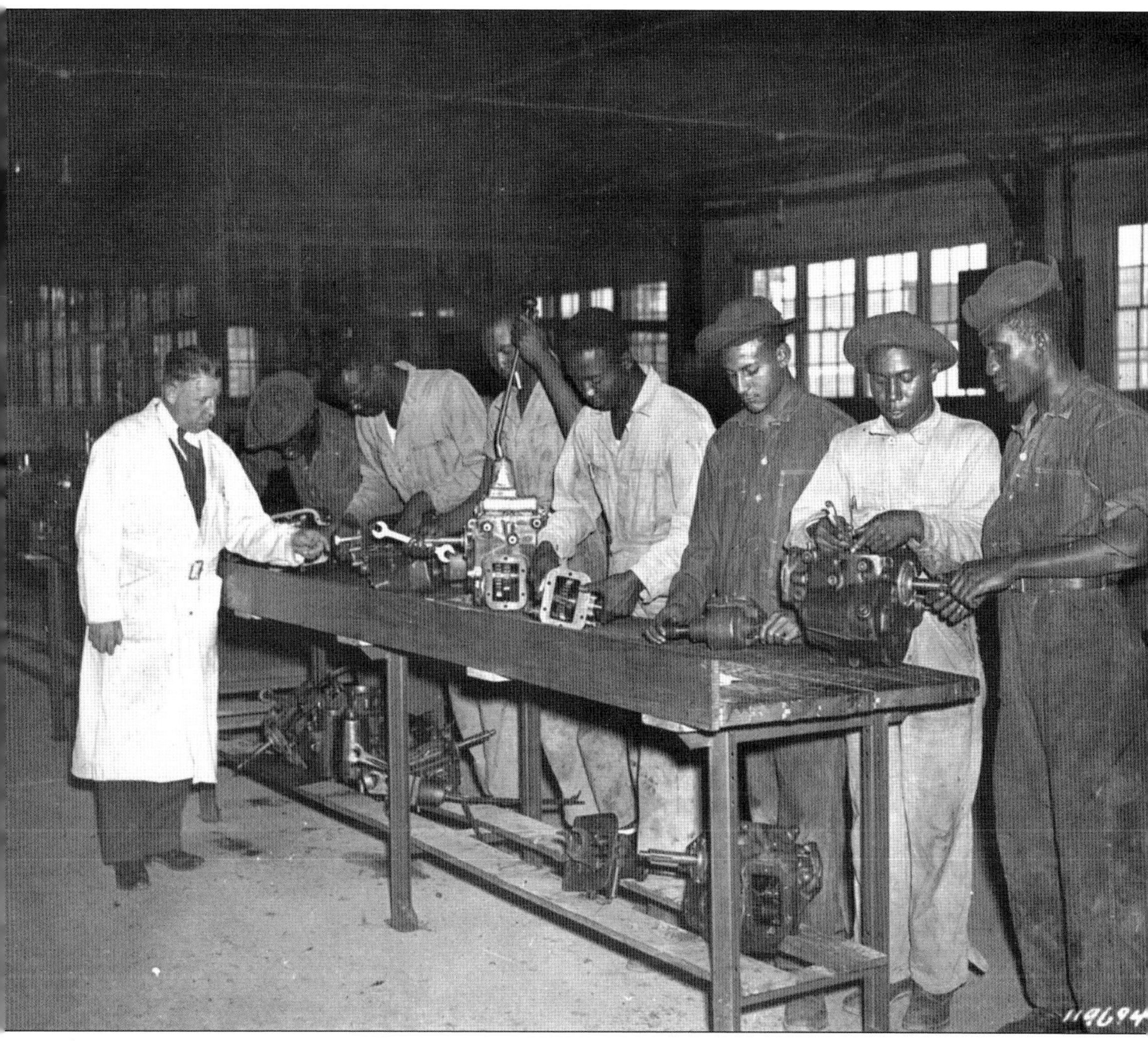

This 1941 image depicts an instructor in a lab coat and seven African American students. The group of students is using the "learn by doing" process" in the transmission section of the Motor Transport School. The transmission is a complex device, and the soldiers appear to be paying close attention to the task at hand. (Courtesy NARA.)

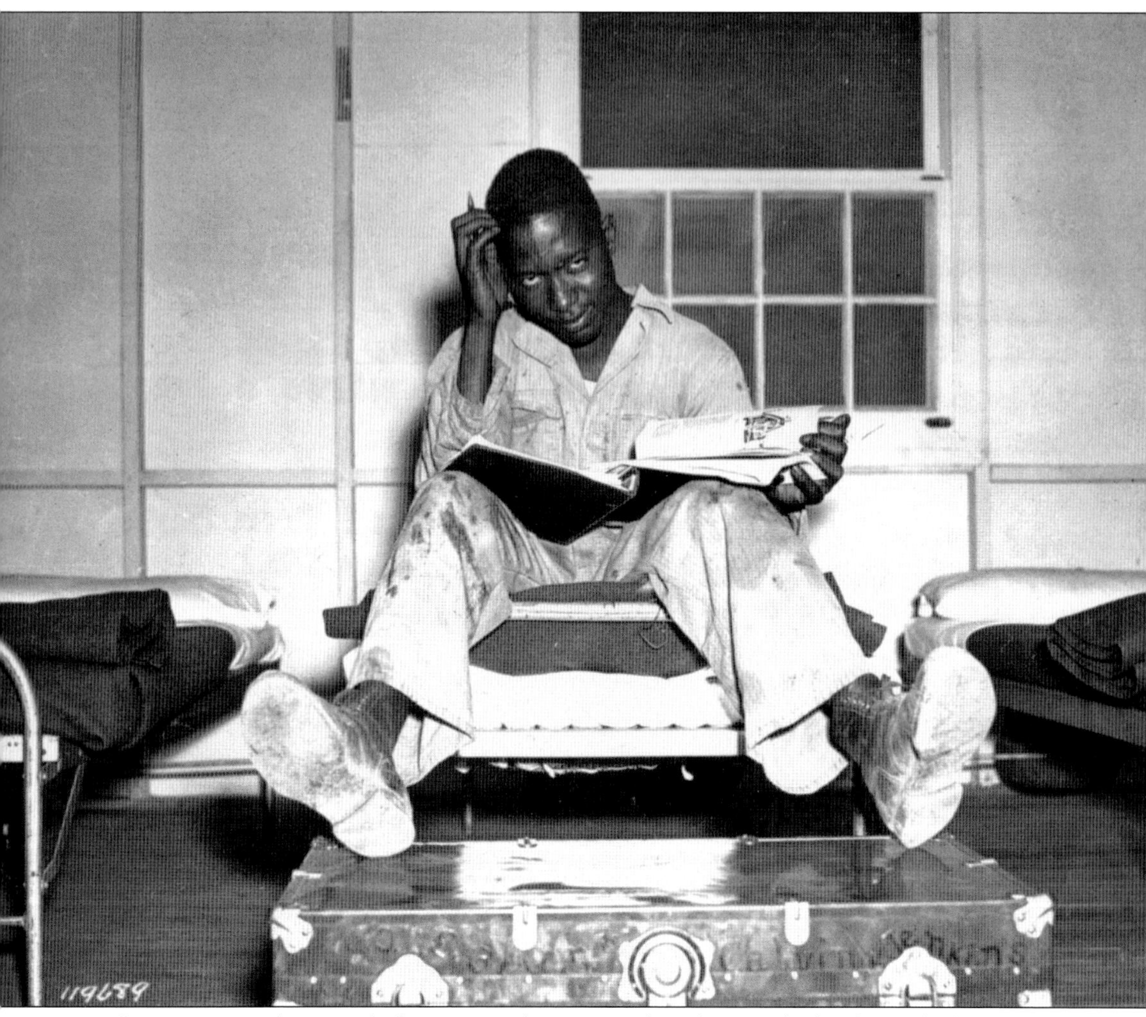

This May 1941 photograph shows Pvt. Clavin V. Jenkins hitting the books in the barracks. The five-month automotive course was challenging, and homework was part of the deal. Private Jenkins is a long way from his home in Shreveport, Louisiana. In a few months, a Navy base in Hawaii will be attacked, and Private Jenkins will be called even farther from home. (Courtesy NARA.)

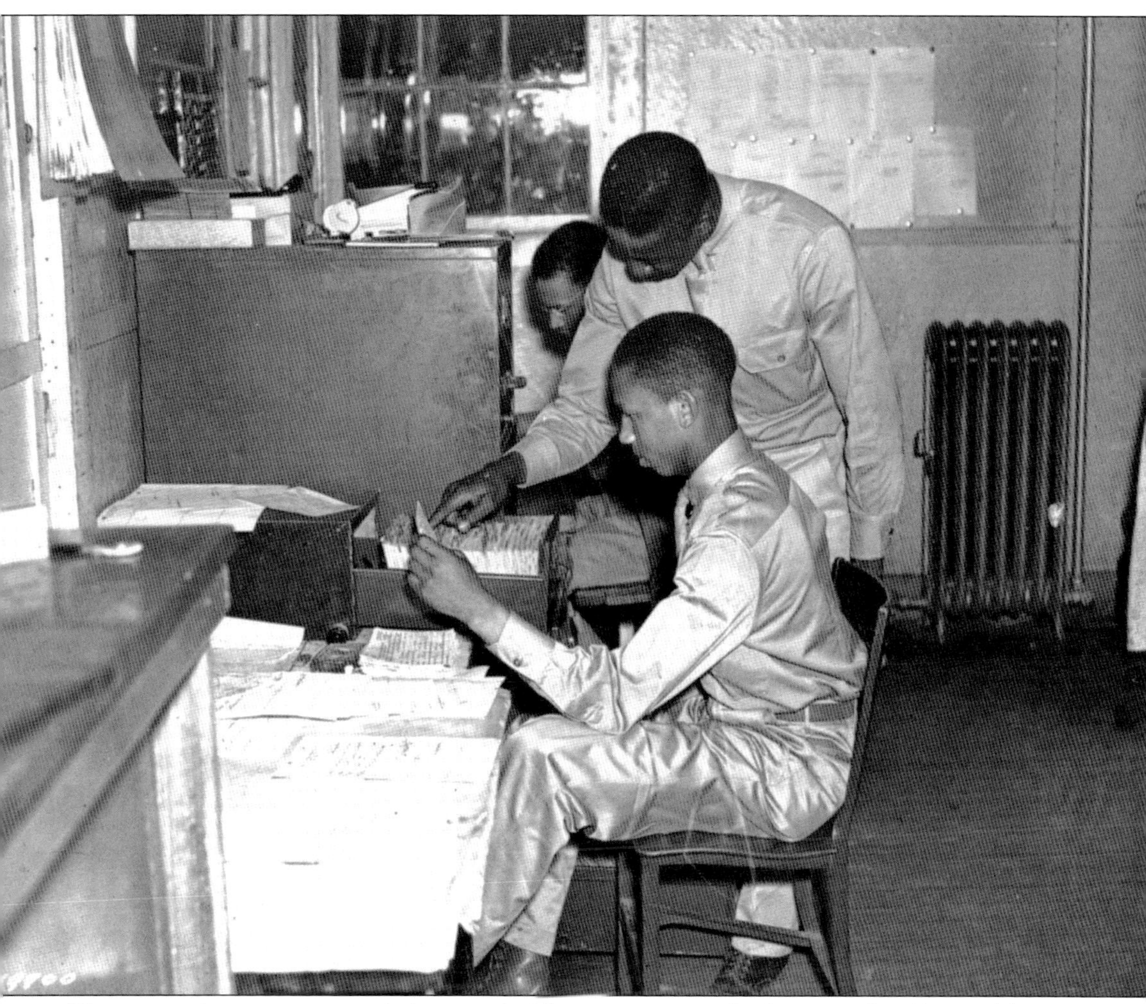

This image shows apprentice clerks at work. The apprentice in the foreground is 19-year-old Pvt. Scott J. George from Richmond, Virginia. The instructor, Cpl. James T. Beach, has been in the Army for five years and comes from Omaha, Nebraska. There was a great deal of paperwork at the Motor Transport School, and clerk training was part of the instruction. (Courtesy NARA.)

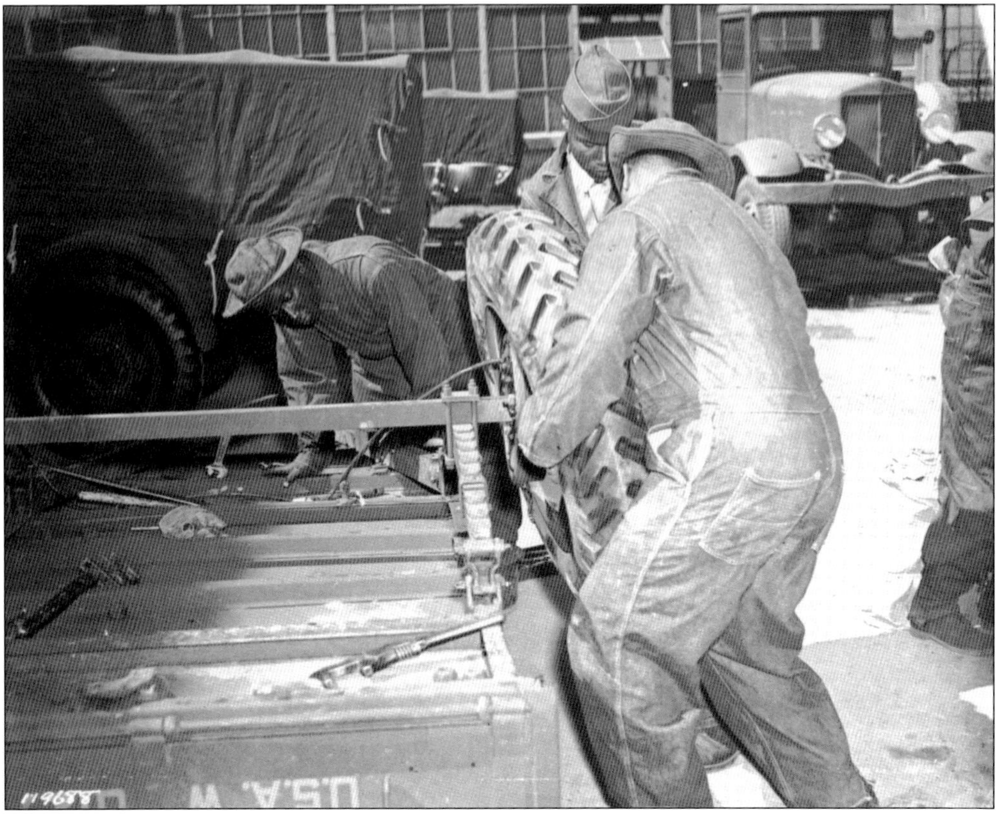

These May 19, 1941, photographs depict student mechanics at the Motor Transport School learning how to assemble trailers. This appears to be a G-518 one-ton cargo trailer, commonly known as the "Ben Hur." The trailers came in many varieties including cargo, generator, water tank, gun carriage, and radar carrier. The above image shows soldiers mounting a wheel; the photograph below shows them tightening lug nuts. These mechanics would make great use of the trailer once deployed. They would be called upon to repair all kinds of vehicles in all kinds of conditions. The trailer with cargo and generator capacity would enable them to function as a repair shop on the go. (Both, courtesy NARA.)

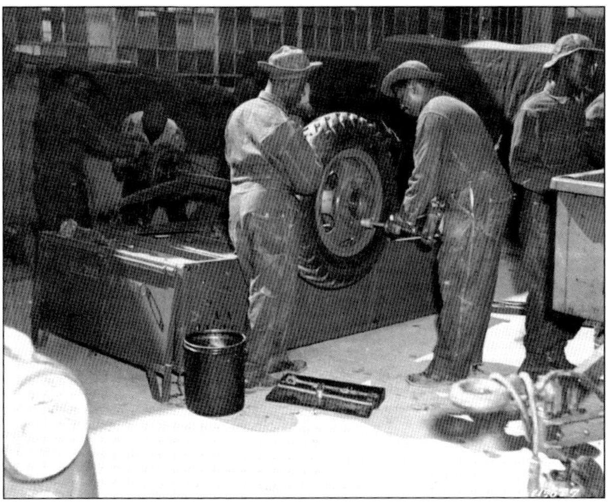

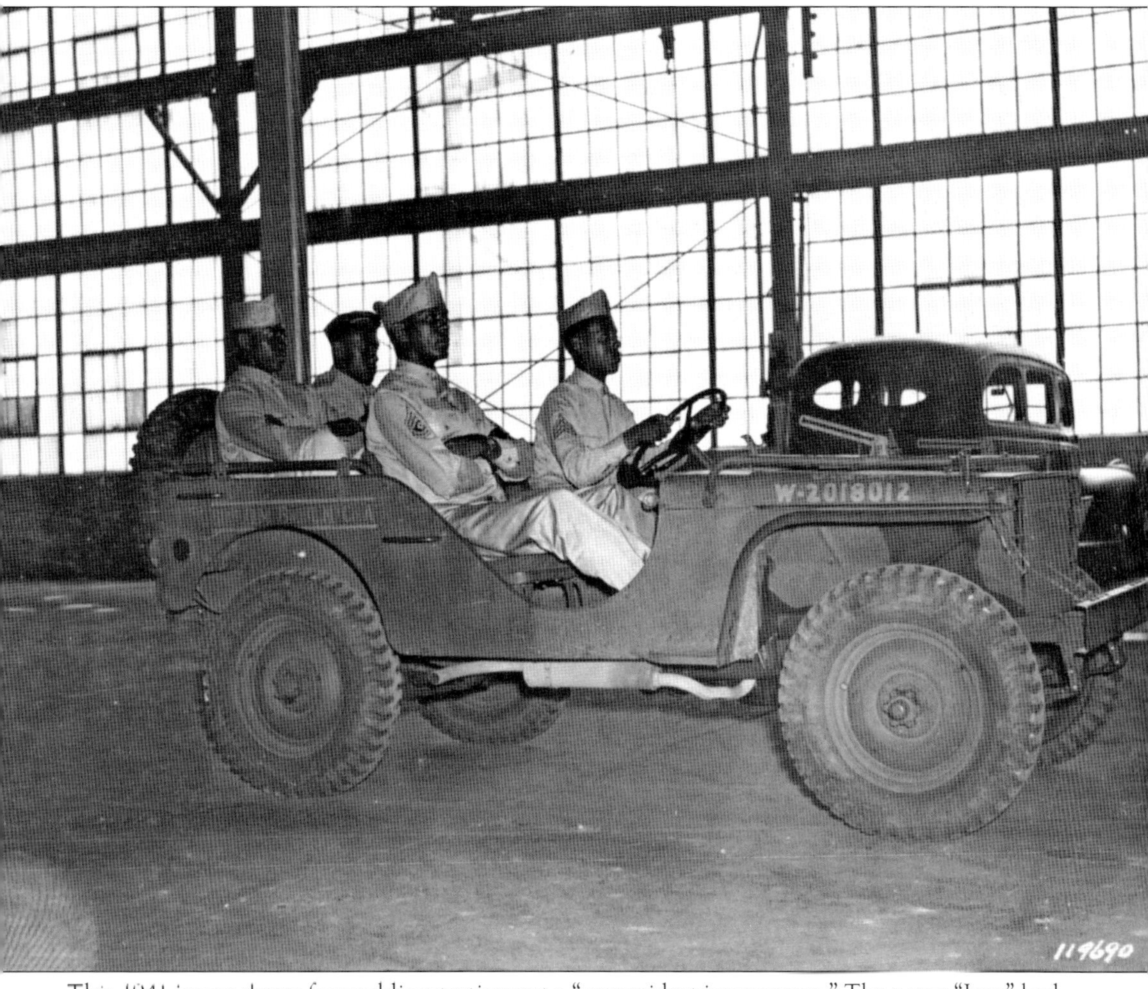

This 1941 image shows four soldiers testing out a "new midget jumpwagon." The name "Jeep" had yet to be applied to this legendary vehicle. The Army called it a quarter-ton 4x4, but the soldiers gave it a litany of nicknames, eventually evolving and settling on "jeep." The soldiers appear to be taking the matter very seriously. (Courtesy NARA.)

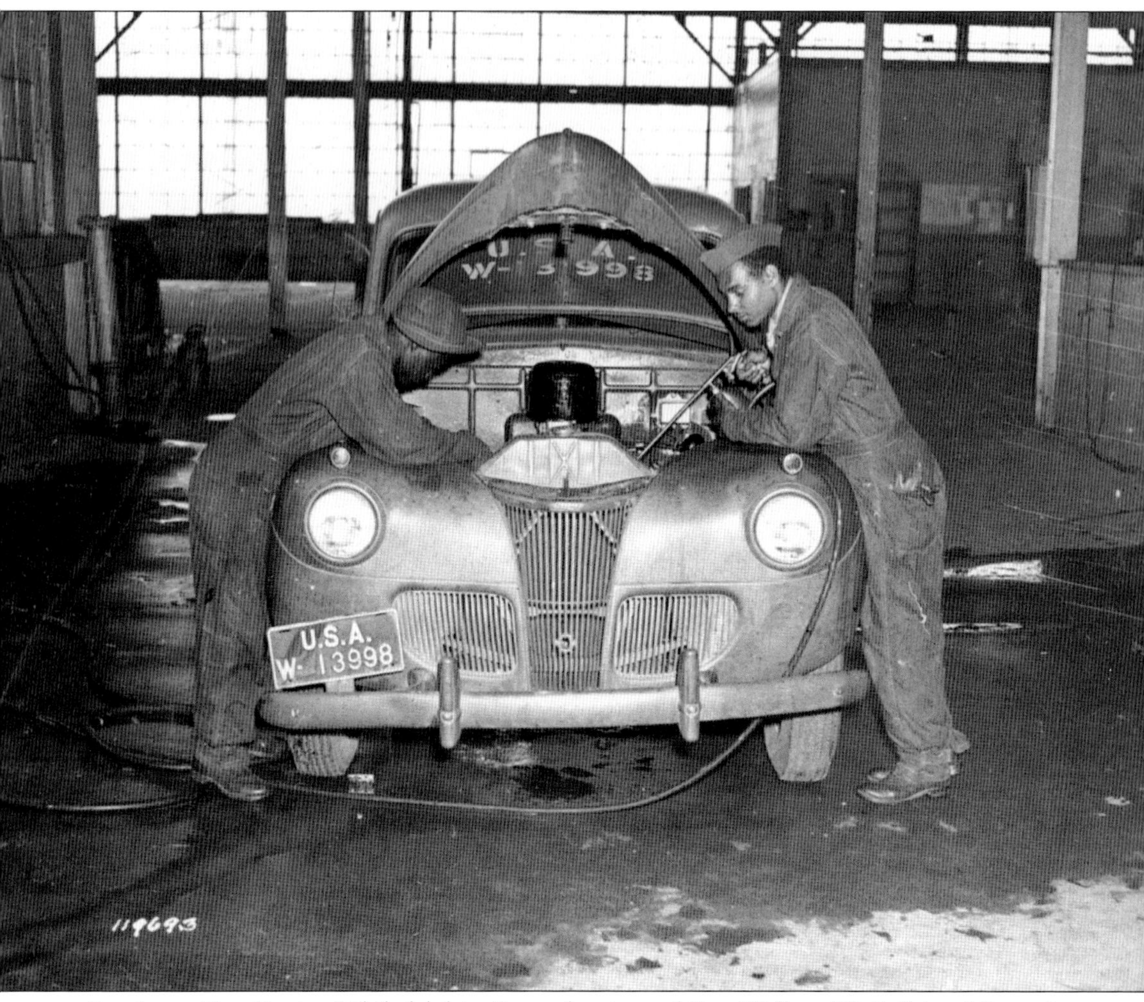

Pvt. James Tate Davis of Philadelphia, Pennsylvania, and Pvt. Wallace W. Colbin of Roanoke, Virginia, are hard at work under the hood of a vehicle. They have both been in the Army for five weeks, and they are well on their way to becoming expert mechanics at the Motor Transport School. (Courtesy NARA.)

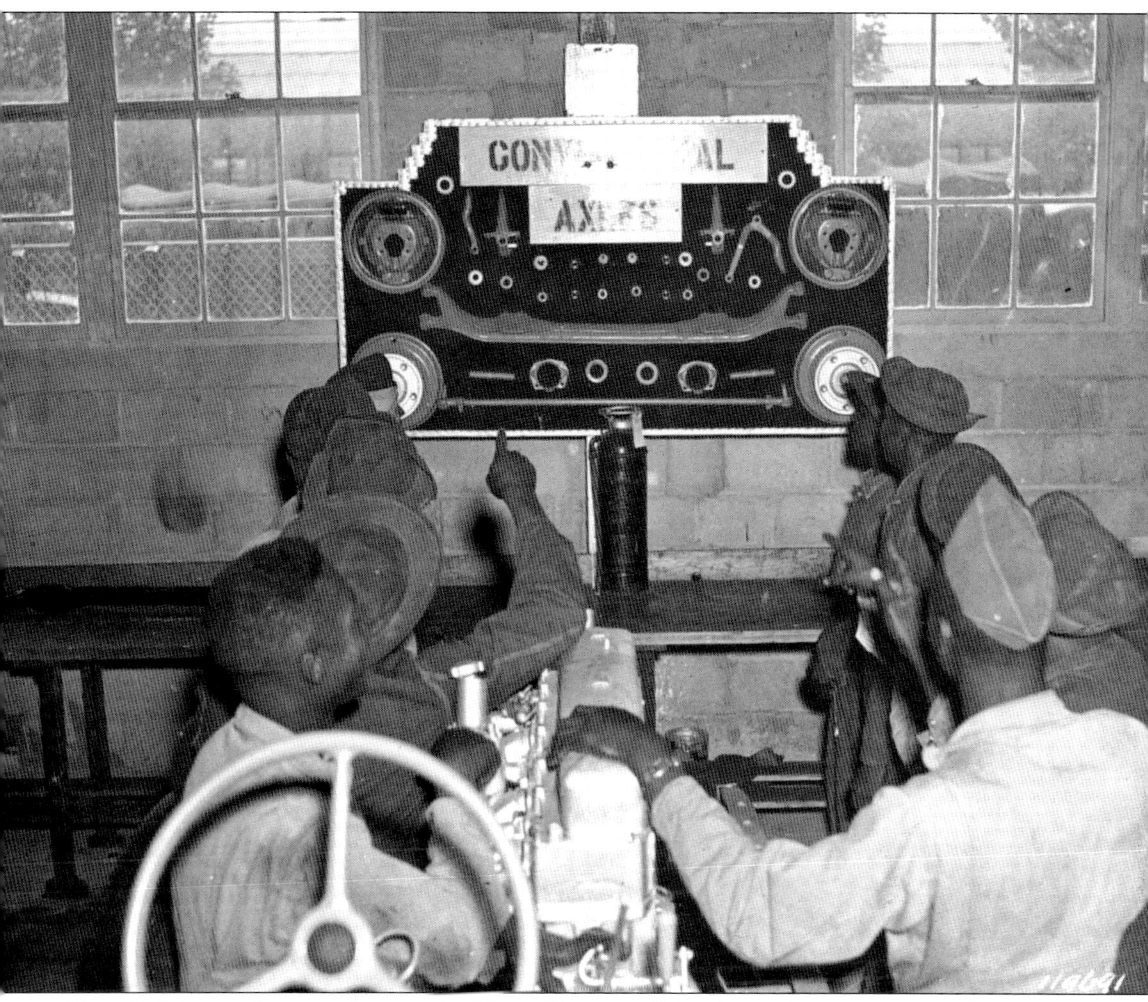

This 1941 image shows students at the Motor Transport School must learn every part of a motor vehicle. These students are employing one of the many training aids. This particular aid shows the vehicle's front axle with the parts mounted and displayed individually. (Courtesy NARA.)

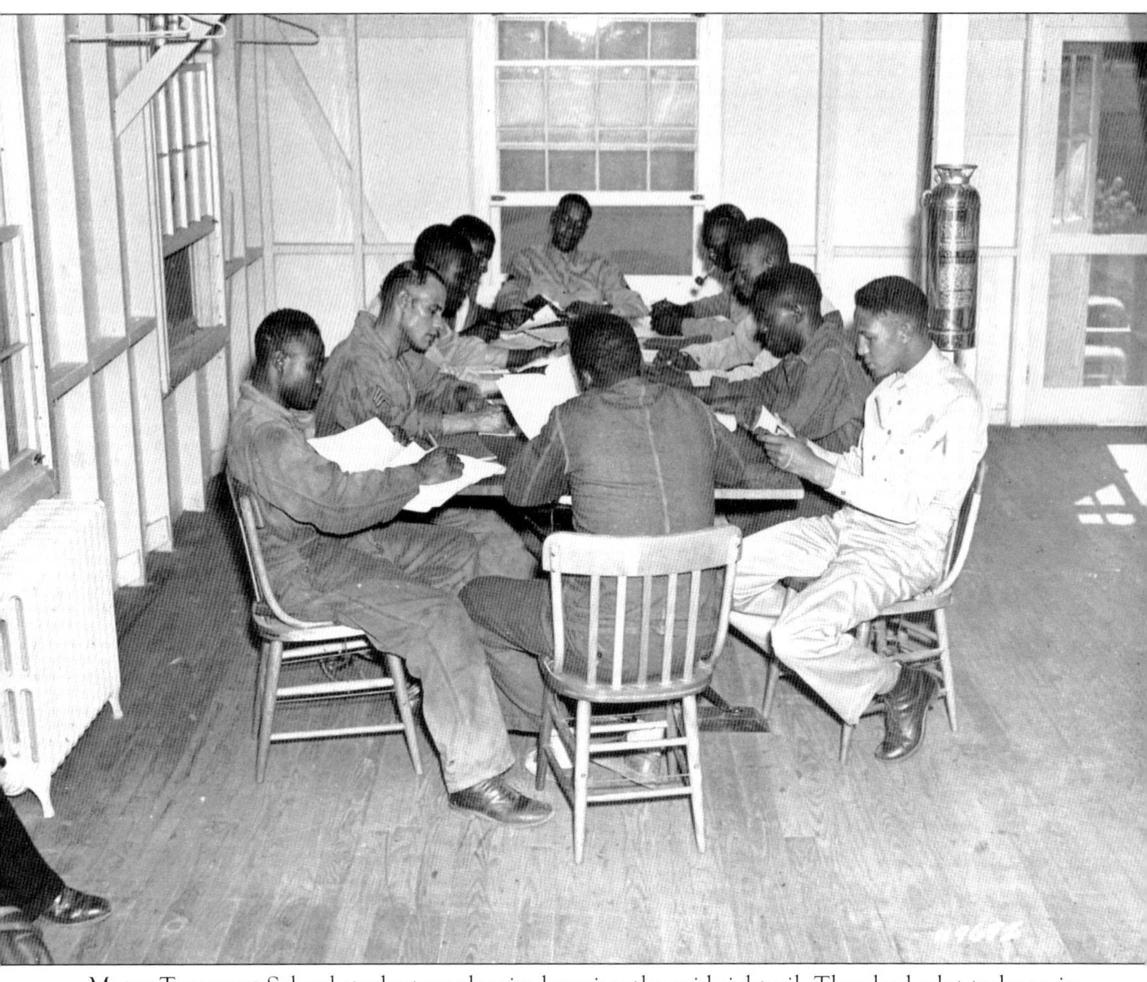

Motor Transport School student mechanics burning the midnight oil. They had a lot to learn in the five-month program, so homework was part of the deal. Most of the students are still clad in coveralls from a long day of mechanic classes. The windows are open; perhaps they are enjoying a cool spring night in 1941. (Courtesy NARA.)

Five

Memorable Events

Fort Holabird was the scene of several memorable events. From the unsolved payroll robbery in 1919 to the housing of German POWs during World War II and most recently the housing of Watergate conspirators in the 1970s.

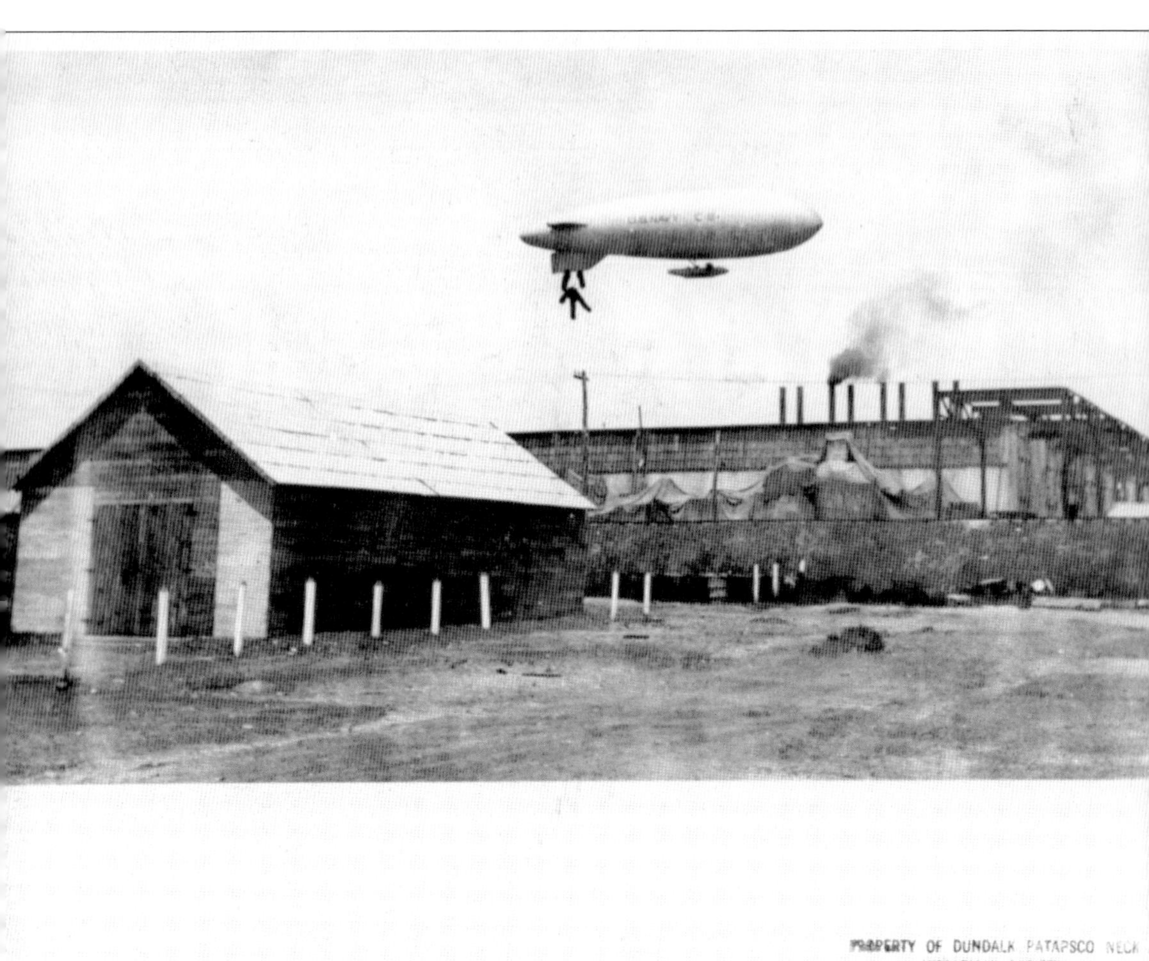

On July 2, 1919, a US Navy C-8 dirigible was en route from Cape May, New Jersey, to Washington, DC. Under the command of US Navy lieutenant N.J. Learned, it was planned as a nonstop trip. However, the airship encountered steering trouble and began looking for a place to put down. Camp Holabird just east of Baltimore was near their flight path. So Holabird was the chosen landing site. (Courtesy Dundalk-Patapsco Neck Historical Society & Museum.)

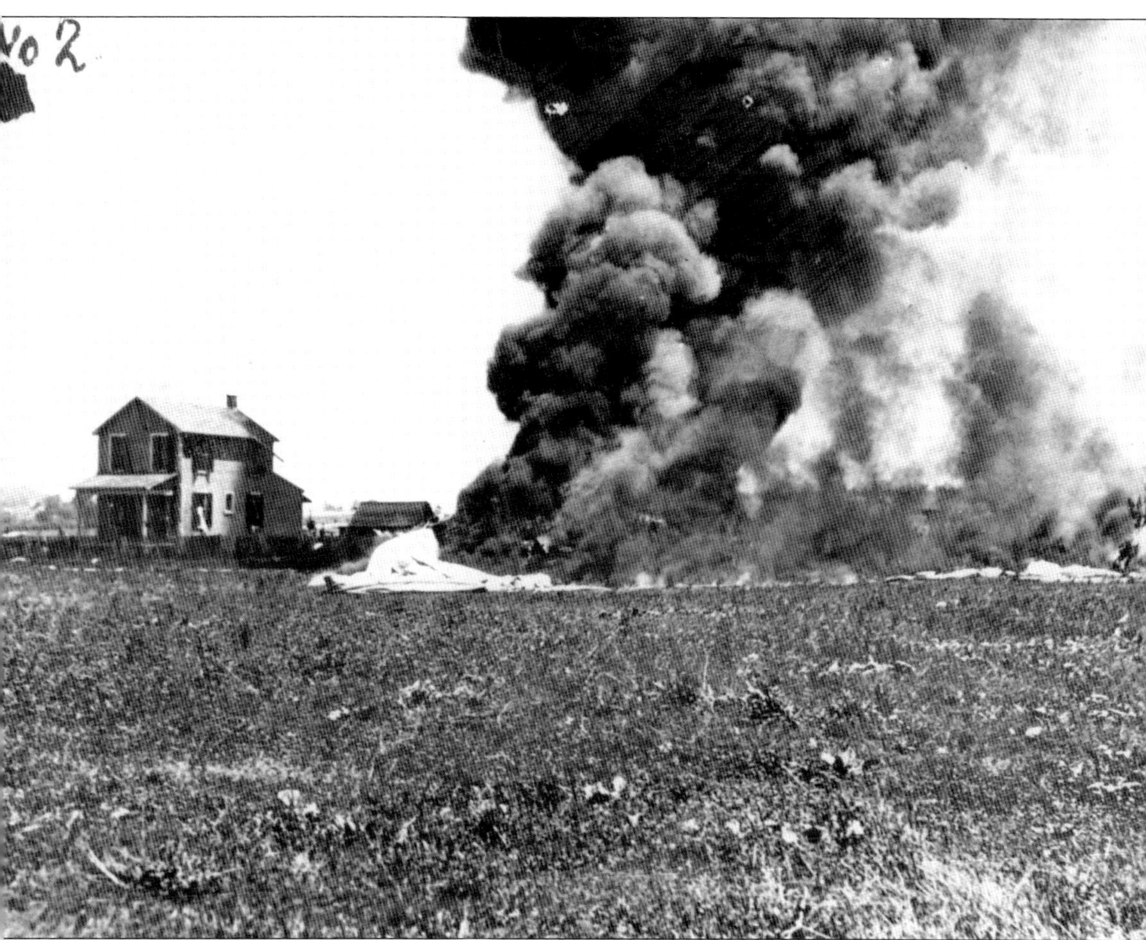

The crew hovered the dirigible over the eastern suburbs of Baltimore looking for a good landing site within the confines of Camp Holabird. While hovering, a large crowd gathered to view the spectacle. Aviation was in its infancy, so an approaching airship was an awe-inspiring event for spectators. A line was dropped to anchor the craft as it touched down. Then suddenly, the dirigible exploded. Spectators were knocked to the ground, windows shattered, and buildings shook. (Courtesy Dundalk-Patapsco Neck Historical Society & Museum.)

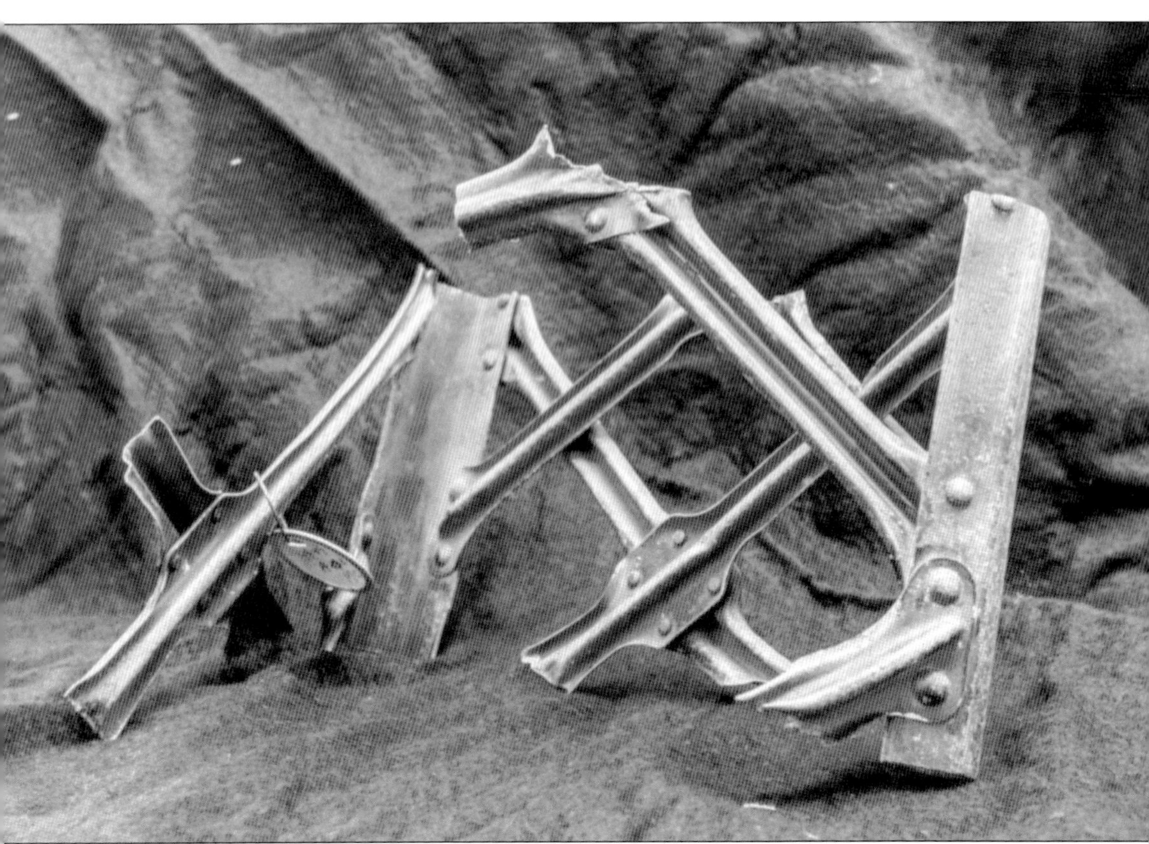

This piece of twisted metal is an artifact of the 1919 Camp Holabird Airship explosion. The explosion was violent and sudden. Seventy-nine people were injured, but mercifully no one was killed. Ens. C.W. Tyndell owes his life to a quick-thinking Holabird Soldier. Ensign Tyndell was entangled in the burning wreckage when Pvt. Andrew Washburn sprinted to the scene to free him. Ensign Tyndell had severe burns on his hands and arms, but he survived. (Courtesy Dundalk-Patapsco Neck Historical Society & Museum.)

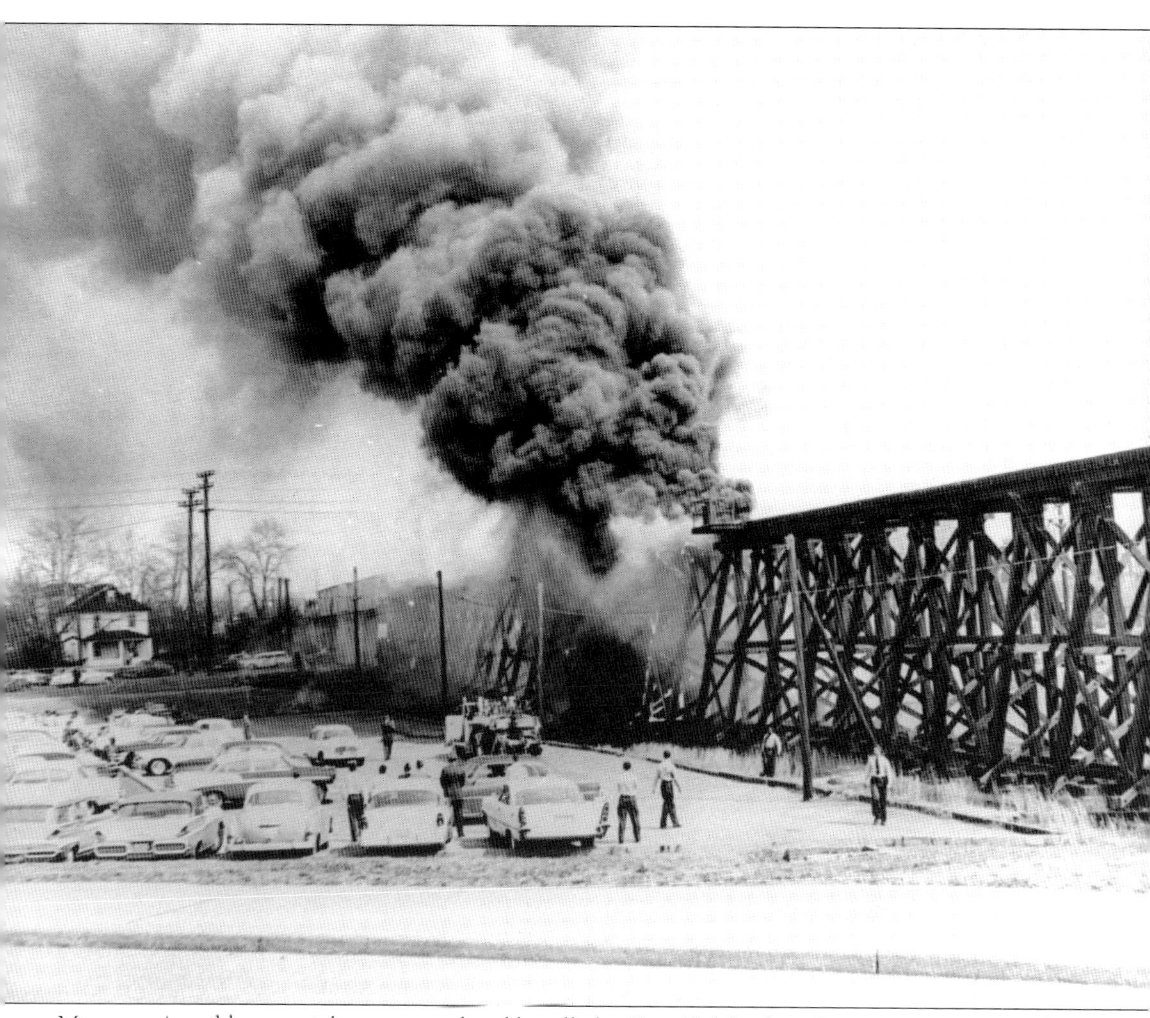

Many combustible materials were stored and handled at Fort Holabird, so fires were an occasional occurrence. This particularly stubborn trestle fire is just one example. The Fort Holabird Fire Department often worked with local fire departments as was the case with this fire. Baltimore County firefighters can be seen in the foreground. (Courtesy Dundalk-Patapsco Neck Historical Society & Museum.)

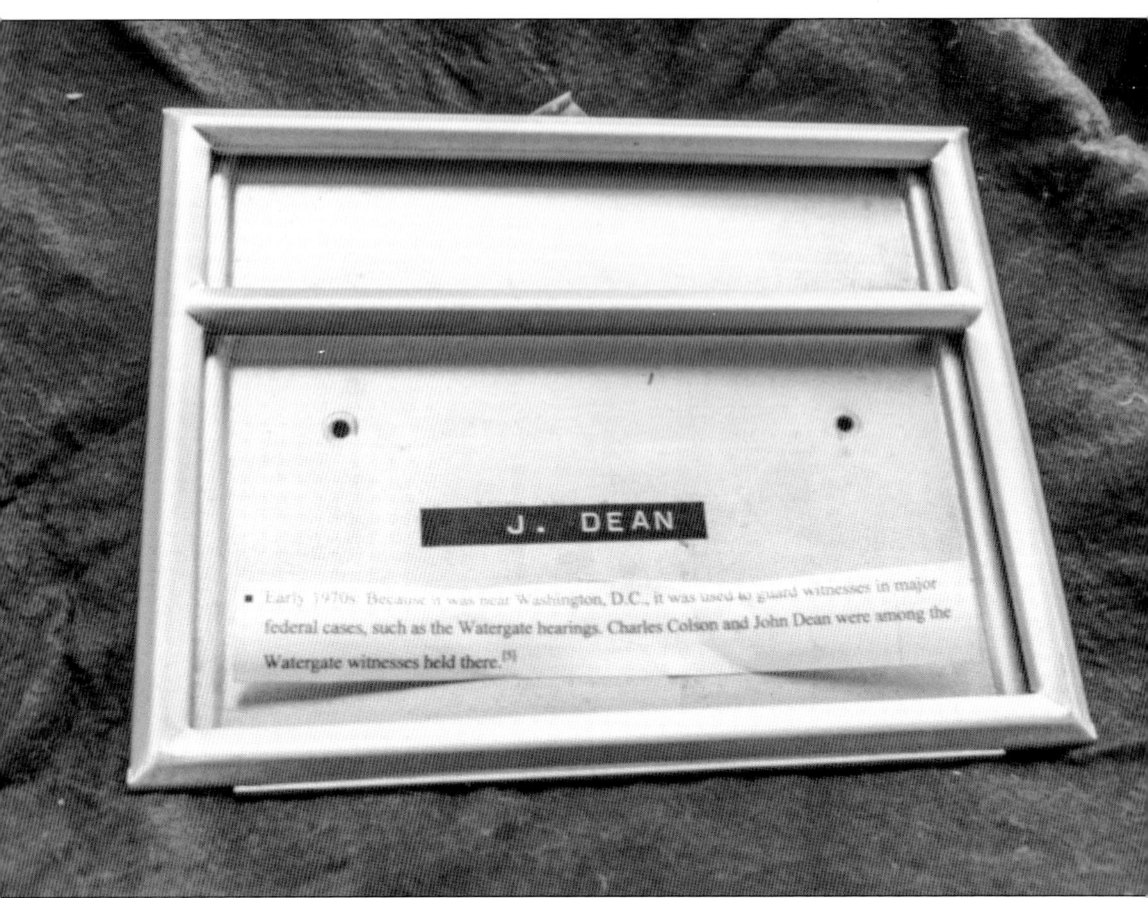

During the Watergate hearings of the 1970s, the federal government was looking for a place to house witnesses. Fort Holabird was their choice. Watergate figures including John Dean, Charles Colson, and E. Howard Hunt were housed there. This image is of the door plate bearing the name "J. Dean." It was the room in the old bachelor officer quarters where John Dean was housed during Watergate. It was retrieved by a local historian who was invited to collect artifacts when Holabird was closed. (Courtesy Charles McClanahan Adapt Creative Co. [photographer], taken with permission by the Dundalk-Patapsco Neck Historical Society & Museum.)

Six

Post Closure

Fort Holabird had a long life and served the country during four wars. It was host to the introduction of the motor vehicle to the military, and later the military intelligence center and school. But eventually, Holabird completed its mission. In 1971, the Intelligence School was moved to Fort Huachuca, and in 1973, Fort Holabird officially closed. The land was handed over to the local government, and Holabird became an industrial park providing jobs and opportunities for many.

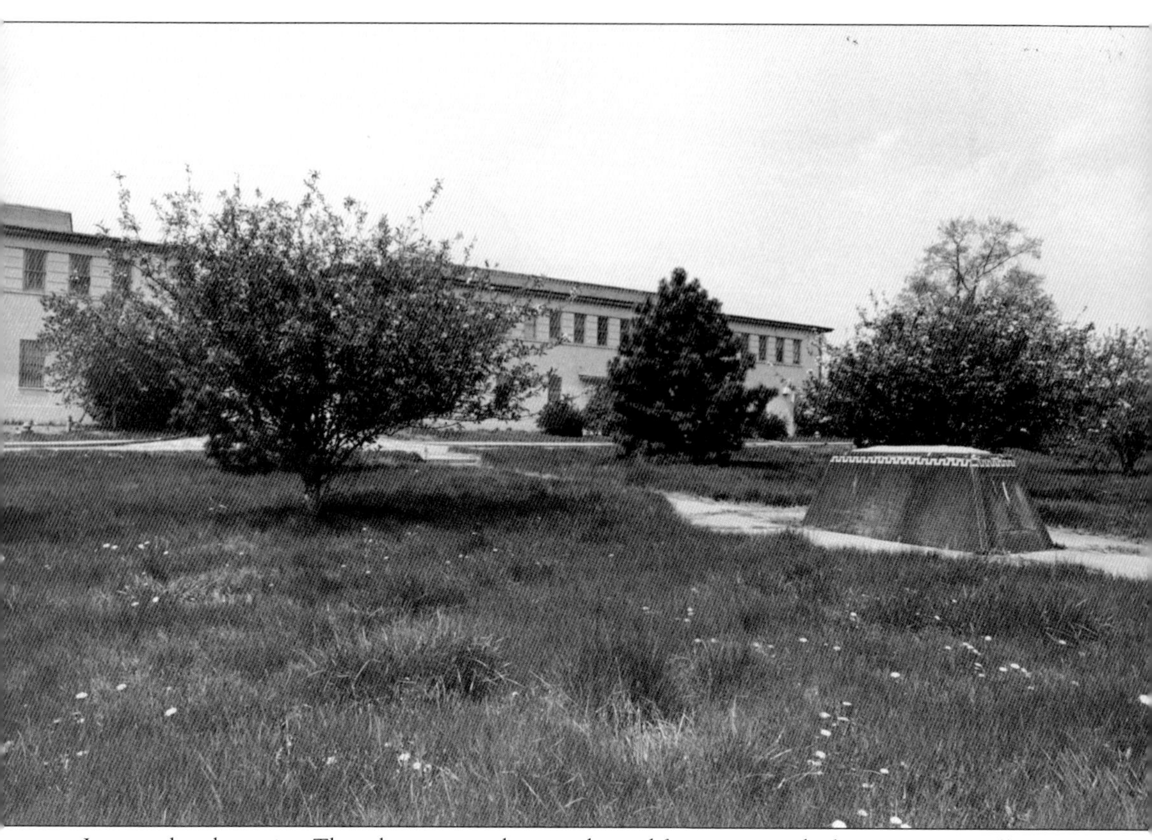

Just a pedestal remains. The sphinx statue that stood guard for years outside the US Army Intelligence Command building is gone. When the intelligence command and school moved to Fort Huachuca in 1971 the sphinx went with them. Some reports indicate the sphinx made a stop at Fort Meade before shipping out to Arizona. (Courtesy Dundalk-Patapsco Neck Historical Society & Museum.)

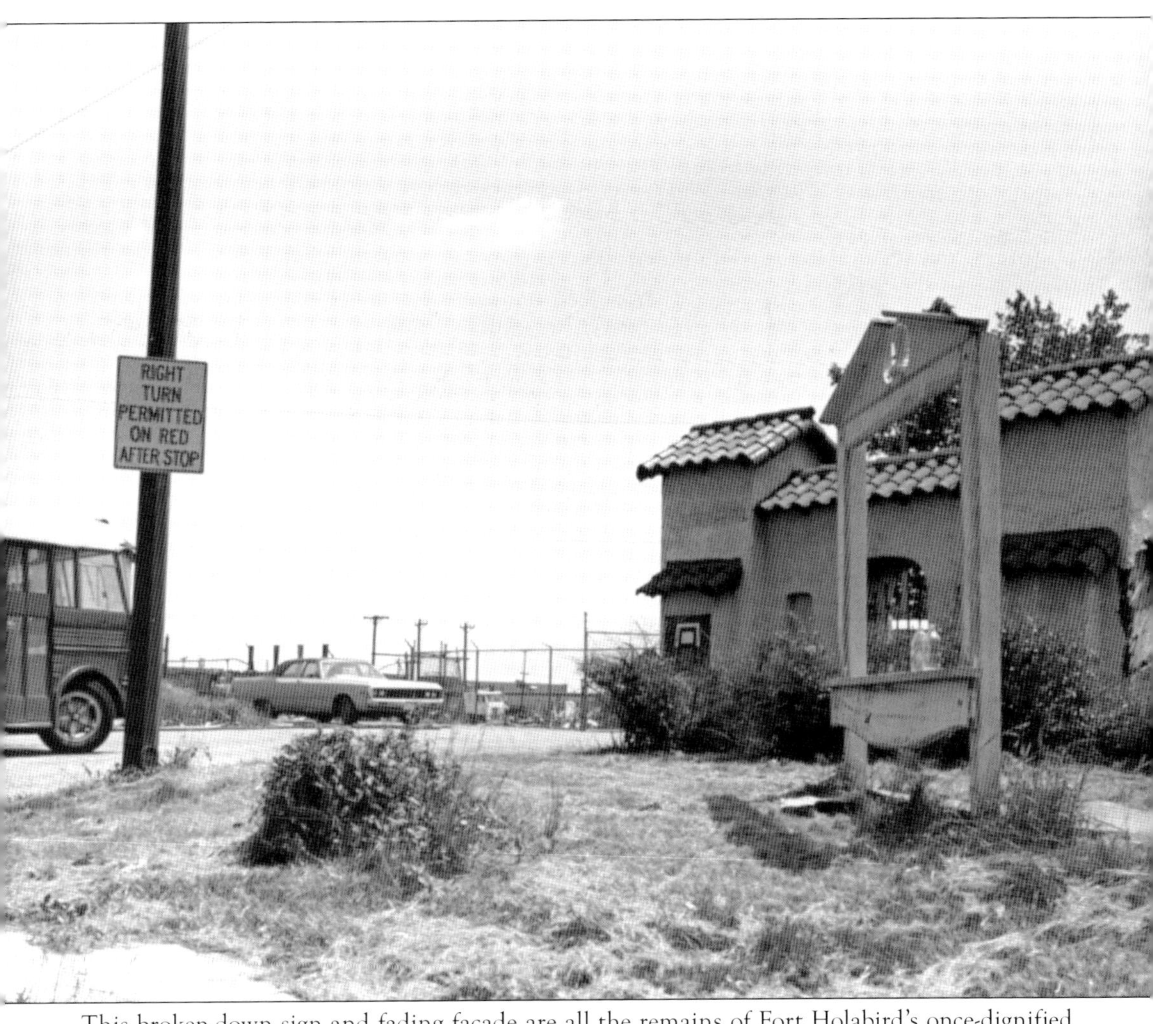

This broken-down sign and fading façade are all the remains of Fort Holabird's once-dignified main gate. Where MPs once welcomed VIPs, now construction trucks rumble through as Fort Holabird transitions to the Holabird Industrial Park. Holabird's mission is still carried on, but now at Fort Huachuca, Arizona. The mission continues; only the land use has changed. (Courtesy Dundalk-Patapsco Neck Historical Society & Museum.)

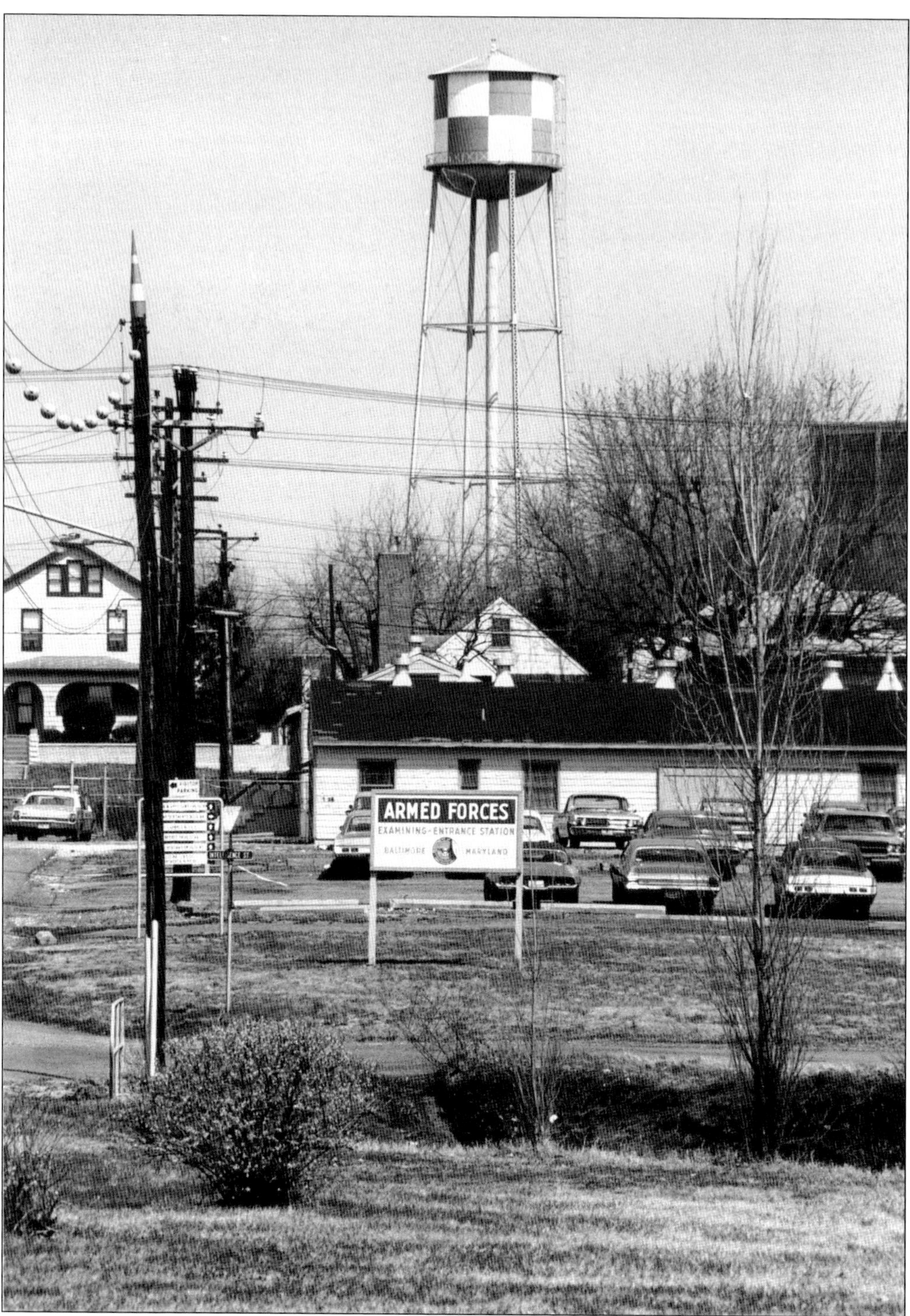

One of Fort Holabird's last missions was as an "Armed Forces Examining-Entrance Station." Holabird had become a draft induction center. Several thousand Baltimore area draftees remember Holabird this way. Holabird closed in 1973, which was the same year the draft ended. So, this was Fort Holabird's last mission. (Courtesy Dundalk-Patapsco Neck Historical Society & Museum.)

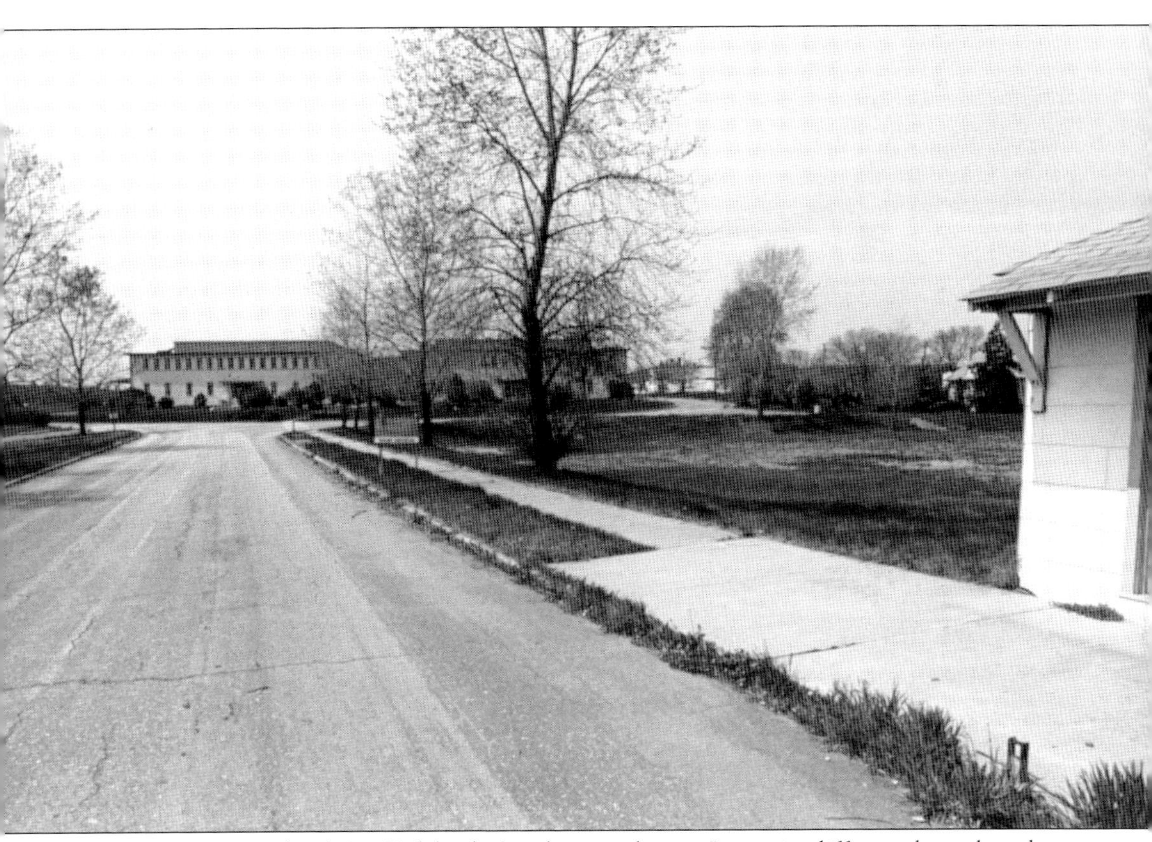

This road is an example of Fort Holabird after the post closure. It is quite different than when the Army was here. The grass is overgrown and unmowed, the pavement is cracked and empty, and the guard shack appears vacant. When the Army was here, Holabird was always neatly manicured and well-painted. (Courtesy Dundalk-Patapsco Neck Historical Society & Museum.)

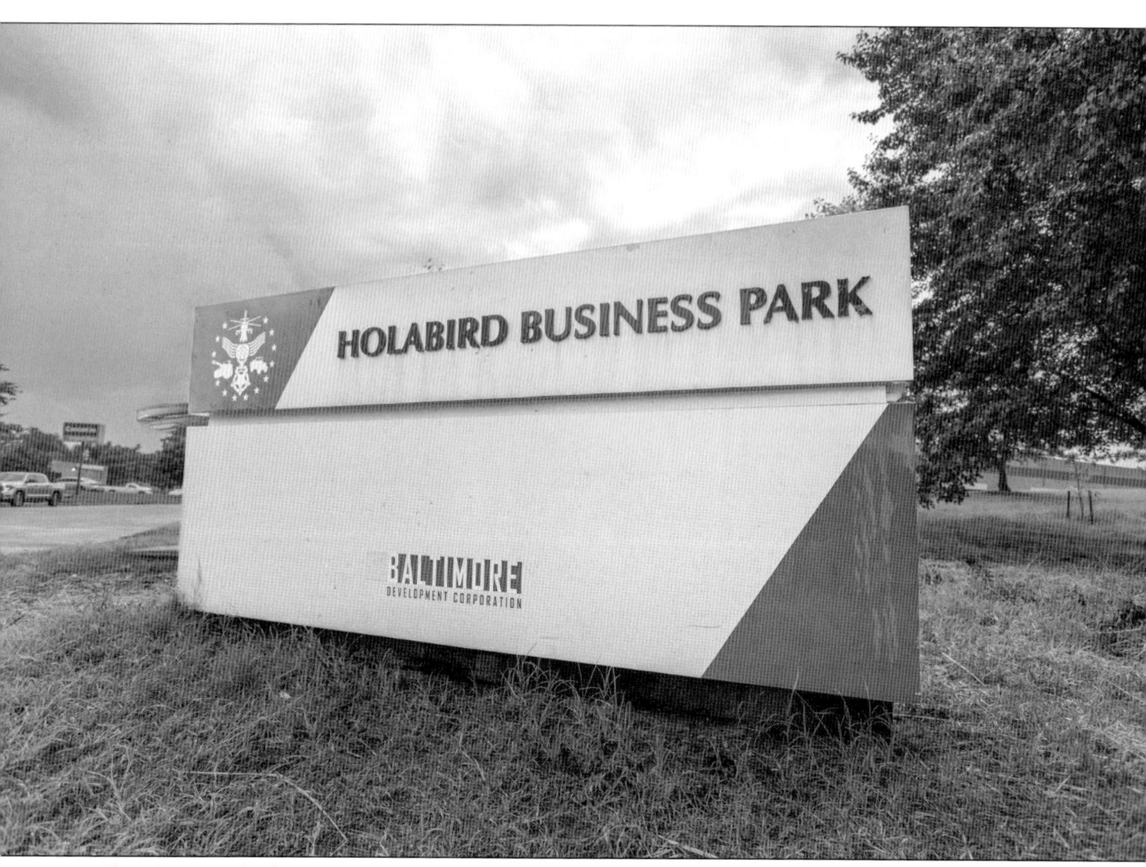

Shortly after the last Fort Holabird sign came down, the "Holabird Business Park" Sign went up. The new owner was the local government, and the land was converted into an industrial park. The land where the legendary jeep was tested, and spies once trained will create jobs and business opportunities for local residents. (Courtesy Dundalk-Patapsco Neck Historical Society & Museum.)

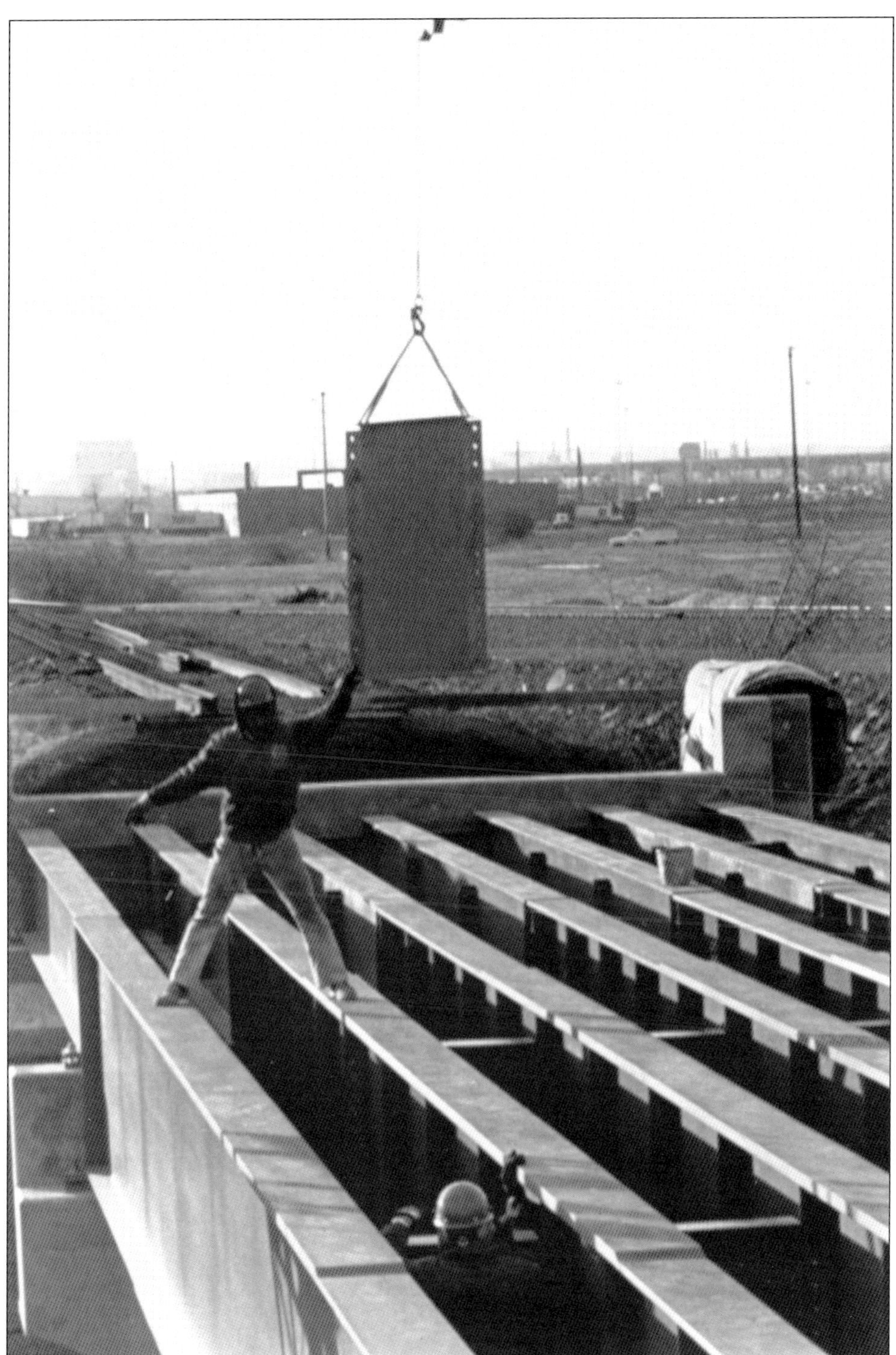

Part of tearing down Fort Holabird is building back up again. As the military buildings were cleared away, new construction was started. This crane and worker are busy at work. The land where motor pools, mess halls, and barracks once stood is occupied by now warehouses, factories, and offices. (Courtesy Dundalk-Patapsco Neck Historical Society & Museum.)

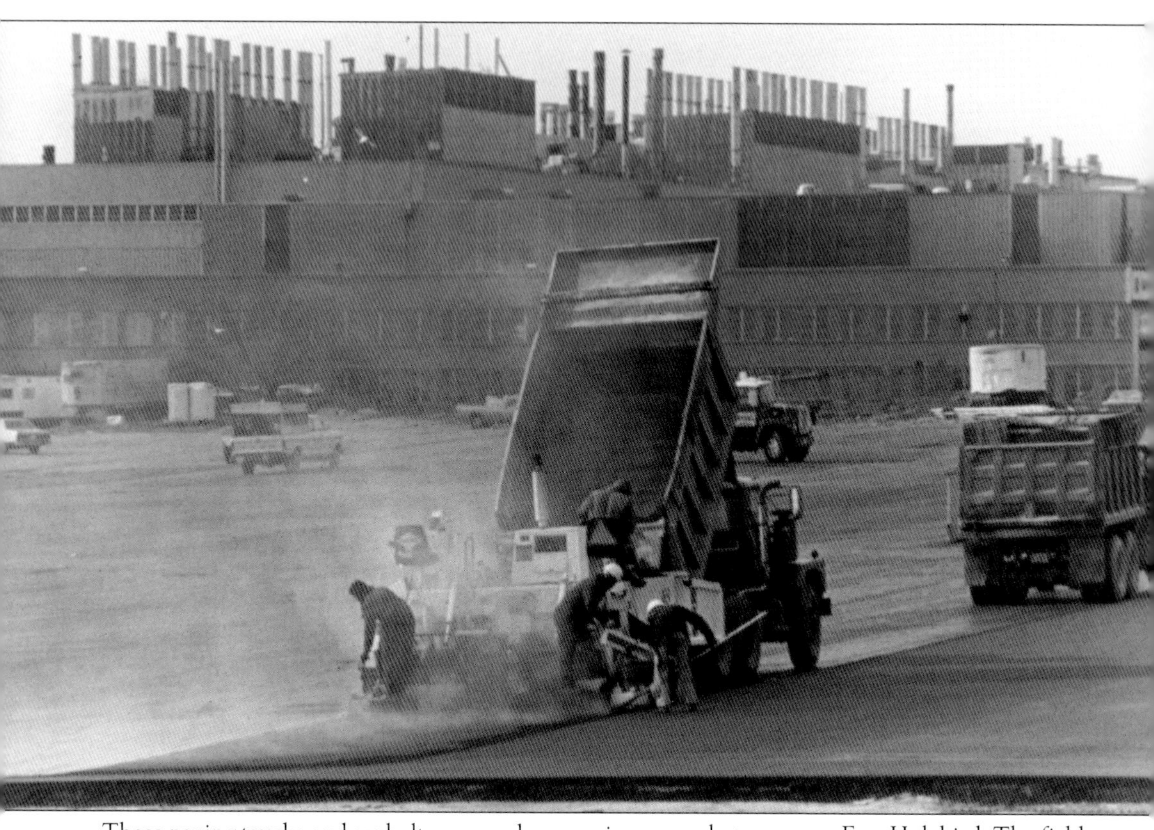

These paving trucks and asphalt crew are busy paving over what was once Fort Holabird. The fields where generations of soldiers once marched and trained will now lie under a layer of blacktop. The acres of paving will now serve as employee parking and truck lots for the Holabird Business Park. (Courtesy Dundalk-Patapsco Neck Historical Society & Museum.)

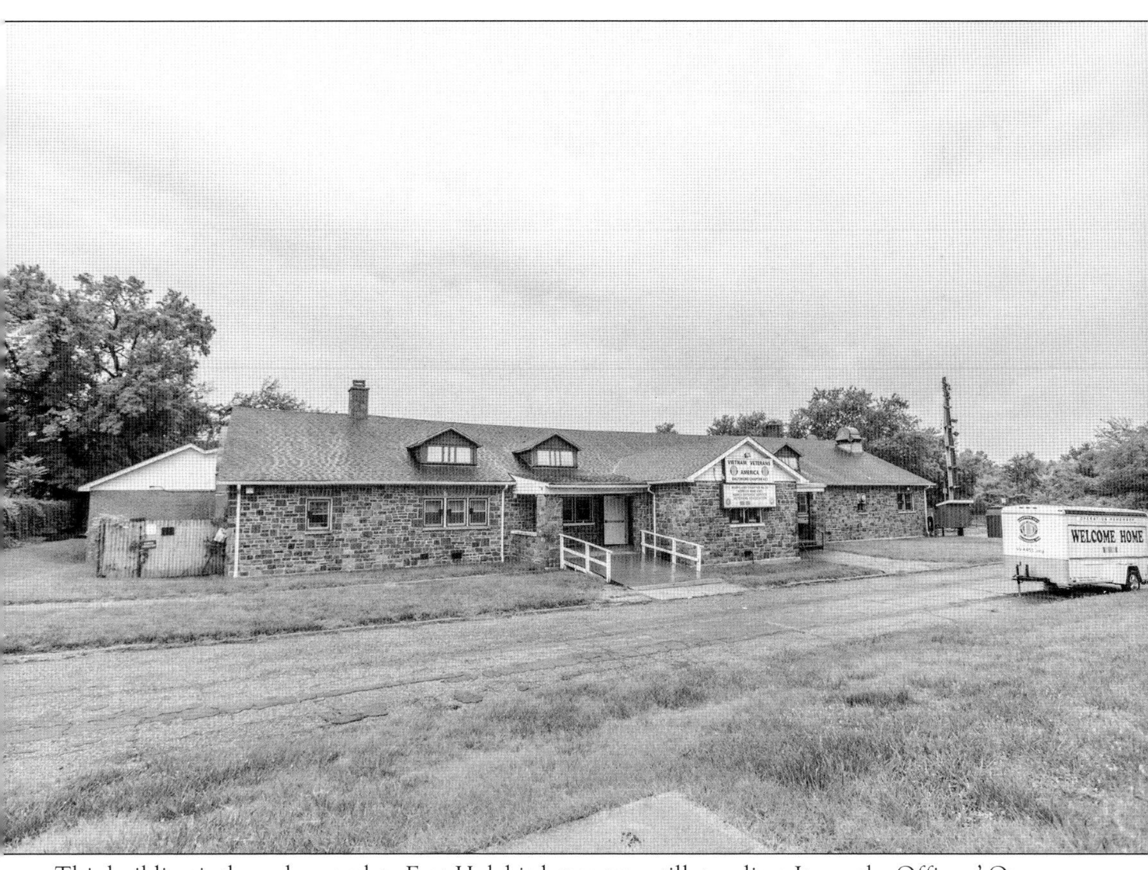

This building is the only complete Fort Holabird structure still standing. It was the Officers' Open Mess, more commonly called the Officers' Club. Today, it is home to Chapter No. 451 of the Vietnam Veterans of America. (Courtesy Charles McClanahan Adapt Creative Co. [photographer], taken with permission by Chapter 451 Vietnam Veterans of America.)

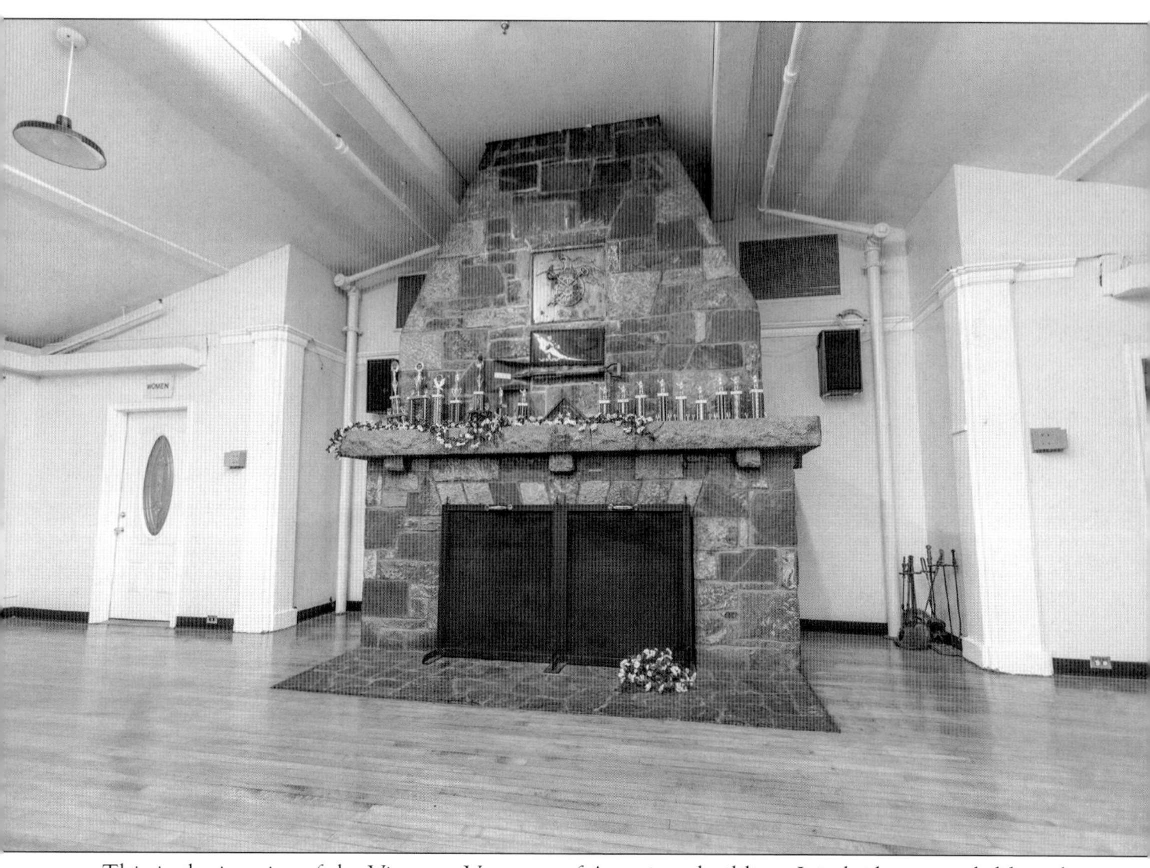

This is the interior of the Vietnam Veterans of American building. It is laid out much like other fraternal groups such as American Legion. The fireplace is huge and dominates the room. It is made of stone much like the building itself. One can only imagine generations of officers stopping by for a drink or meal and enjoying the roaring fireplace. (Courtesy Charles McClanahan Adapt Creative Co. [photographer], taken with permission by Chapter 451 Vietnam Veterans of America.)

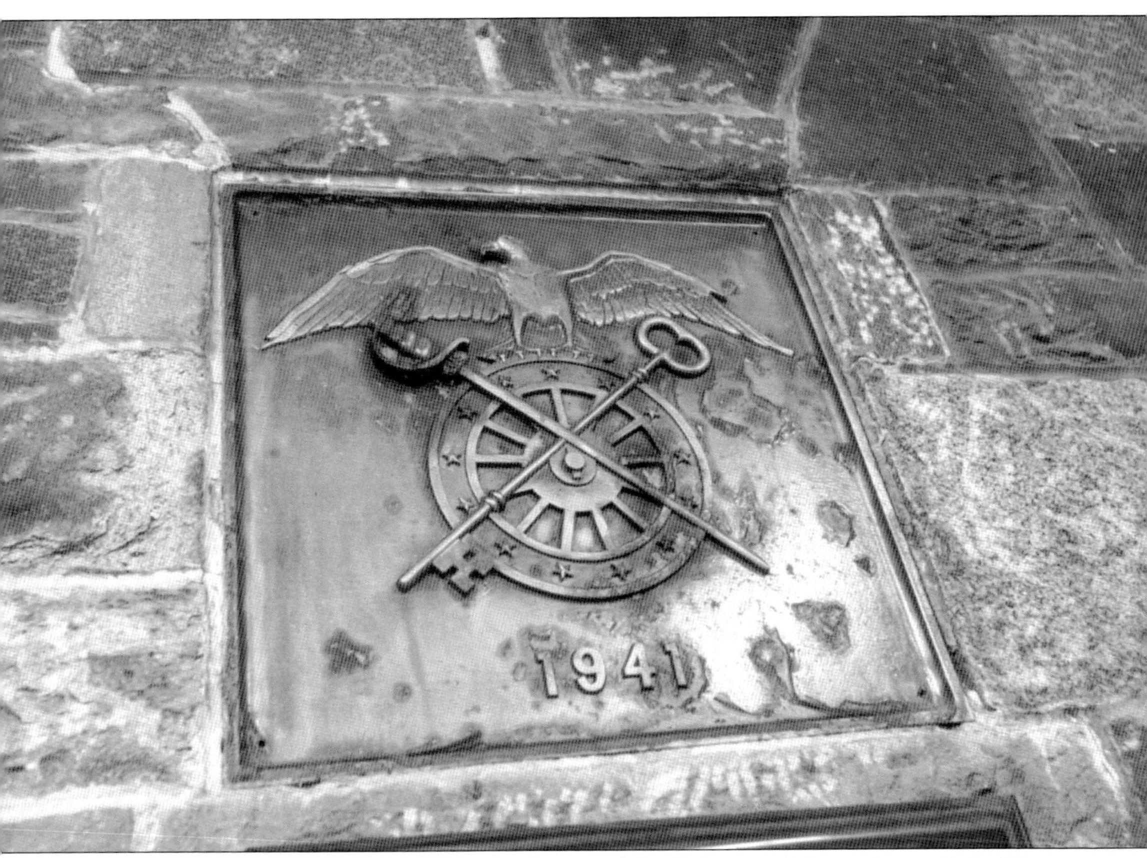

This brass plaque on the fireplace tells much of Fort Holabird's history. It bears the symbol of the Quartermaster Corps as well as the year 1941. This plaque stood watch through Holabird's Motor Transport School years, the Intelligence School years, and now the Vietnam Veterans of America chapter. Soldiers who served the country in four wars have drank and dined under this plaque. (Courtesy Charles McClanahan Adapt Creative Co. [photographer], taken with permission by Chapter 451 Vietnam Veterans of America.)

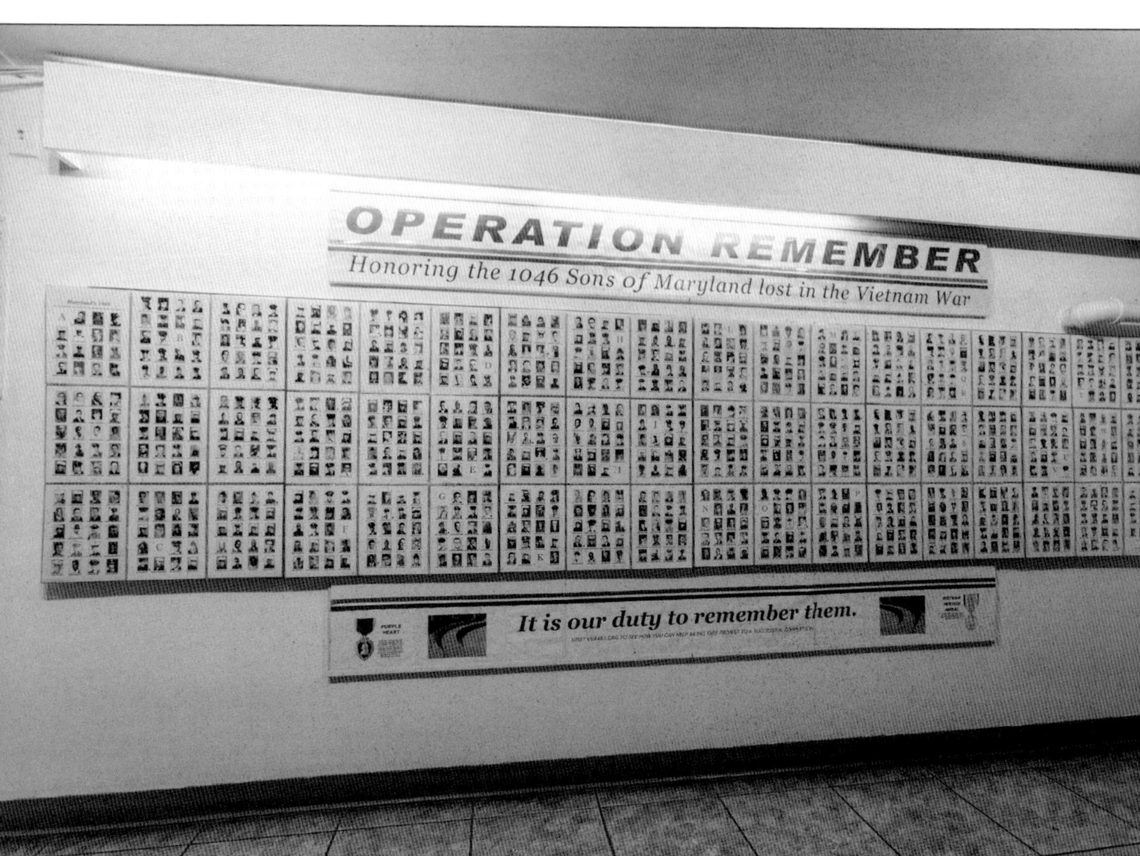

Chapter No. 451 of the Vietnam Veterans of America use the facility for meeting and social purposes, but their mission is not forgotten. One wall inside the facility bears the names and images of the 1,046 Marylanders who died in the Vietnam Conflict. It is an honorable gesture to their memory. (Courtesy Charles McClanahan Adapt Creative Co. [photographer], taken with permission by Chapter 451 Vietnam Veterans of America.)

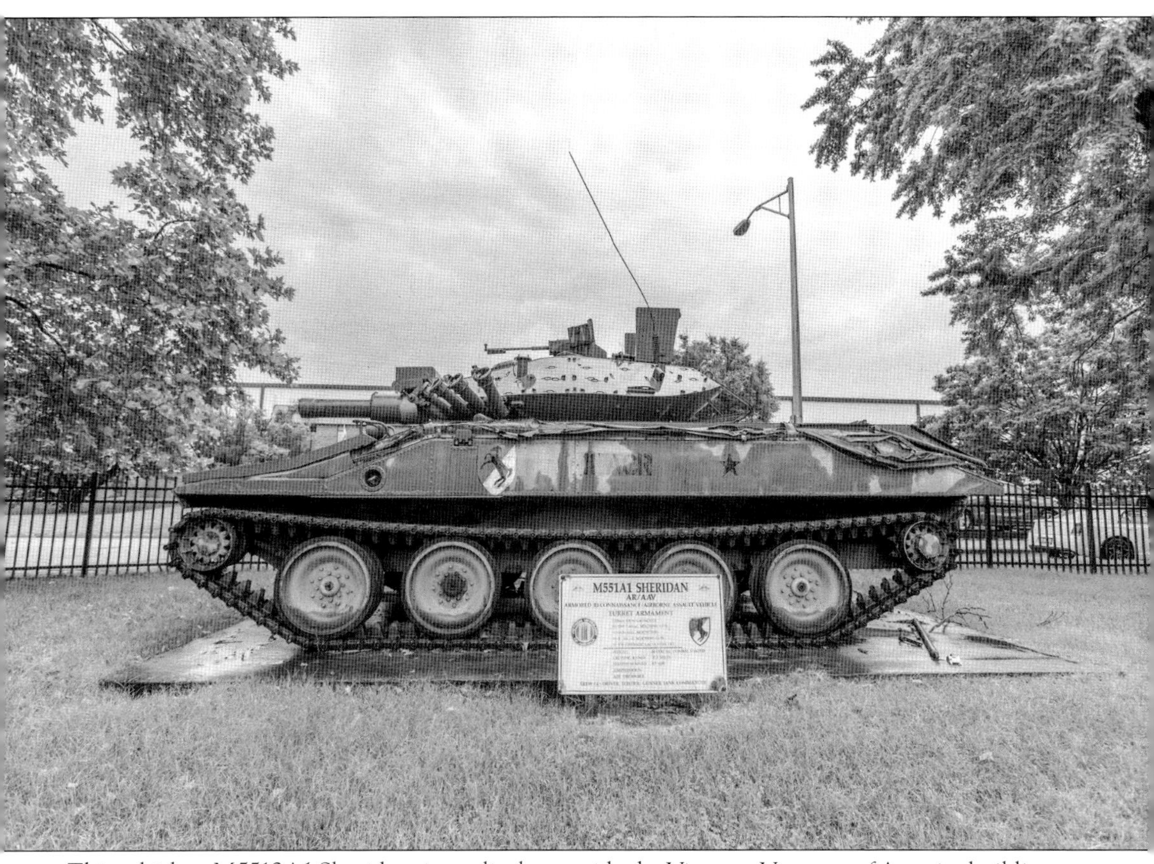

This vehicle, a M5512A1 Sheridan, is on display outside the Vietnam Veterans of America building. It bears the marking of the 11th Armored Cavalry Regiment, a unit that served bravely in Vietnam. Thousands of military vehicles have rumbled across Fort Holabird's ground. Now, there is only one military vehicle left on that land that was once Fort Holabird. (Courtesy Charles McClanahan Adapt Creative Co. [photographer], taken with permission by Chapter 451 Vietnam Veterans of America.)

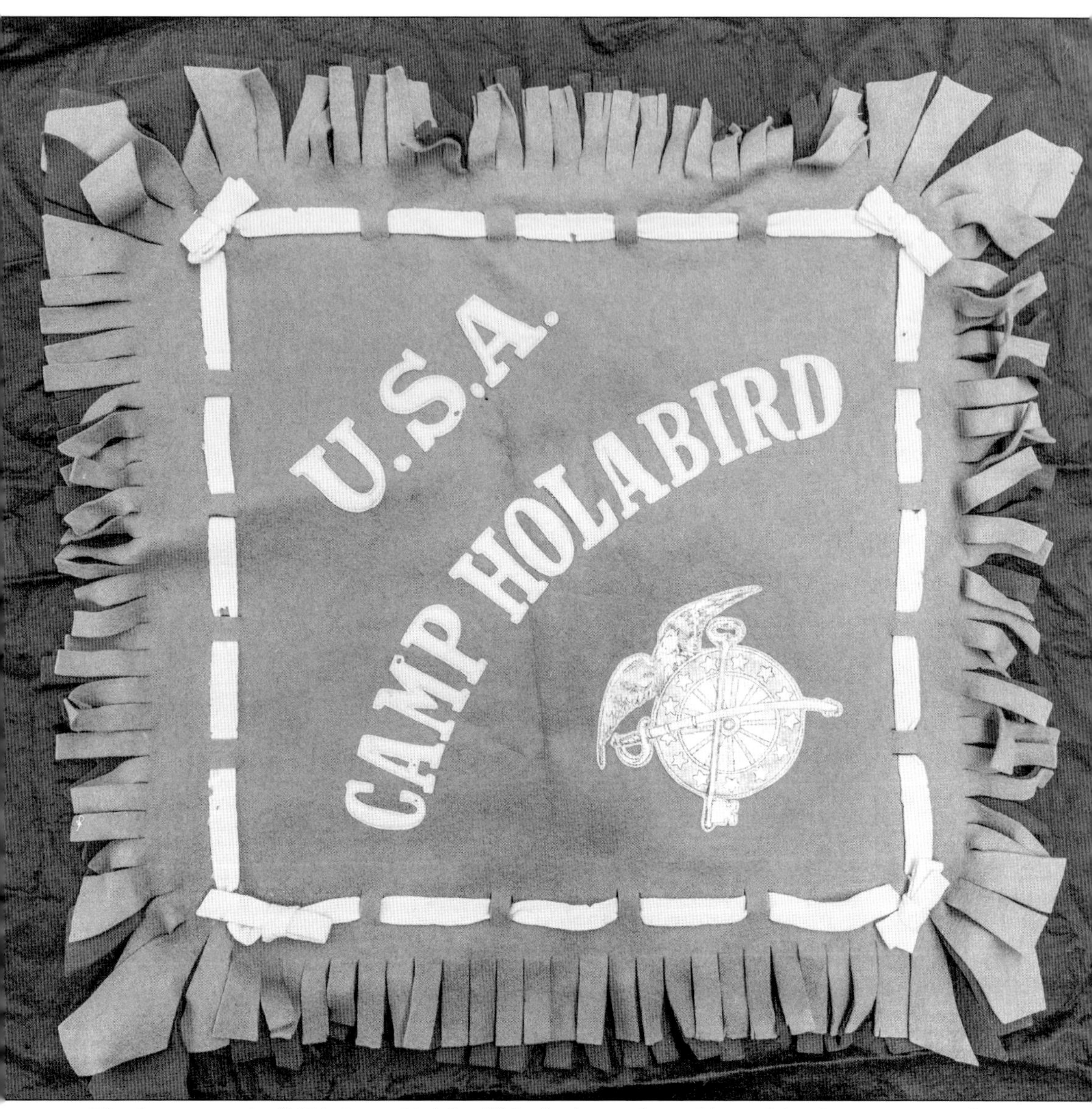

This banner reads, "USA Camp Holabird." It also bears the emblem of the Quartermaster Corps. Its history is uncertain, but it is believed to date to World War I. Perhaps it rode atop a guidon as soldiers proudly marched. Perhaps it rested atop an informal flagpole in an orderly room. This banner and other artifacts are among all that is left as a reminder of Camp Holabird. (Courtesy Charles McClanahan Adapt Creative Co. [photographer], taken with permission by the Dundalk-Patapsco Neck Historical Society & Museum.)

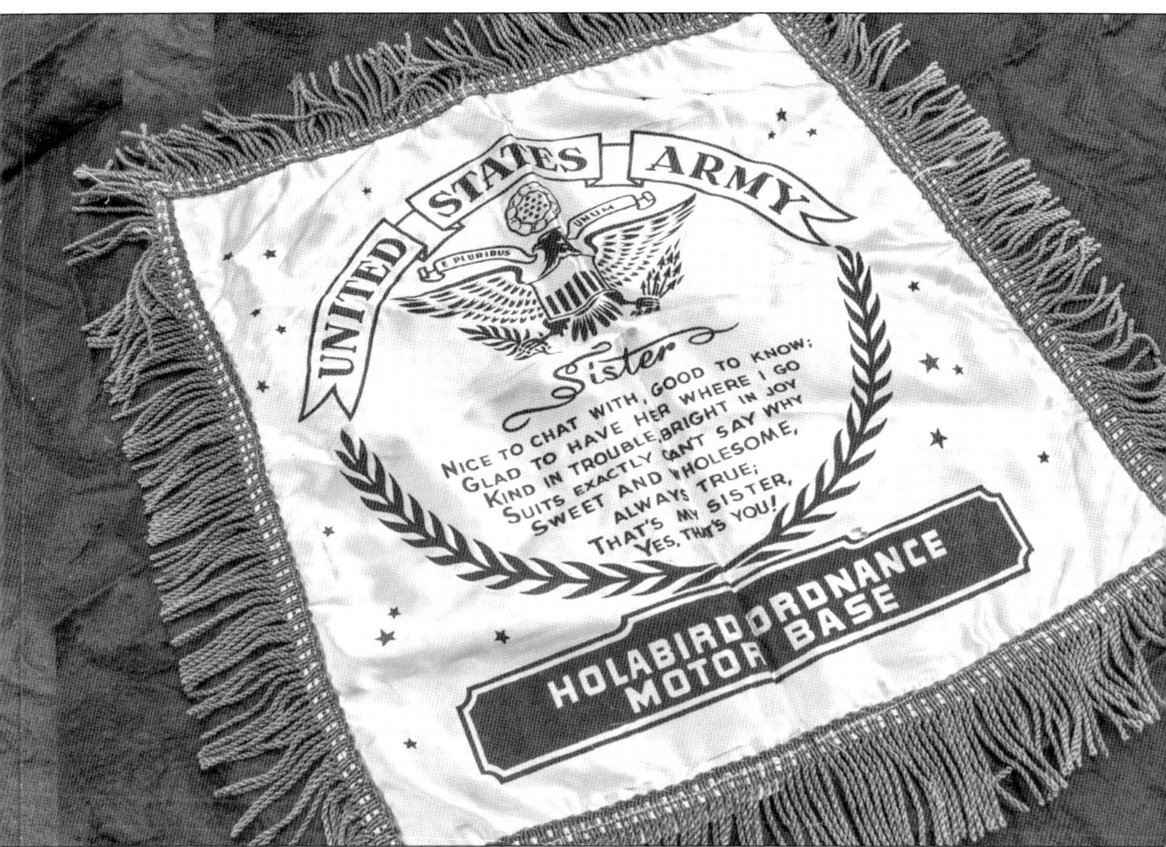

This is one of the few remaining artifacts of old Camp Holabird. It is a pillow sham, and these were at one time a popular souvenir for soldiers. They could be purchased at the post exchange in many varieties and sent home to friends and family. This particular sham is labeled "Sister." (Courtesy Charles McClanahan Adapt Creative Co. [photographer].)

Consistent with our mission to preserve history on a local level, this book was printed in South Carolina on American-made paper and manufactured entirely in the United States. Products carrying the accredited Forest Stewardship Council (FSC) label are printed on 100 percent FSC-certified paper.

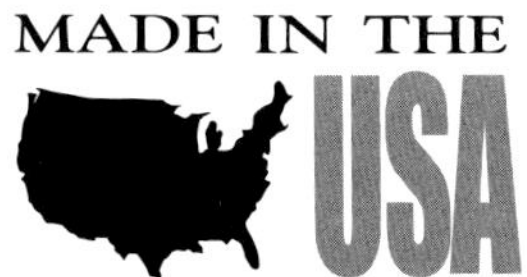